MILITARY
AIRCRAFT
MARKINGS
& PROFILES

LT COL ALAIN KAME
SERVICE THIS AIRCRAFT
WITH GRADE JP-4
PER MIL-J-5624
1.PUSH BUTTON TO OPEN DOO
2.PULL RING OUT 6 FEET TO
JETTISON CANOPY

MILITARY AIRCRAFT MARKINGS & PROFILES

BARRY C WHEELER

GALLERY BOOKS
An Imprint of W. H. Smith Publishers Inc.
112 Madison Avenue
New York City 10016

This edition published in 1990 by Gallery Books,
an imprint of W H Smith Publishers Inc.,
112 Madison Avenue, New York 10016

Copyright © 1990 The Hamlyn Publishing Group
Copyright © 1990 Pilot Press – colour profiles

This edition was originally published in Great Britain in
1990 by The Hamlyn Publishing Group Limited,
a division of the Octopus Publishing Group,
Michelin House, 81 Fulham Road, London SW3 6RB

ISBN 0 8317 6002 8

Produced by Mandarin Offset

Printed and bound in Hong Kong

CONTENTS

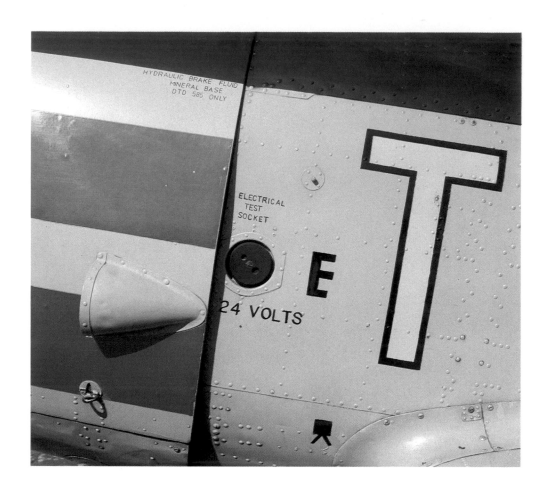

PREFACE

"If I was in charge of tactics, I would spray all fighter aircraft light gray, reduce the size of the national insignia and delete *all* unnecessary external colors and markings and that includes all those bright squadron badges!" That quote is by an official UK camouflage specialist who has the survivability of the aircrews as his first priority and on reviewing the current trend in color schemes on modern military aircraft he has almost achieved his aim.

Counter-shaded gray has become the principal paint scheme for many types of Western Alliance-operated combat aircraft, and trials have proved that of all the schemes considered in recent years, this one provides the most concealment, both air-to-air and air-to-ground. However, *esprit de corps* remains an essential part of military life and in peacetime, colorful markings are still widely used.

Aircraft markings and colors hold a fascination for enthusiast and casual observer alike. The design is limitless and is almost an art form. Although conformity is a military watchword and most squadron commanders try to achieve a uniform standard of finish on their aircraft, virtually no two are identical. This may be because of different paint schemes, a change of unit markings from one machine to the next, air and ground crew names applied on the fuselage sides or maintenance and safety stenciling applied in slightly different places on the airframe.

Esoteric perhaps, but to an aircraft enthusiast, these differences form the spur which extends his interest. It makes the aircraft individual and lifts the subject out of the boring sameness which can haunt other hobbies. Even officialdom now realizes that there is much to gain in goodwill and support by encouraging these enthusiasts. So much so that there are an increasing number of Western air forces that paint military aircraft in special "one-off" schemes to commemorate anniversaries or particular events.

Like the knights of old, markings on aircraft have become heraldic symbols of ownership and have developed steadily since the airplane first went to war in 1914. Alongside the story of the markings is the evolution of camouflage for the two subjects are interrelated, and to concentrate more on one than the other would be to tell only half the story.

Why are aircraft painted and marked? The answer is, for a number of reasons, but basically to protect the airframe against corrosion, assist in concealment from an enemy and to provide some form of national or unit identity. Markings were the first to appear, followed by camouflage, the latter being a derivation of the French *camoufler* – to disguise. Most of the color schemes have been the result of particular requirements such as for aircraft operating over certain types of terrain like the jungle or the desert, or for special roles.

Given today's modern, high-performance combat aircraft, it would perhaps be logical to think that there is no real need for camouflage. After all, missiles are fired at targets beyond visual range and most tacticians argue that the day of the old-fashioned dogfight is now long past. That may be so, but at low level, under the radar, a fast-moving aircraft will need all the protection it can get if it is to reach its target, deliver its weapons and escape unde-tected. An enemy on patrol will be looking out for just such an intruder, and if he is painted in the wrong color scheme, the old clichéd "Mk 1 eyeball" could more easily pick him out against the background clutter.

Markings as well as camouflage have changed over the last 70 years. Basic national insignia, the most obvious and widespread form of marking to indicate ownership, was first used in the early years of this century and continues to be applied, mainly to the wings, fuselage and tail. Some insignia remain almost unaltered in design since they were first adopted during the First World War, others have changed either to reflect a move to a new national political status, or the size has diminished to provide a less visible marking which would not compromise the camouflaged finish.

In addition to the national insignia, aircraft often carry badges, both official and unofficial. Also airframe stenciling, from the very basic NO STEP warning, to large panels giving detailed instructions for arming or maintaining the aircraft.

The first part of this book looks at the background to current marking and camouflage and is related to the aircraft's role. Since color is task orientated the sections highlight the various changes undergone by the types over the last 70 years or so.

The second part is a reference to the colors themselves in the form of profiles showing the often wide-ranging types of camouflage applied to different aircraft. The profiles have been chosen to give as broad a view as possible and where it is considered relevant, official color specifications are included in the captions.

COLORS OF WAR AND PEACE

Single seat fighters have always been regarded as the *elite* among aircraft and from the earliest days of military flying, flamboyant markings have often been the hallmark of the breed. The forerunners of fighters were called scouts and the British Expeditionary Force took some to France at the outbreak of the First World War in August 1914, attached to reconnaissance units of the Royal Flying Corps. Their markings were limited to a black number applied to the tail over buff-colored, clear-doped linen fabric. Nobody had seriously considered the use of camouflage at that stage and generally national markings were not thought necessary. This all changed in the first weeks of the conflict when any aircraft flying over the lines attracted ground fire from friend and foe alike.

The French and the Germans introduced the first practical national markings; one meter diameter roundels of red, white and blue had appeared on French military aircraft as early as 1912, and the black and white cross *patée* was adopted by the German Air Service from the first weeks of the war.

Two months after the start of the war, Field HQ in France directed that British aircraft were to have the Union Jack marking painted under the lower wings. This insignia might have survived if the St George's Cross in the flag had not appeared similar to the German cross at a distance.

The RFC finally decided that the concentric circle marking was by far the best form of insignia and following agreement with the French, the roundel was adopted but with the colors reversed, red in the center, white and a blue outer ring. During the changeover period, aircraft on the Western Front were often noted with both roundels and 24in × 18in flags painted under the wings. Eventually the roundel remained and was also applied to the sides of the fuselage – clear of the cockpit after the crews felt it provided an ideal target for enemy gunners to aim at – and supplemented with rudder striping, blue being next to the rudder post followed by equal width bands of white and red.

Despite changes of color shade and marking size over the years, the three countries – Britain, France and Germany – still retain the basic insignia.

Camouflage came late in 1915, when the German Air Service introduced a two-color disruptive scheme of green and brown with a light blue on the under surfaces; mauve or purple replaced the brown later in the war.

The RFC adopted camouflage early in 1916, usually with a dark top surface color varying from green to khaki and natural finish under surfaces. This may seem an obvious combination now, but in those early days, nothing like it had been tried before and it involved hundreds of aircraft. Size was also a factor when it came to the wing roundel, which was quite often painted the full width of the upper and lower wings, thereby almost totally negating the effect of concealment.

The German's flying circus

Something more radical came towards the end of 1916. This was the "Circus". Groups of brightly painted fighting aircraft flown by ace pilots operated along the Front and concealment was set aside as individual pilots tried to outdo each other by way of color and design. As many as four *Jagdstaffeln* ("Jastas", or scout squadrons), with perhaps 50 aircraft, combined to achieve local superiority and most were flamboyantly marked, as shown in combat reports made at the time covering such types as Fokker Triplanes, Albatros and Pfalz scouts. For example *Jagdstaffel* 1 – red noses and wings; *Jagdstaffel* 2 – bright yellow bellies; *Jagdstaffel* 3 – black and white checks on fuselage; *Jagdstaffel* 4 – black snake-line over gray on fuselage.

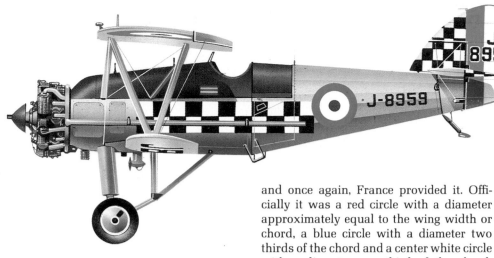

France too chose a two-color camouflage for its front-line scouts, although the fuselage sides were saved for unit or personal insignia (hardly of the same caliber as their German counterparts). With the United States entry into the war in 1917, an appropriate national insignia was required and once again, France provided it. Officially it was a red circle with a diameter approximately equal to the wing width or chord, a blue circle with a diameter two thirds of the chord and a center white circle with a diameter one third of the chord. Vertical equally spaced rudder stripes were added, red leading, and commonality with other Allied aircraft was complete. It was to be 1919 before the US Air Service readopted the star-and-red-disc design first used within the United States from May 1917.

The years after 1918 saw the consolidation of national markings among the major powers and in many cases unit insignia were ordered to be applied in particular sizes, styles and locations to obtain some orderliness. For example, in September 1923, the US Army issued an order governing formation of unit insignia placed on aircraft and designs to be officially approved. A year later the US Navy standardized on a number-letter-number form of squadron marking for ease of identity. In March 1927, the Air Ministry decreed that serial numbers were to be marked under the wings of all RAF aircraft and to be read from opposite ways, port and starboard.

Some markings came and went as the fortunes of the countries changed. Estonia, Latvia and Lithuania all had air forces until these countries disappeared, while conflicts such as the Spanish Civil War produced insignia for both sides. Unless a nation was at war, camouflage was not high on the list of official priorities. In the USA, bright colors were widely adopted by the pursuit squadrons, while the British fighter units retained a more sober appearance of a silver finish with carefully applied squadron markings on wings and fuselages.

Fighter colors and markings during the Second World War were of almost infinite variety and the diversity of both can be seen in the color pages. Considerable research was undertaken by a number of countries to try and establish the best types of camouflage for particular areas of operation. For day fighters, most research

Above: Union Jack insignia on a Shorts 184 seaplane.

Below: The white dumbell on these Sopwith Camels was a form of quick identification.

showed that light colors such as white, sky-blue, blue-green and light gray best suited the under surfaces, but top surface colors varied considerably between air forces as different solutions were arrived at. Green was a common color, often combined with other shades to form a disruptive scheme for overland operations.

The RAF decided on brown and green initially, changing to gray and green in 1942 for offensive operations over the English Channel. To reduce mis-identification, a light-colored band was painted around the rear fuselage and was later supplemented by yellow bands along the leading edges of the wings. Large code letters were applied to the fuselage sides and the basic RAF roundel took on various forms with yellow being added in some cases and the white being deleted in others. Desert colors – two shades of brown – tended to be used in North Africa. Late in the war, "southern Pacific" schemes were predominantly white.

Gray fighter schemes

German thoroughness had deduced that gray formed a useful neutral color and this was introduced onto fuselages of Luftwaffe fighters quite early in the conflict, combined with a "splinter" or hard edged pattern of two greens applied to the upper surfaces of the wings and tailplanes. The cross *patée* of the First World War gave way to a straight edged design and the swastika insignia of the National Socialist party was painted on the fins or rudders of all aircraft. The Luftwaffe used a number and symbol system to identify aircraft in a unit and badges were widely employed. However, as the war progressed and fighter units were moved around the gradually diminishing Reich, so camouflage took on a much more *ad hoc* appearance with units in the field adopting schemes which were felt to be most applicable to the terrain over which they flew. Quite often the black was painted out of the national insignia or plain black outline markings were used, depending on the background camouflage of the aircraft, the individual pilot or the local unit commander. Units operating in North Africa followed the Italian example and sprayed their aircraft in a desert finish comprising a brown usually with a mottled darker color to give a disruptive finish. "Theater bands" showed operational areas.

Germany's allies, Italy and Japan both used distinctive markings to identify their nationality. The former had a prominent white cross on the tail and three black fasces in a circle on the wings. A white fuselage band was an added feature on which many units painted their squadron number and individual aircraft number.

On the other side of the world, Japan's blood red "meatball" as the Americans were to call it, appeared on all Army and Navy-operated aircraft and apart from

US aircraft carrier Langley during the interwar period.

outlining variations, remained consistent throughout the war and continues in use today. Green was a dominant color in Japanese camouflage although towards the end of the war unpainted fighters were regularly encountered by the Allies as the urgent need for replacement aircraft prevented the standard application of protective camouflage.

Before the United States entered the Second World War, orders were issued to change some of the basic national markings. This included the positioning of the star insignia above the port and below the starboard wings, applying it on the fuselage sides and abolishing the rudder striping on Army Air Corps aircraft. Later orders called for the deletion of the red center in the insignia to prevent any confusion with the Japanese marking and, because shape is dominant to color, white rectangles were added to the sides of the blue circular field and a red border was painted around the whole design. The red was changed shortly afterwards to blue and this marking was retained until after the war. American camouflage centered generally around green upper surfaces and gray underneath. Fighter units in Europe using a squadron letter code for identification fell in line with RAF practice. Unofficial personal nose art was a particularly American speciality. In the early days, concealment on the ground from marauding Luftwaffe intruders was a requirement, but as the Allied domination of the skies became more widespread, so the need for camouflage faded and early in 1944, a natural finish for USAAF aircraft was

ordered. Against Japan in the Far East, USAAF fighters retained similar colors to those in other war theaters. However, US Navy fighters used blue as a basic camouflage for Pacific island-hopping operations, starting with quite light shades but ending in 1945 with a scheme of dark glossy sea blue overall.

In the post-war years, natural finishes appeared again with squadron markings applied on the fuselages of the RAF's early jet fighters together with some revision to the sizes of the national insignia. As the Cold War increased tension, so there was a general move back towards disruptive schemes and from the early 1950s, green and gray camouflage returned and with some variations, has remained on RAF tactical aircraft to the present day. Consistent

Bristol Fighter in post-war finish.

with high speed, the RAF Lightning force retained the polished natural metal finish of previous years until the mid 1970s, when these aircraft received a coat of gray and green to undertake the low-level intercept role.

During this period, research in the UK showed that if an aircraft was painted light gray overall it would be better camouflaged against the sky than with the green/gray scheme. In 1979, an RAF Phantom was sprayed in a counter-shaded gray scheme, the top surface of the inner wing section being a darker shade of gray than on the outer sections with an even lighter shade

Silver-doped Bulldog fighters of the RAF.

on the undersurfaces. Detection of this aircraft at a distance was significantly more difficult compared with others with existing schemes. To complete the effect, markings were toned down and reduced in size. RAF Phantom, Tornado and Hawk air defense aircraft are now finished in gray and similar colors have been adopted by a number of other air forces.

The United States Air Force also concluded that gray was the answer to reduced detection for fighter aircraft. Air superiority blue was tried initially, but gray eventually won the day and today, both USAF and US Navy types fly in this scheme. Unlike the toned-down colors used by the RAF, American aircraft have just a simple gray or black outline national insignia, small enough to be virtually undetectable at combat ranges.

BOMBERS

As an instrument of power, the bomber aircraft has played a major role in international affairs and in its highly advanced form today continues to command a healthy respect from potential enemies. The heyday of the conventional bomber was undoubtedly the Second World War when fleets of large four-engined aircraft contributed substantially to the defeat of the Axis forces in Europe and Asia. During that period, bombers operated both day and night and colors and markings reflected this.

The RAF adopted night bombing in the belief that under the cover of darkness, aircraft and crews would stand a greater chance of success. To help provide some form of visual protection, Black was applied to all aircraft engaged in these operations with dark green and dark earth forming a disruptive pattern over the top surfaces. This color combination replaced the overall dark green or "Nivo" scheme which the Service had used on its heavy bombers in the inter-war period. Rather strangely this coloration was found to be ideal for night use, given the slight luminescence which is usually present at night and even more so on moonlit nights.

America's strategic bombing campaign from 1942 was almost entirely flown in daylight, but camouflage gave the B-17s and B-24s virtually no protection and had it not been for the development of the long-range escort fighter, losses would have

Dauntless dive-bombers of the USMC in 1943 colors.

eventually halted this element of the offensive against Germany. What the olive drab paint did achieve on the aircraft's top surfaces was to help conceal the big aircraft on the ground from occasional forays by Luftwaffe intruders, but even this threat was thought negligible by 1944 and new aircraft were delivered from the USA in a natural finish. Both RAF and USAAF bombers carried identifying codes and in the case of the latter, bright tail markings to assist with unit identification when flying in the large combat box formations.

The Luftwaffe had conducted a number of trials to determine the best color and patterning for its warplanes and had concluded that a combination of greens would form the ideal daylight camouflage. *Schwarzgrün* and *dunkelgrün* applied in a splinter pattern over the top surfaces and a light blue or *hellblau* underneath became standard by the beginning of the war and remained in use with certain variations until 1945. The bomber units were essentially daylight orientated until the night blitz of London in 1940; for this black under surfaces were adopted and the white in the

national markings was painted out. Four letter codes applied at the factory were changed to comply with a unit identification system when aircraft were delivered to squadrons and examples of these can be found in the color section. Official unit badges were another form of identity.

Some units did adopt non-standard camouflage, such as the Heinkel He 111 unit in France which painted large white clouds over the green upper surfaces of its aircraft and Ju88s appeared with areas of light gray over the factory finish. A white finish was usual for most types of German aircraft on the Russian Front when the winter snows began and by the time it had ended, those aircraft that had survived often looked extremely worn and shabby with the basic undersurface color showing through.

Post-war colors

In the post-war period, the RAF found it difficult to shake off its wartime image and Bomber Command Lancasters, Lincolns and Mosquitos all retained black undersurfaces but with gray replacing the green-brown scheme on the top. The dull red squadron code letters now appeared in white and white also reappeared in the roundels while serials were marked large under the wings. Even the first Canberras took on the black-gray colors until natural metal finish became standard. American supplied B-29s (known in the RAF as Washingtons), were delivered unpainted and remained so except for small areas of color on the fintip indicating the squadron.

Anti-flash white was the color used on the V bombers (Valiant, Victor and Vulcan) to protect them from the results of a nuclear explosion rather than for any reason of concealment (on the ground the white aircraft stood out dramatically). This finish complete with its low-visibility markings, gave way in 1964 to a scheme in keeping with the switch from high-level to low-level bombing – dark green and medium sea gray over all top surfaces while white was retained underneath. Other changes ensued during the following years and all were to reflect the need for reduced visibility in the air.

Above: USAF F-15 fin with the Bitburg base code.

Above: Royal Navy Sea Harrier in pre-Falklands color scheme.

Below: RAF Jaguar with 2 Sqn marking on the intake.

Above: Nose markings, old and new – B-17F; (*inset*) a KC-10A.

Large codes identified WWII bombers like this 91st BG B-17; *Below* 8th AF B-24.

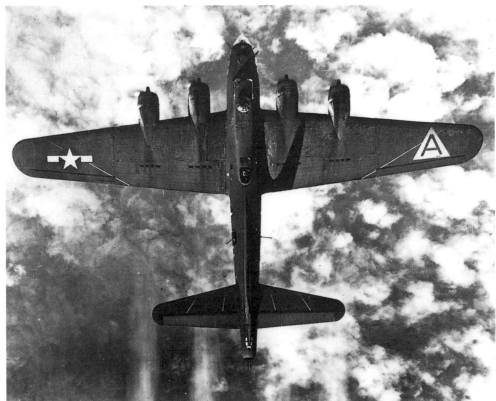

The V-bombers gave way to the Tornado and the dullness of their appearance is an indication of the need for survival in a world where potential aggressors have large numbers of modern and very capable low-level surface-to-air missiles and radar-directed guns. The bright squadron markings displayed on the fuselages and fins of RAF Tornados in peacetime would very quickly be removed in wartime! Having ended the war with fleets of silver bombers, the United States retained natural metal finish for its Strategic Air Command (SAC) force of new B-47s and B-52s in the 1950s and early 1960s. In 1947, red reappeared in the national marking after its deletion during the war. It was now added as a stripe to each of the white rectangles so that all the colors of the US flag would be represented. This form of insignia was to remain prominently displayed until the Vietnam war prompted a change more in keeping with the dark camouflage which was adopted.

On the silver and gray bombers, SAC and Wing badges were a feature of the time and the large black letters: US AIR FORCE were displayed on the fuselage of the aircraft.

A shrinking Star and Bar

Tactical bombers in SE Asia acquired a three-tone camouflage after initial operations in light gray and soon this Vietnam coloring was to be found on the top surfaces of B-52s engaged in conventional carpet bombing of Viet Cong bases and targets in North Vietnam. For night operations, black was sprayed over the undersurfaces and tails of the aircraft and this finish was also applied to the new F-111 when it was first deployed to SE Asia in 1968. The national insignia began to diminish in size during this period and many markings were deleted altogether in an effort to reduce visibility. However, there was still a need to identify the unit to which an aircraft belonged so those involved in tactical operations like the F-105 and F-4 used a series of two-letter codes which were marked prominently on the fins.

In the 1970s, SAC B-52s were assigned to the low-level nuclear attack role alongside the faster FB-111s and received a disruptive three-color camouflage to reduce the chances of their being spotted by higher-flying enemy fighters. Later trials by SAC

showed that the typical terrain reflectance value for the earth (ignoring desert and snow) is approximately 11 per cent and this became the reflectance target value for a new paint scheme which blended the aircraft outline more effectively into the background. The result was two shades of gray and one of green, low contrast, counter-shaded markings and minimal maintenance instructions over the airframe. At a distance, the current SAC camouflage appears one color, but it is not and trials have proved that it is quite effective over different terrains. Until there is another change, this scheme will remain the current standard for US bombers although radar absorbent paint on the Northrop B-2 and probably the Rockwell B-1B would do more for the combat survival of these types than the visual aspects of the schemes on older aircraft like the B-52 and FB-111.

INTERDICTION

"To deny the enemy the use of his rear areas" is the modern definition of interdiction. In an air power context, the word was most widely used when the Royal Air Force chose to insert it into the Canberra designations B(I)6 and B(I)8 in the late 1950s to better describe the particular roles of these two versions. The conventional interdiction task involves low-flying operations, usually by single aircraft, against such targets as supply dumps, assembly points, command centers and airfields. As well as hitting the target, the mission is also intended to spread as much confusion and disruption as possible in areas where attack is least expected.

Some of the earliest "interdiction" sorties could probably be credited to 100 Sqn, Royal Flying Corps, whose FE2b bombers flew missions behind the German lines in the early part of the First World War. The aircraft were painted in black night camouflage, often without national markings. More than 40 years later, Canberras had black as their protective coloring with gray-green camouflage on the upper surfaces and fin, but they were never destined to go to war so their unit markings remained colorfully intact.

In the Second World War intruder operations were conducted by both Allied and Axis Powers with the Luftwaffe achieving some success with individual bombers operating against airfields and factories engaged in war production. He 111s and Ju 88s were the main types used and their finish was much the same as that on the standard bomber aircraft with all the light colors overpainted black. It was only a matter of time before the RAF hit back and with the introduction of the Mosquito into service, the ideal intruder aircraft became available. The Mosquito proved to be an excellent night fighter and early machines started operations in 1942 painted all black, initially in a color known as Special Night finish RDM 2A which later gave way to Smooth Night DTD308 from late in 1942. For the intruder role, aircraft retained the Smooth Night underneath but carried a dark green-medium sea gray camouflage

on the top surface with dull red squadron codes on the sides of the fuselage; serial numbers were black.

Towards the end of the war, many Allied aircraft took part in interdiction-type operations over Europe, mostly in daylight and usually as part of fighter sweeps to search for targets of opportunity such as trains, airfields and river supply barges. Standard colors were retained for these missions

Top: RAF **Victor – originally a bomber, later an airborne tanker.**
Above: USAF **F-111, probably the finest all-weather strike aircraft of them all.**

Tornado colors for strike (*above*) and intercept (*below*) missions.

1950s bombers still flying — USAF B-52 (*top*) and Soviet Bear — escorted by USAF F-15.

although individual aircraft were sometimes given "modified" paint schemes to confuse ground gunners and break up the aircraft outline at low level.

After the war, the US Air Force operated the B-26 Invader in the interdiction role, covering the aircraft's natural finish with overall gloss black (later a dull matt finish) with red serials and "buzz-numbers", the latter being another form of identification. Aircraft in this form flew missions in Korea and also conducted numerous reconnais-

sance operations over Communist territory. The type was again called up for service during the Vietnam war when modified Invaders, redesignated A-26As, conducted night interdiction missions from Thailand over Laos, Cambodia and North Vietnam in attempts to disrupt the supply routes to the south. Markings were minimal and sometimes were not carried at all, while the

camouflage was the standard SE Asia three-color finish with flat black under surfaces.

Today, the low-level attack role is the one that offers the best chance of survival for aircraft and crew. The F-111, 20 years on from its baptism of fire in Vietnam, still remains one of the few aircraft which is capable of penetrating the sophisticated defenses of an enemy, find the target no matter what the weather is, by day or by night, stand a good chance of hitting it and gain the safety of friendly territory. The majority of the F-111s are currently based in the UK and their colors and markings have remained almost unchanged with the three-tone Vietnam-style camouflage still considered acceptable for the European theater and the black signifying their preferred operational scenario.

MARITIME AIRCRAFT

Camouflaging aircraft for maritime use is as involved as coloring aircraft for overland operations. The essential criteria is to resist as far as possible salt-water corrosion of the vulnerable metal airframes and engines, while at the same time affording some visual protection by giving the aircraft a color scheme in keeping with the surrounding environment. Given that different climatic conditions can produce

World War One and After

1914-1935

AVRO 504

One of the most famous biplane trainers, the Avro 504 first appeared in 1913 and in the opening stages of World War I operated in bombing and reconnaissance roles with the Royal Flying Corps and the Royal Naval Air Service. However, from 1915 the Avro was assigned the training task for which this aircraft was ideally suited: its docile handling quality endeared it to all who flew it. The main variants were the 504J, 504K, and the postwar 504N. Production exceeded 8600.

504K, ROYAL FLYING CORPS TRAINING UNIT, 1918
This aircraft has a khaki-green finish with clear-doped undersurfaces.

504K, No 8 TRAINING SQUADRON, RFC/RAF, 1918
A clear-doped finish with unit marking and aluminum nose cowling distinguish this aircraft. The small D prefix indicates an Avro-built machine.

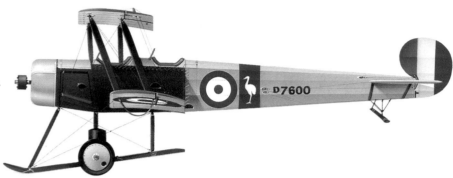

504R, ESTONIAN AIR FORCE, TALLIN, 1928
Only a small number of this variant, known as the Gosport, were built.

504N, OXFORD UNIVERSITY AIR SQUADRON, UPPER HEYFORD, UK, MID-1930s
This was widely used by RAF flying-training schools between the wars. It also saw service with the Cambridge University Air Squadron.

504N, DANISH NAVY, 1927
A converted 504K, it is shown with a blind-flying hood closed over the rear cockpit.

S.E.5a

One of the outstanding single-seat fighters or scouts of World War I, the S.E.5 was designed by the Royal Aircraft Factory at Farnborough and was superior in most respects to its enemy contemporaries. Armament was a single Vickers gun in the fuselage and a Lewis gun above the wing. The type entered service with 56 Squadron in France in April 1917. Unreliability forced a switch from the 200-hp Hispano-Suiza engine to the 200-hp Wolseley Viper. Production totalled 5205.

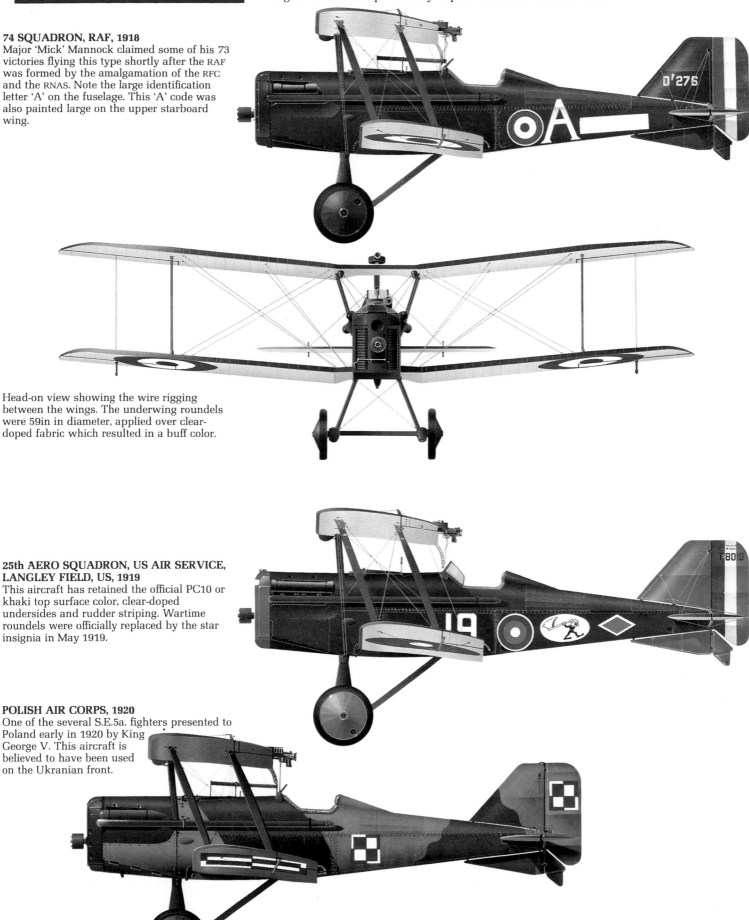

74 SQUADRON, RAF, 1918
Major 'Mick' Mannock claimed some of his 73 victories flying this type shortly after the RAF was formed by the amalgamation of the RFC and the RNAS. Note the large identification letter 'A' on the fuselage. This 'A' code was also painted large on the upper starboard wing.

Head-on view showing the wire rigging between the wings. The underwing roundels were 59in in diameter, applied over clear-doped fabric which resulted in a buff color.

25th AERO SQUADRON, US AIR SERVICE, LANGLEY FIELD, US, 1919
This aircraft has retained the official PC10 or khaki top surface color, clear-doped undersides and rudder striping. Wartime roundels were officially replaced by the star insignia in May 1919.

POLISH AIR CORPS, 1920
One of the several S.E.5a. fighters presented to Poland early in 1920 by King George V. This aircraft is believed to have been used on the Ukranian front.

SOPWITH CAMEL

Invariably linked with air stories of World War I, the Sopwith Camel was a tricky and temperamental little fighter for a novice pilot, but in maneuverability it had no equal and overcame its lack of speed with this vital asset. Armament usually comprised twin Vickers guns with provision, on naval versions, for a Lewis gun above the wing to replace one of the Vickers. The Camel entered service in July 1917 and 32 squadrons had the type by the end of the war. Production totalled 5490.

A FLIGHT, 10 (NAVAL) SQUADRON, ROYAL NAVAL AIR SERVICE, TREIZENNES, BELGIUM, 1917
The khaki-green camouflage is almost totally compromised by Canadian William Alexander's personal markings.

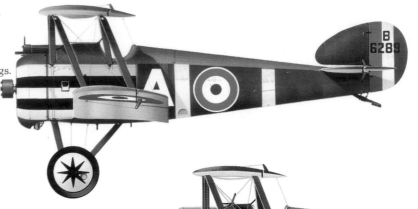

65 SQUADRON, ROYAL FLYING CORPS, 1917
This Camel (F6314) still survives and can be seen in the RAF Museum, Hendon. Colors and markings are typical. Note the polished aluminum cowling.

PERSONAL COLORS, 1919
Just after the war, in 1919, a Capt C. M. McEwen flew this Boulton & Paul-built Camel while based in Italy. The serial had been wrongly marked – it should be D8239.

GROUPE DE CHASSE BELGE, BELGIAN AIR SERVICE, 1918
A Camel in Belgian markings with what appears to be polished wood around the cockpit area. The pilot was the Belgian ace, Jan Oleislagen, and the plane sports a resplendent thistle insignia just aft of the cockpit.

F1 CAMEL, POSSIBLY SLAVO-BRITISH AVIATION GROUP, 1919
Apart from the leaping bear marking, this machine is quite anonymous although it has evidence of previous RFC/RAF ownership on the rudder and fuselage side. It is believed to have been one of a number used against the Russians in 1919–20.

ALBATROS DV

Originally designed by the Albatros company in an attempt to contain the ascendancy of the growing numbers of Allied fighters arriving at the Front in the spring of 1917. The D.V, however, was not a success. Little better than its D-III predecessor, the new aircraft suffered from structural weakness of the lower wing and accidents as well as enemy action befell, what was aesthetically, a very streamlined design. With well over 1000 serving on the Western Front in May 1918, production probably exceeded 3000 by the end of World War I.

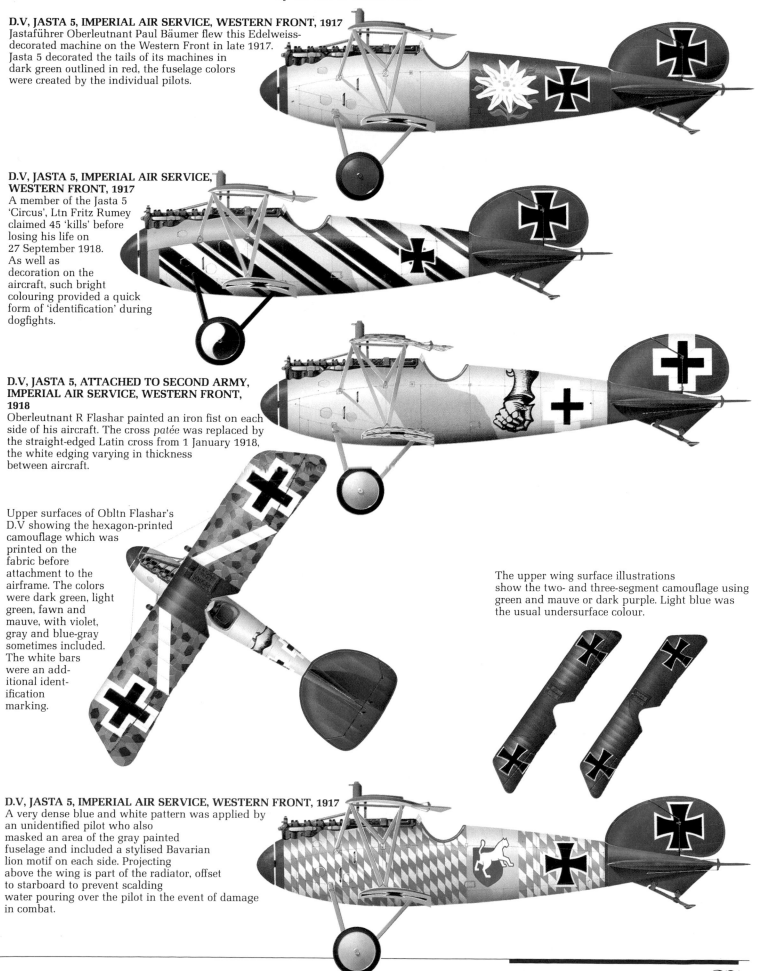

D.V, JASTA 5, IMPERIAL AIR SERVICE, WESTERN FRONT, 1917
Jastaführer Oberleutnant Paul Bäumer flew this Edelweiss-decorated machine on the Western Front in late 1917. Jasta 5 decorated the tails of its machines in dark green outlined in red, the fuselage colors were created by the individual pilots.

D.V, JASTA 5, IMPERIAL AIR SERVICE, WESTERN FRONT, 1917
A member of the Jasta 5 'Circus', Ltn Fritz Rumey claimed 45 'kills' before losing his life on 27 September 1918. As well as decoration on the aircraft, such bright colouring provided a quick form of 'identification' during dogfights.

D.V, JASTA 5, ATTACHED TO SECOND ARMY, IMPERIAL AIR SERVICE, WESTERN FRONT, 1918
Oberleutnant R Flashar painted an iron fist on each side of his aircraft. The cross *patée* was replaced by the straight-edged Latin cross from 1 January 1918, the white edging varying in thickness between aircraft.

Upper surfaces of Obltn Flashar's D.V showing the hexagon-printed camouflage which was printed on the fabric before attachment to the airframe. The colors were dark green, light green, fawn and mauve, with violet, gray and blue-gray sometimes included. The white bars were an additional identification marking.

The upper wing surface illustrations show the two- and three-segment camouflage using green and mauve or dark purple. Light blue was the usual undersurface colour.

D.V, JASTA 5, IMPERIAL AIR SERVICE, WESTERN FRONT, 1917
A very dense blue and white pattern was applied by an unidentified pilot who also masked an area of the gray painted fuselage and included a stylised Bavarian lion motif on each side. Projecting above the wing is part of the radiator, offset to starboard to prevent scalding water pouring over the pilot in the event of damage in combat.

FOKKER Dr 1

Apart from the Sopwith Camel, the only World War I fighter to hold the imagination of the public was Fokker's diminutive triplane, the Dr I. Its fame was due in great part to the exploits of Germany's leading ace, Baron Manfred von Richthofen, who fought and died flying the type. The Dr I was inspired by the Sopwith Triplane, and Fokker designer Reinhold Platz produced a lightly loaded, fast-climbing, highly maneuverable fighter which in one period on the Western Front equipped some 12 Jagdstaffeln. Production was about 320 aircraft.

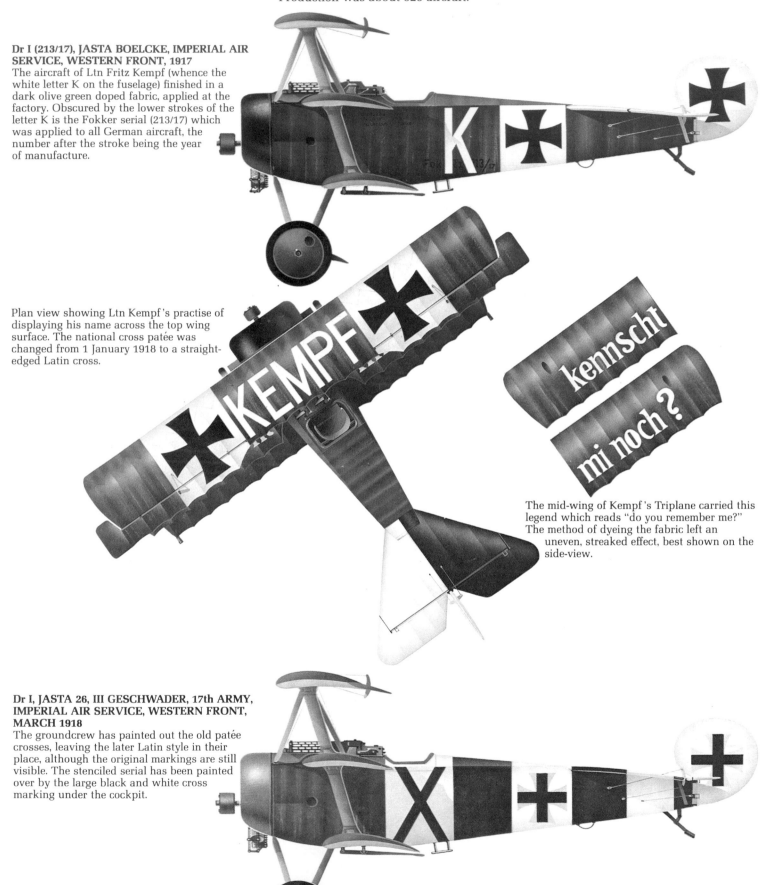

Dr I (213/17), JASTA BOELCKE, IMPERIAL AIR SERVICE, WESTERN FRONT, 1917
The aircraft of Ltn Fritz Kempf (whence the white letter K on the fuselage) finished in a dark olive green doped fabric, applied at the factory. Obscured by the lower strokes of the letter K is the Fokker serial (213/17) which was applied to all German aircraft, the number after the stroke being the year of manufacture.

Plan view showing Ltn Kempf's practise of displaying his name across the top wing surface. The national cross patée was changed from 1 January 1918 to a straight-edged Latin cross.

The mid-wing of Kempf's Triplane carried this legend which reads "do you remember me?" The method of dyeing the fabric left an uneven, streaked effect, best shown on the side-view.

Dr I, JASTA 26, III GESCHWADER, 17th ARMY, IMPERIAL AIR SERVICE, WESTERN FRONT, MARCH 1918
The groundcrew has painted out the old patée crosses, leaving the later Latin style in their place, although the original markings are still visible. The stenciled serial has been painted over by the large black and white cross marking under the cockpit.

Dr I rear fuselage of an unidentified Jasta. The remainder of the aircraft was similar to that flown by Kempf (see opposite), with streaked dark olive green dope.

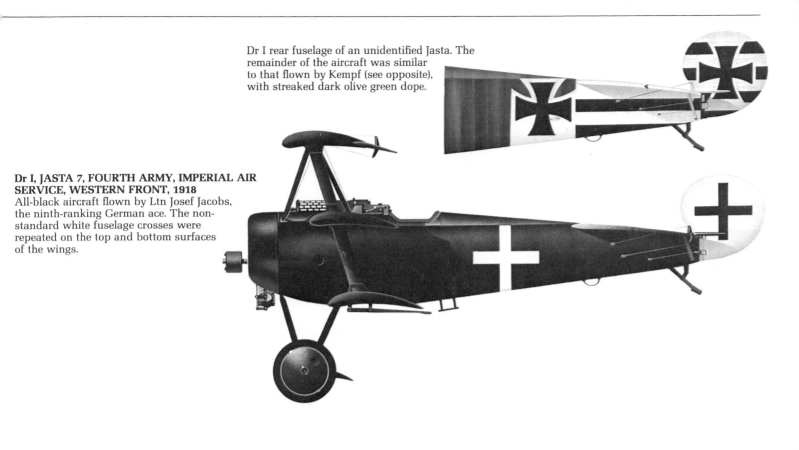

Dr I, JASTA 7, FOURTH ARMY, IMPERIAL AIR SERVICE, WESTERN FRONT, 1918
All-black aircraft flown by Ltn Josef Jacobs, the ninth-ranking German ace. The non-standard white fuselage crosses were repeated on the top and bottom surfaces of the wings.

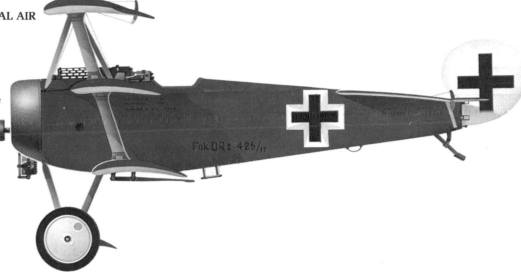

Dr I 425/17, JAGDGESCHWADER I, IMPERIAL AIR SERVICE, CAPPY, WESTERN FRONT, 21 APRIL 1918
Famous as the vermilion-doped Triplane in which Rittmeister Manfred von Richthofen lost his life. The 110hp Oberursel rotary engine is now among the exhibits of the Imperial War Museum, London. The old style cross can be seen under the later marking.

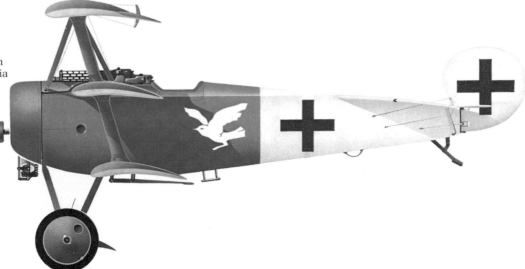

Dr I, JASTA 18, IMPERIAL AIR SERVICE, WESTERN FRONT, LATE 1918
Acquired by the French after the Armistice in November, this machine carries a bird insignia of the unknown pilot. Standard Triplane armament comprised two fixed 7.92mm MG and 1000 rounds of ammunition.

BRISTOL BULLDOG

The epitome of the interwar biplane fighter, the Bulldog made its first flight on 17 May 1927 and entered RAF service with 3 Squadron at Upavon, Wiltshire, in May 1929. At one stage during the mid-1930s, this nimble machine represented some 70 per cent of the UK's fighter force. Production models of the Bulldog were the II, IIA and IVA, and Bristol built a total of 441, just under half being exported to customers such as Denmark, Latvia, Estonia and Finland.

Mk IIA, 17 SQUADRON, RAF UPAVON, UK, 1934
The yellow represented on the spinner, wheels and rudder is the flight leader's color. Black zigzags seen on the fuselage were also applied over the silver-finished top wing surface.

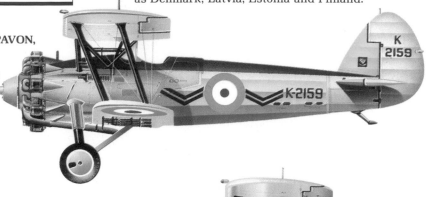

Mk IIA, VASTERAS FLYGKAR (F1), SWEDISH AIR FORCE, 1935
Painted with an overall silver finish; the two black marks on the lower rear fuselage are hand-holds for lifting the aircraft. Later IIa's had their tail skids replaced by a rear wheel.

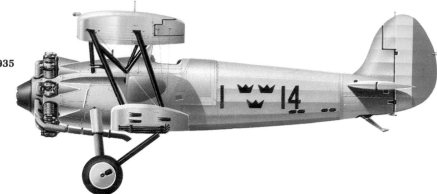

Mk IIA (BRISTOL TYPE 105D), 1 ESKADRILLE, DANISH ARMY, 1932
This aircraft equipped Denmark's first fighter unit. The badge on the fin is a small 'Bulldog' insignia applied by the Bristol Company and is not a unit badge.

Mk IVA, TLELV 35, FINNISH AIR FORCE, 1942
The yellow band and yellow wingtips were a standard identification feature. The Finnish Air Force bought 17 of this type in 1935 – the last Bulldogs to be built.

Mk II, SPANISH REPUBLICAN FORCES, LAMIACO, SPAIN, 1936–7
This example was a former Latvian aircraft. The hastily applied camouflage was over-painted on the fuselage with a large red identification panel and was flown by foreign volunteer pilots operating with Basque forces.

HAWKER HART

One of the most successful inter-war biplanes, the Hart light bomber was advanced for its time in both construction and performance. When it flew in June 1928 it could outdistance any fighter then in service – and most of those on order! The bombload of some 520lb was carried underwing; behind the pilot was a rear gunner armed with a single .303 MG. From the Hart was developed a range of similar aircraft including the Demon, Hector, Audax, Hardy and Osprey, to take production of all types to more than 2700.

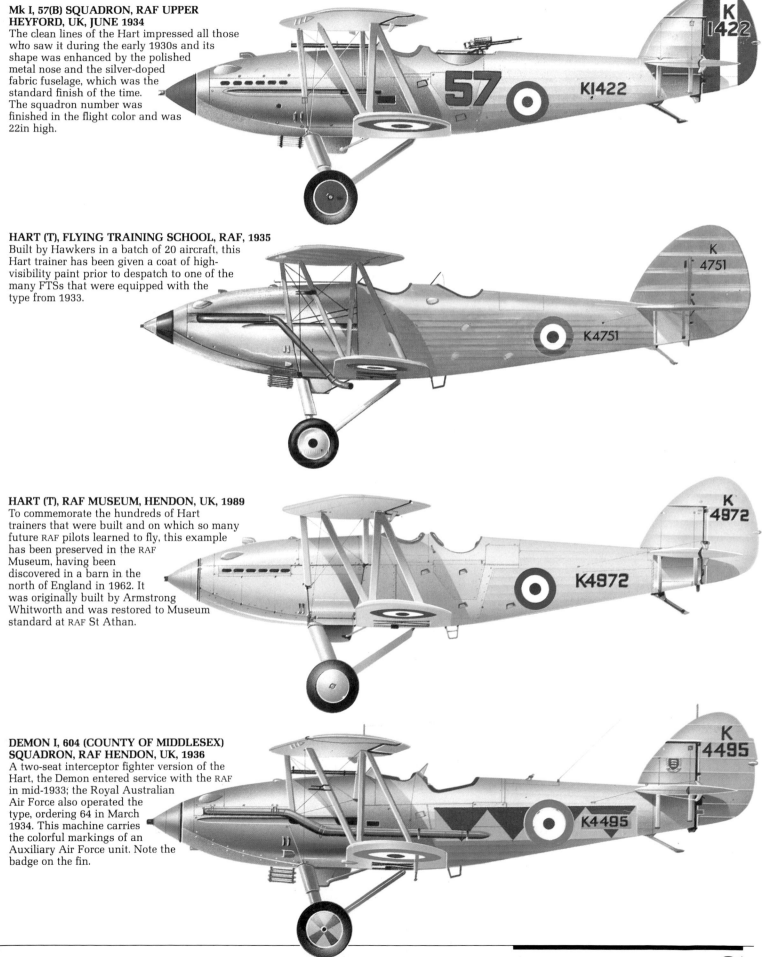

Mk I, 57(B) SQUADRON, RAF UPPER HEYFORD, UK, JUNE 1934
The clean lines of the Hart impressed all those who saw it during the early 1930s and its shape was enhanced by the polished metal nose and the silver-doped fabric fuselage, which was the standard finish of the time. The squadron number was finished in the flight color and was 22in high.

HART (T), FLYING TRAINING SCHOOL, RAF, 1935
Built by Hawkers in a batch of 20 aircraft, this Hart trainer has been given a coat of high-visibility paint prior to despatch to one of the many FTSs that were equipped with the type from 1933.

HART (T), RAF MUSEUM, HENDON, UK, 1989
To commemorate the hundreds of Hart trainers that were built and on which so many future RAF pilots learned to fly, this example has been preserved in the RAF Museum, having been discovered in a barn in the north of England in 1962. It was originally built by Armstrong Whitworth and was restored to Museum standard at RAF St Athan.

DEMON I, 604 (COUNTY OF MIDDLESEX) SQUADRON, RAF HENDON, UK, 1936
A two-seat interceptor fighter version of the Hart, the Demon entered service with the RAF in mid-1933; the Royal Australian Air Force also operated the type, ordering 64 in March 1934. This machine carries the colorful markings of an Auxiliary Air Force unit. Note the badge on the fin.

31

HAWKER FURY

Ordered by the Air Ministry as a fast bomber interceptor, the Fury was the most elegant of fighting biplanes. Originally named Hornet, the prototype flew in March 1929 and Hawker received an order for 118 Fury Is for the RAF. These were followed by 112 of the more powerful Fury II. Exports were made to a number of countries and Yugoslavia built the type under license. Total production was 264.

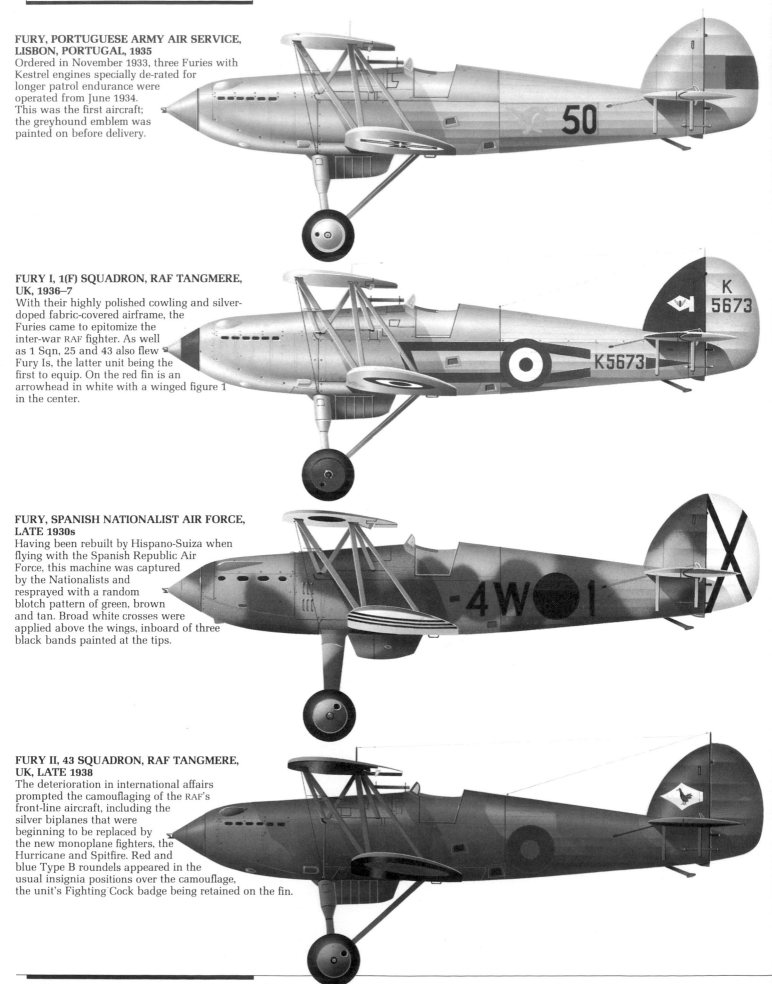

FURY, PORTUGUESE ARMY AIR SERVICE, LISBON, PORTUGAL, 1935
Ordered in November 1933, three Furies with Kestrel engines specially de-rated for longer patrol endurance were operated from June 1934. This was the first aircraft; the greyhound emblem was painted on before delivery.

FURY I, 1(F) SQUADRON, RAF TANGMERE, UK, 1936–7
With their highly polished cowling and silver-doped fabric-covered airframe, the Furies came to epitomize the inter-war RAF fighter. As well as 1 Sqn, 25 and 43 also flew Fury Is, the latter unit being the first to equip. On the red fin is an arrowhead in white with a winged figure 1 in the center.

FURY, SPANISH NATIONALIST AIR FORCE, LATE 1930s
Having been rebuilt by Hispano-Suiza when flying with the Spanish Republic Air Force, this machine was captured by the Nationalists and resprayed with a random blotch pattern of green, brown and tan. Broad white crosses were applied above the wings, inboard of three black bands painted at the tips.

FURY II, 43 SQUADRON, RAF TANGMERE, UK, LATE 1938
The deterioration in international affairs prompted the camouflaging of the RAF's front-line aircraft, including the silver biplanes that were beginning to be replaced by the new monoplane fighters, the Hurricane and Spitfire. Red and blue Type B roundels appeared in the usual insignia positions over the camouflage, the unit's Fighting Cock badge being retained on the fin.

GRUMMAN G-5

This was the aircraft in which observers with strong arms were needed because it was their job to operate the long jackscrew which retracted the main undercarriage into the belly of the portly "Fifi" after take-off. The first US Navy aircraft to have this feature, the prototype XFF-1 flew in December 1931 and proved a sprightly performer for its day, exceeding 200mph with a Wright Cyclone engine in later production aircraft. It entered service in mid 1933, but was relegated to the Reserve three years later. Canada built 57 under license, some seeing service with the RCAF as the Goblin.

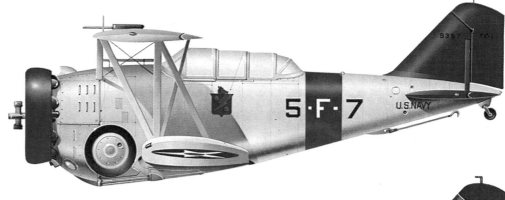

FF-1, VF-5B "RED RIPPERS," US NAVY, USS *LEXINGTON*, 1934–5
One of the 27 FF-1s ordered for use aboard Navy carriers and finished in the colors of the 3rd Section Leader of the Squadron. The blue tail denoted the *Lexington*, while under the cockpit is the boar's head unit insignia. From this ungainly looking Grumman design stemmed a range of aircraft that was to culminate in the Mach 2 Tomcat interceptor of today's Navy.

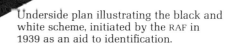

GOBLIN, 118 (F) SQUADRON, ROYAL CANADIAN AIR FORCE, DARTMOUTH, NOVA SCOTIA, CANADA, 1941
The Canadian machines were assembled by Canadian Car & Foundry, Grumman producing the fuselages and Brewster the wings and tail surfaces. Sixteen were taken on charge by the RCAF, this machine receiving the standard Dark Green and Dark Earth disruptive camouflage.

Plan view of No 344, RCAF, showing the upper surface pattern and positioning of the Type B wing roundels.

Underside plan illustrating the black and white scheme, initiated by the RAF in 1939 as an aid to identification.

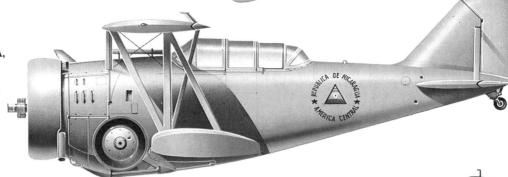

GE-23, NICARAGUAN AIR ARM, MANAGUA, NICARAGUA, 1938
The sole example of its type supplied to the Nicaraguan Government, it retained its natural light alloy finish. Basic armament of the production FF-1 comprised a single .30in MG on top of the forward fuselage and two .30in guns in a flexible mount in the rear cockpit and fired by the observer.

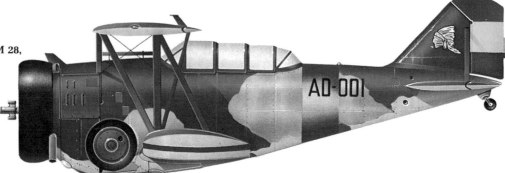

GE-23 DELFIN, 1 ESCUADRILLA, GRUPO NUM 28, SPANISH REPUBLICAN AIR FORCE, SPAIN, 1938
Named Dolphin in Republican use, this aircraft appears to have received a half-hearted attempt at a camouflage scheme. From its number it was probably the first of 34 actually delivered of a planned order for 50. The red band was painted above and below both wings as well as round the center fuselage.

BOEING P-26

America's switch from biplane to monoplane fighters is best exemplified by the P-26, or Peashooter, as it became known in the Air Corps. Conservative features still held sway and the USAAC accepted an open cockpit, external wire bracing and a fixed undercarriage. However, it was an all-metal airplane. Delivery of 136 began in 1934 and exports were made to Panama, the Philippines and Guatemala. The similar Model 281 was sold to China.

P-26B, US ARMY AIR CORPS, JUNE 1934
One of two aircraft given the B sub-type designation, this machine has a fuel-injection system and also incorporated wing flaps, which the Army considered necessary owing to the P-26A's high landing speed.

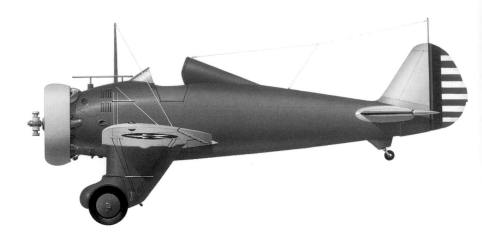

P-26A, 17th PURSUIT SQUADRON, 1st PURSUIT GROUP, USAAC, 1935
Even post-war USN markings didn't better the USAAC pre-war colors, typified by the aircraft shown on these pages. The underwing markings were divided into "U.S." under the starboard side and "ARMY" under the port side.

Emblem of the 17th Pursuit Sqn.

P-26A, 94th PURSUIT SQUADRON, 1st PURSUIT GROUP, USAAC, SELFRIDGE, USA, 1937
All aircraft of this group incorporated a diagonal fuselage band painted in the squadron color with the unit emblem superimposed.

Indian Head emblem of the 94th Pursuit Sqn.

P-26A, 34th PURSUIT SQUADRON, 17th PURSUIT GROUP, USAAC, MARCH FIELD, USA, 1934
The standard USAAC Olive Drab fuselage was repainted Blue during the course of the year. Under the fuselage the unit number (34) can just be made out; on the top is the individual aircraft number (5).

Thunderbirds insignia of the 34th Pursuit Sqn.

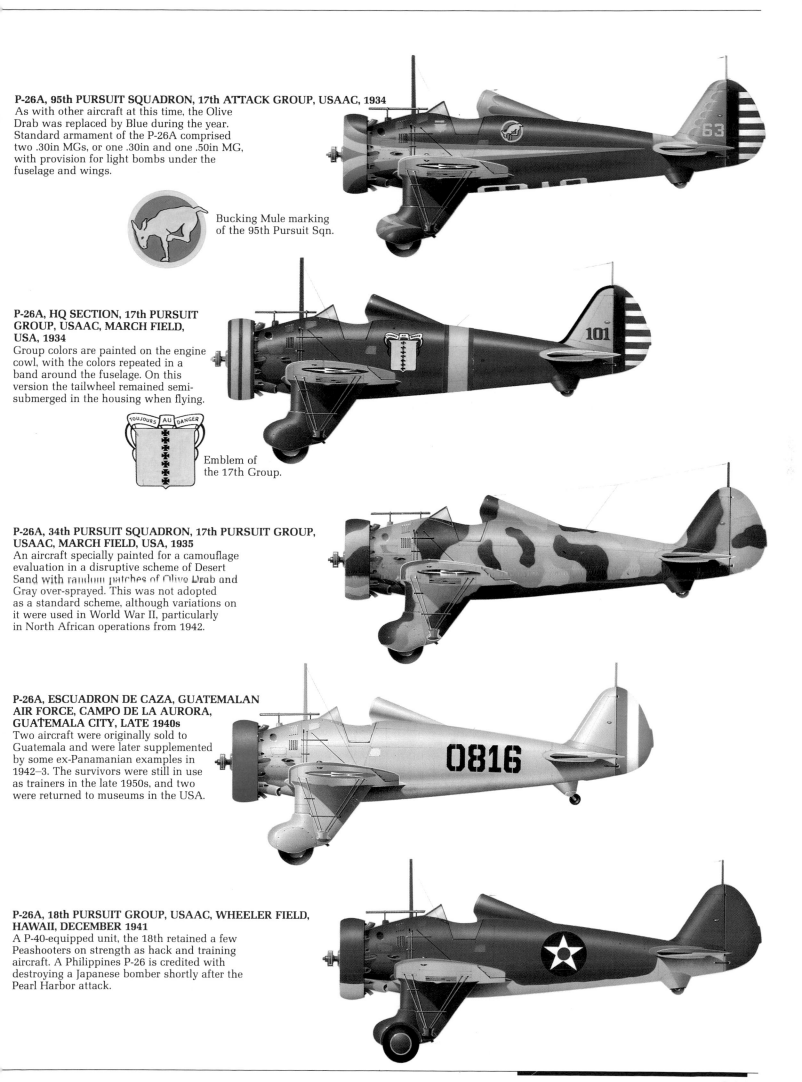

P-26A, 95th PURSUIT SQUADRON, 17th ATTACK GROUP, USAAC, 1934
As with other aircraft at this time, the Olive Drab was replaced by Blue during the year. Standard armament of the P-26A comprised two .30in MGs, or one .30in and one .50in MG, with provision for light bombs under the fuselage and wings.

Bucking Mule marking of the 95th Pursuit Sqn.

P-26A, HQ SECTION, 17th PURSUIT GROUP, USAAC, MARCH FIELD, USA, 1934
Group colors are painted on the engine cowl, with the colors repeated in a band around the fuselage. On this version the tailwheel remained semi-submerged in the housing when flying.

Emblem of the 17th Group.

P-26A, 34th PURSUIT SQUADRON, 17th PURSUIT GROUP, USAAC, MARCH FIELD, USA, 1935
An aircraft specially painted for a camouflage evaluation in a disruptive scheme of Desert Sand with random patches of Olive Drab and Gray over-sprayed. This was not adopted as a standard scheme, although variations on it were used in World War II, particularly in North African operations from 1942.

P-26A, ESCUADRON DE CAZA, GUATEMALAN AIR FORCE, CAMPO DE LA AURORA, GUATEMALA CITY, LATE 1940s
Two aircraft were originally sold to Guatemala and were later supplemented by some ex-Panamanian examples in 1942–3. The survivors were still in use as trainers in the late 1950s, and two were returned to museums in the USA.

P-26A, 18th PURSUIT GROUP, USAAC, WHEELER FIELD, HAWAII, DECEMBER 1941
A P-40-equipped unit, the 18th retained a few Peashooters on strength as hack and training aircraft. A Philippines P-26 is credited with destroying a Japanese bomber shortly after the Pearl Harbor attack.

35

Into the Abyss
1935-1945

BRISTOL BLENHEIM 1

The RAF's first all-metal, stressed-skin monoplane to enter production. The Blenheim outshone most biplane fighters then in service when the early squadrons formed in the late 1930s. However, like many aircraft of its day, it had been overtaken by monoplane fighter development and it stood little chance of surviving against the German Bf 109 during the early daylight operations. Production of the Mk I topped the 1450 mark before the lines were switched to the long-nose Mk IV series.

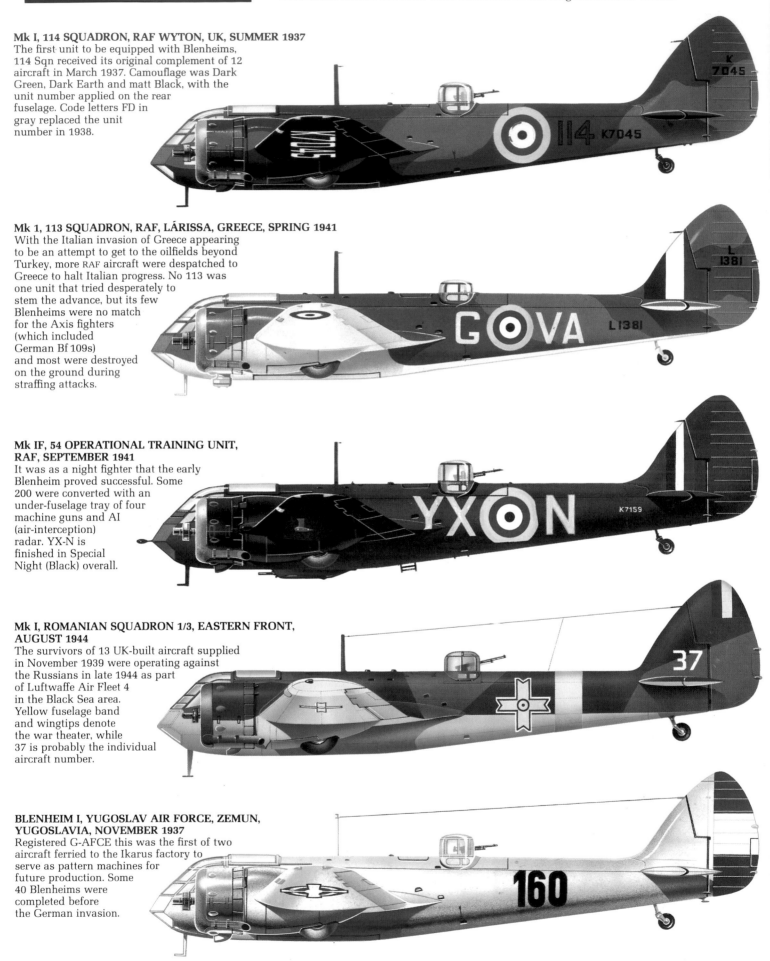

Mk I, 114 SQUADRON, RAF WYTON, UK, SUMMER 1937
The first unit to be equipped with Blenheims, 114 Sqn received its original complement of 12 aircraft in March 1937. Camouflage was Dark Green, Dark Earth and matt Black, with the unit number applied on the rear fuselage. Code letters FD in gray replaced the unit number in 1938.

Mk 1, 113 SQUADRON, RAF, LÁRISSA, GREECE, SPRING 1941
With the Italian invasion of Greece appearing to be an attempt to get to the oilfields beyond Turkey, more RAF aircraft were despatched to Greece to halt Italian progress. No 113 was one unit that tried desperately to stem the advance, but its few Blenheims were no match for the Axis fighters (which included German Bf 109s) and most were destroyed on the ground during straffing attacks.

Mk IF, 54 OPERATIONAL TRAINING UNIT, RAF, SEPTEMBER 1941
It was as a night fighter that the early Blenheim proved successful. Some 200 were converted with an under-fuselage tray of four machine guns and AI (air-interception) radar. YX-N is finished in Special Night (Black) overall.

Mk I, ROMANIAN SQUADRON 1/3, EASTERN FRONT, AUGUST 1944
The survivors of 13 UK-built aircraft supplied in November 1939 were operating against the Russians in late 1944 as part of Luftwaffe Air Fleet 4 in the Black Sea area. Yellow fuselage band and wingtips denote the war theater, while 37 is probably the individual aircraft number.

BLENHEIM I, YUGOSLAV AIR FORCE, ZEMUN, YUGOSLAVIA, NOVEMBER 1937
Registered G-AFCE this was the first of two aircraft ferried to the Ikarus factory to serve as pattern machines for future production. Some 40 Blenheims were completed before the German invasion.

GLOSTER GAUNTLET

Still influenced by the scouts of World War I, the RAF continued to fly open-cockpit fighters until the late 1930s, the last being the sprightly Gauntlet. This was designed to an Air Ministry specification issued in 1926, but it was not until May 1935 that the type entered RAF service, having been developed through a series of prototypes using a variety of engines. Powered by a Bristol Mercury, the Gauntlet could reach 230mph, making it the fastest fighter in RAF service between 1935 and 1937. Production totaled 228.

Mk II, 151 SQUADRON, RAF NORTH WEALD, UK, 1937
Compared with the Mk I, this version had constructional changes to rationalize production methods, and some machines were fitted with a three-bladed propeller in place of the more usual two-bladed wooden type. All-over silver with unit markings on fuselage and across the top wing between the roundels.

Mk II, 17 SQUADRON, RAF KENLEY, UK, 1938
Based at one of the defensive airfields positioned around London, this unit along with others at the time was instructed to apply a Dark Green/Dark Earth camouflage over the top surfaces of its aircraft. Codes were Medium Sea Gray and roundels were Type B converted from 25in Type A.

GAUNTLET, 1 ESCADRILLE, ARMY AVIATION TROOPS, VAERLOSE, DENMARK, EARLY 1940
Seventeen license-built aircraft plus one pattern example from Glosters were acquired by the Danish air arm, entering service in 1938. Prior to the brief defense of the country in April 1940, the Gauntlets were given this hastily applied camouflage. Few survived the initial German attack.

Mk II, T/LeLv 35, FINNISH AIR FORCE, KAUHAVA, FINLAND, SPRING 1942
South Africa donated 24 examples to Finland via the UK, these being used as fighter-trainers between 1940 and 1945. They were coded GT-395 to -418 and during the Continuation War carried the black and green upper-surface camouflage seen here, with yellow Eastern Front markings. This example is ski-equipped for winter use.

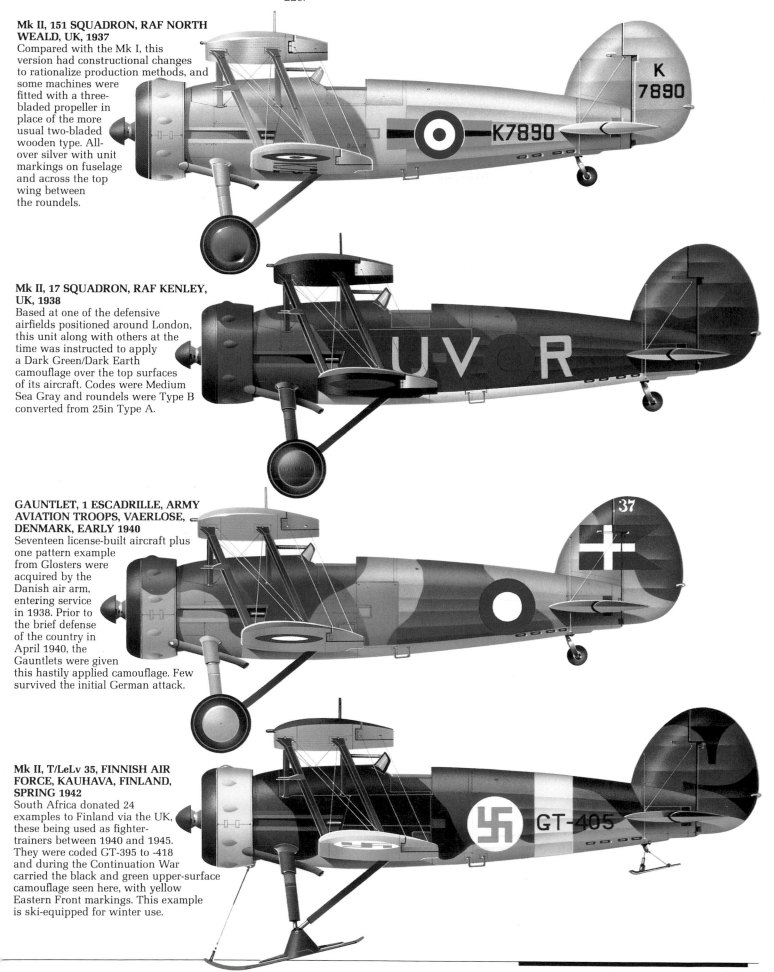

DOUGLAS DC-3

Unlikely ever to be deprived of its unofficial title, "The greatest transport aircraft ever made", the DC-3 or C-47 or Dakota or Skytrain or whatever other names it went by, has been the logistical backbone of most of the world's air arms at one time or another over the past 50 years. In 1988 there were still more than 300 in airline use, 53 years since the first Douglas Sleeper Transport first took to the air. US production totaled 10,655, the Japanese built a further 485, while Soviet lines are believed to have turned out nearly 3000.

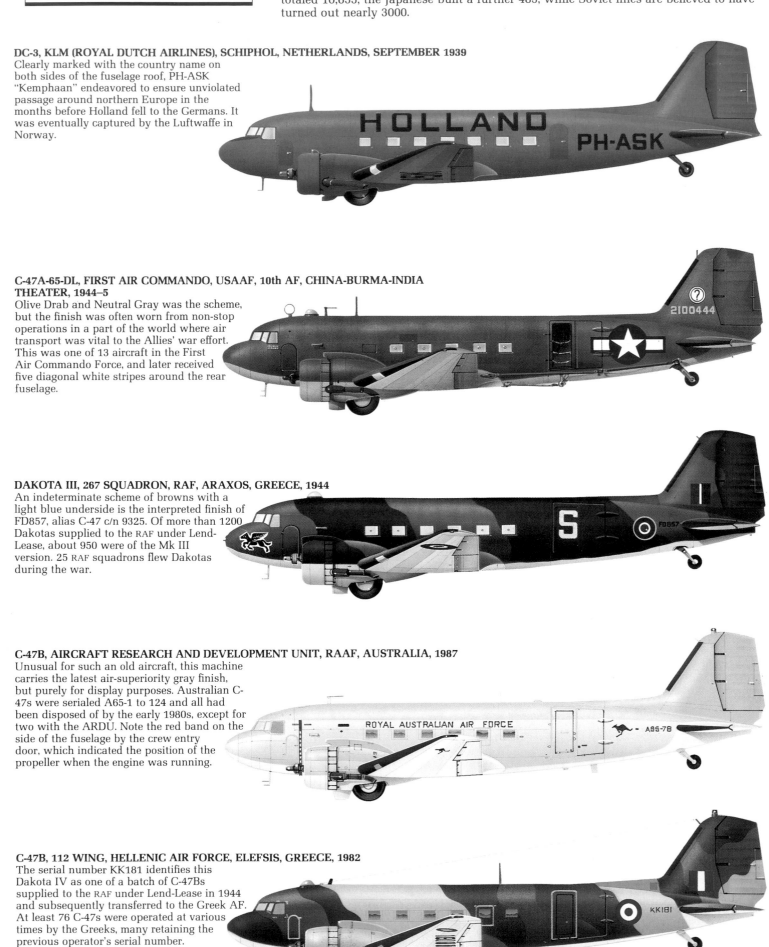

DC-3, KLM (ROYAL DUTCH AIRLINES), SCHIPHOL, NETHERLANDS, SEPTEMBER 1939
Clearly marked with the country name on both sides of the fuselage roof, PH-ASK "Kemphaan" endeavored to ensure unviolated passage around northern Europe in the months before Holland fell to the Germans. It was eventually captured by the Luftwaffe in Norway.

C-47A-65-DL, FIRST AIR COMMANDO, USAAF, 10th AF, CHINA-BURMA-INDIA THEATER, 1944–5
Olive Drab and Neutral Gray was the scheme, but the finish was often worn from non-stop operations in a part of the world where air transport was vital to the Allies' war effort. This was one of 13 aircraft in the First Air Commando Force, and later received five diagonal white stripes around the rear fuselage.

DAKOTA III, 267 SQUADRON, RAF, ARAXOS, GREECE, 1944
An indeterminate scheme of browns with a light blue underside is the interpreted finish of FD857, alias C-47 c/n 9325. Of more than 1200 Dakotas supplied to the RAF under Lend-Lease, about 950 were of the Mk III version. 25 RAF squadrons flew Dakotas during the war.

C-47B, AIRCRAFT RESEARCH AND DEVELOPMENT UNIT, RAAF, AUSTRALIA, 1987
Unusual for such an old aircraft, this machine carries the latest air-superiority gray finish, but purely for display purposes. Australian C-47s were serialed A65-1 to 124 and all had been disposed of by the early 1980s, except for two with the ARDU. Note the red band on the side of the fuselage by the crew entry door, which indicated the position of the propeller when the engine was running.

C-47B, 112 WING, HELLENIC AIR FORCE, ELEFSIS, GREECE, 1982
The serial number KK181 identifies this Dakota IV as one of a batch of C-47Bs supplied to the RAF under Lend-Lease in 1944 and subsequently transferred to the Greek AF. At least 76 C-47s were operated at various times by the Greeks, many retaining the previous operator's serial number.

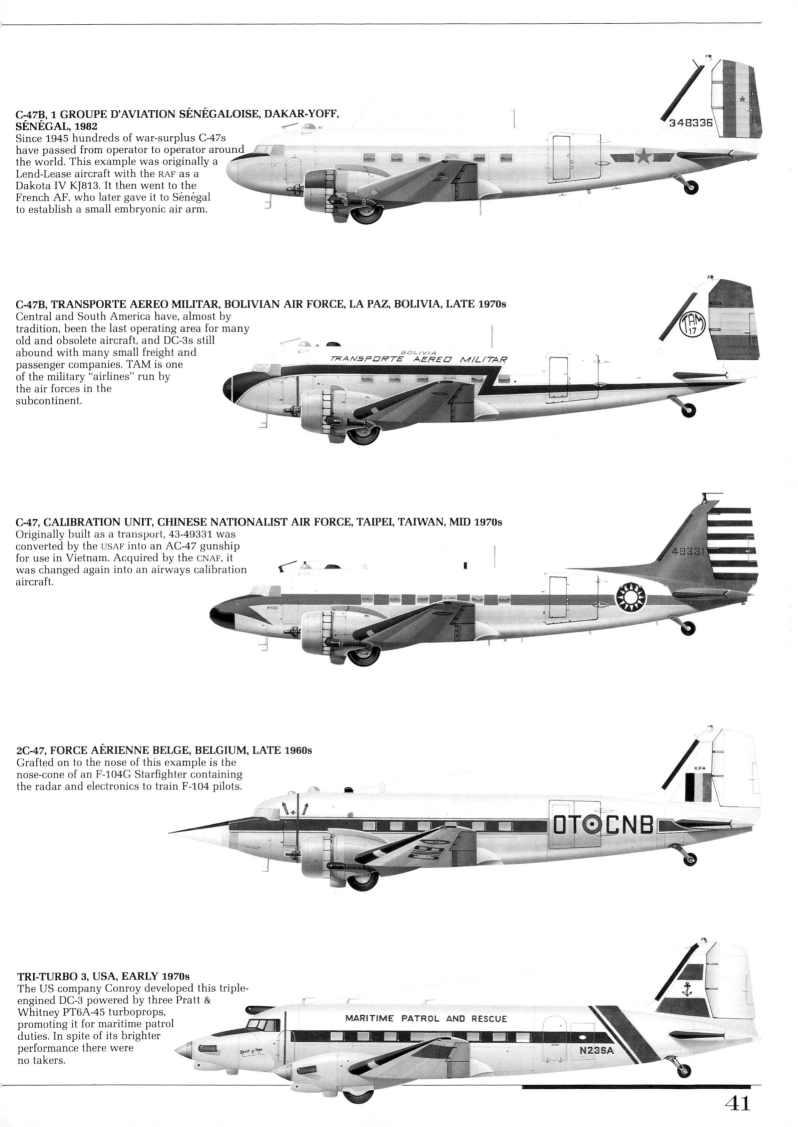

C-47B, 1 GROUPE D'AVIATION SÉNÉGALOISE, DAKAR-YOFF, SÉNÉGAL, 1982
Since 1945 hundreds of war-surplus C-47s have passed from operator to operator around the world. This example was originally a Lend-Lease aircraft with the RAF as a Dakota IV KJ813. It then went to the French AF, who later gave it to Sénégal to establish a small embryonic air arm.

C-47B, TRANSPORTE AEREO MILITAR, BOLIVIAN AIR FORCE, LA PAZ, BOLIVIA, LATE 1970s
Central and South America have, almost by tradition, been the last operating area for many old and obsolete aircraft, and DC-3s still abound with many small freight and passenger companies. TAM is one of the military "airlines" run by the air forces in the subcontinent.

C-47, CALIBRATION UNIT, CHINESE NATIONALIST AIR FORCE, TAIPEI, TAIWAN, MID 1970s
Originally built as a transport, 43-49331 was converted by the USAF into an AC-47 gunship for use in Vietnam. Acquired by the CNAF, it was changed again into an airways calibration aircraft.

2C-47, FORCE AÉRIENNE BELGE, BELGIUM, LATE 1960s
Grafted on to the nose of this example is the nose-cone of an F-104G Starfighter containing the radar and electronics to train F-104 pilots.

TRI-TURBO 3, USA, EARLY 1970s
The US company Conroy developed this triple-engined DC-3 powered by three Pratt & Whitney PT6A-45 turboprops, promoting it for maritime patrol duties. In spite of its brighter performance there were no takers.

JUNKERS Ju 52

Probably unfairly judged as outmoded at the beginning of the Second World War, Junkers' all-metal Ju 52 served the Luftwaffe well throughout the conflict, flying in all theaters and proving to be docile and undemanding to its crews. First flown in 1932, it entered military service in 1933 and no less than 230 were eventually registered to the German airline Lufthansa. During World War II it took part in all the major operations, including Crete, Stalingrad and the Kuban Peninsular. More than 5000 were built, including at least 500 in France and Spain.

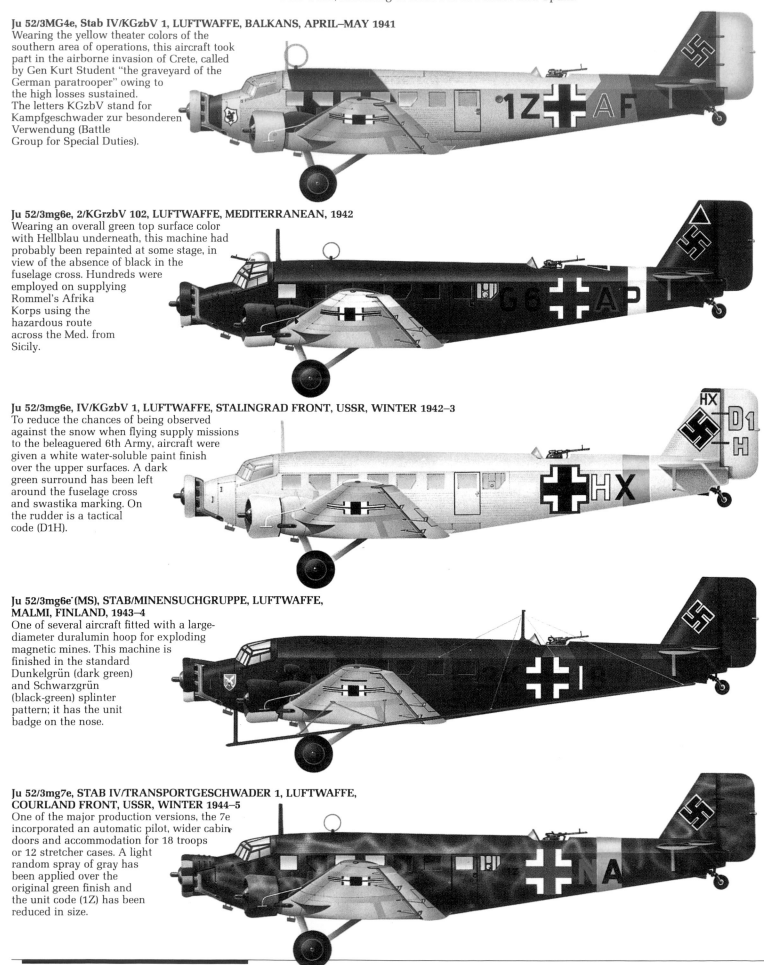

Ju 52/3MG4e, Stab IV/KGzbV 1, LUFTWAFFE, BALKANS, APRIL–MAY 1941
Wearing the yellow theater colors of the southern area of operations, this aircraft took part in the airborne invasion of Crete, called by Gen Kurt Student "the graveyard of the German paratrooper" owing to the high losses sustained. The letters KGzbV stand for Kampfgeschwader zur besonderen Verwendung (Battle Group for Special Duties).

Ju 52/3mg6e, 2/KGrzbV 102, LUFTWAFFE, MEDITERRANEAN, 1942
Wearing an overall green top surface color with Hellblau underneath, this machine had probably been repainted at some stage, in view of the absence of black in the fuselage cross. Hundreds were employed on supplying Rommel's Afrika Korps using the hazardous route across the Med. from Sicily.

Ju 52/3mg6e, IV/KGzbV 1, LUFTWAFFE, STALINGRAD FRONT, USSR, WINTER 1942–3
To reduce the chances of being observed against the snow when flying supply missions to the beleaguered 6th Army, aircraft were given a white water-soluble paint finish over the upper surfaces. A dark green surround has been left around the fuselage cross and swastika marking. On the rudder is a tactical code (D1H).

Ju 52/3mg6e (MS), STAB/MINENSUCHGRUPPE, LUFTWAFFE, MALMI, FINLAND, 1943–4
One of several aircraft fitted with a large-diameter duralumin hoop for exploding magnetic mines. This machine is finished in the standard Dunkelgrün (dark green) and Schwarzgrün (black-green) splinter pattern; it has the unit badge on the nose.

Ju 52/3mg7e, STAB IV/TRANSPORTGESCHWADER 1, LUFTWAFFE, COURLAND FRONT, USSR, WINTER 1944–5
One of the major production versions, the 7e incorporated an automatic pilot, wider cabin doors and accommodation for 18 troops or 12 stretcher cases. A light random spray of gray has been applied over the original green finish and the unit code (1Z) has been reduced in size.

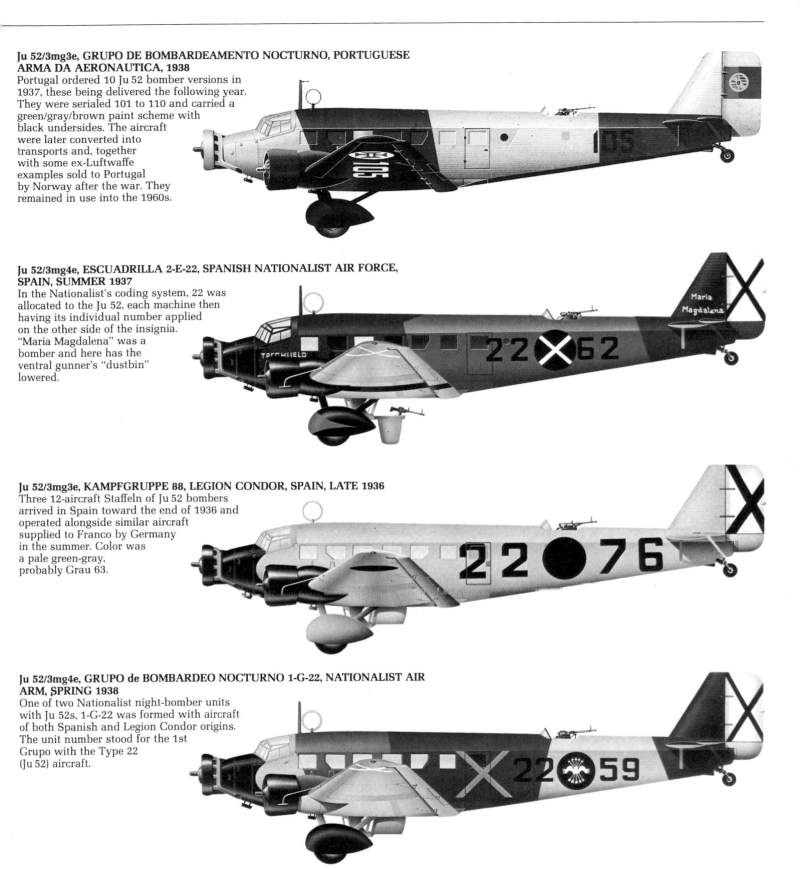

Ju 52/3mg3e, GRUPO DE BOMBARDEAMENTO NOCTURNO, PORTUGUESE ARMA DA AERONAUTICA, 1938

Portugal ordered 10 Ju 52 bomber versions in 1937, these being delivered the following year. They were serialed 101 to 110 and carried a green/gray/brown paint scheme with black undersides. The aircraft were later converted into transports and, together with some ex-Luftwaffe examples sold to Portugal by Norway after the war. They remained in use into the 1960s.

Ju 52/3mg4e, ESCUADRILLA 2-E-22, SPANISH NATIONALIST AIR FORCE, SPAIN, SUMMER 1937

In the Nationalist's coding system, 22 was allocated to the Ju 52, each machine then having its individual number applied on the other side of the insignia. "Maria Magdalena" was a bomber and here has the ventral gunner's "dustbin" lowered.

Ju 52/3mg3e, KAMPFGRUPPE 88, LEGION CONDOR, SPAIN, LATE 1936

Three 12-aircraft Staffeln of Ju 52 bombers arrived in Spain toward the end of 1936 and operated alongside similar aircraft supplied to Franco by Germany in the summer. Color was a pale green-gray, probably Grau 63.

Ju 52/3mg4e, GRUPO de BOMBARDEO NOCTURNO 1-G-22, NATIONALIST AIR ARM, SPRING 1938

One of two Nationalist night-bomber units with Ju 52s, 1-G-22 was formed with aircraft of both Spanish and Legion Condor origins. The unit number stood for the 1st Grupo with the Type 22 (Ju 52) aircraft.

Ju 52/3mg4e, GRUPO DE BOMBARDEO NOCTURNO 2-G-22, NATIONALIST AIR ARM, SPRING 1938

An aircraft of the other night-bomber unit, but with a different segmented camouflage and the dark blue cross moved farther along the fuselage. Note the tail skid on this machine compared with the tailwheel on the 1-G-22 aircraft.

FAIREY SWORDFISH

Unlike other aircraft that were clearly obsolete at the beginning of World War II, the Swordfish was not withdrawn from service (it probably would have been had there been a replacement). As it turned out, this venerable biplane torpedo-bomber earned glory for itself and the Royal Navy, winning battle honors which eluded more modern carrier-based aircraft. Among its most famous was the crippling of the Italian Fleet at Taranto, the torpedoing of the *Bismarck*, and the attacks on the German battleships engaged in the "Channel Dash" in February 1942. Production totaled 2391.

Mk I, 823 SQUADRON, FLEET AIR ARM, HMS *GLORIOUS*, 1936
Developed initially from the TSR I (Torpedo-Spotter-Reconnaissance) and the modified TSR II which flew in April 1934, the Swordfish entered service in July 1936; by 1939 13 squadrons were equipped. Early aircraft were finished in silver overall with a color/number code on the fuselage side (yellow for *Glorious*, 804 call sign code number). Black fuselage decking and fin.

Mk I, 821 SQUADRON, FLEET AIR ARM, HMS *ARK ROYAL*, 1940
Early war markings on a carrier-based aircraft with Sky color undersides extending up to a line along the fuselage to meet the temperate gray/green pattern which was painted on the top surfaces. Eight inch serial and large figure/letter code indicate a carrier-based aircraft.

Mk I, 820 SQUADRON, FLEET AIR ARM, HMS *ARK ROYAL*, 1939
An all-silver finished aircraft with revised markings after the style shown on the aircraft at the top of the page. Colored bands indicated the carrier, in this case blue-red-blue for *Ark Royal* and a letter/number/letter (A4G) identifying the carrier, the aircraft's role (torpedo-spotter) and the individual aircraft within its squadron.

Mk I, 824 SQUADRON, FLEET AIR ARM, HMS *EAGLE*, 1940.
An example of how aircraft with the same colors could differ in terms of the area camouflaged and the position of the markings. Compare this machine with 5L in View No. 2. About the only item to maintain continuity is the serial number on the rear fuselage.

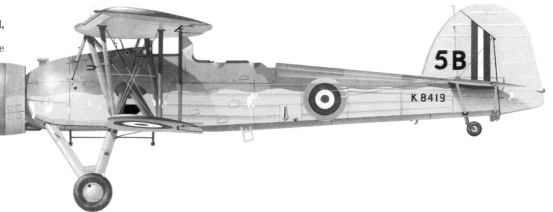

Mk I, CATAPULT FLIGHT, ROYAL NAVY, HMS *MALAYA*, 1940
About 70 floatplane versions were built and operated from the battleships and cruisers of the Home and Mediterranean fleets. This aircraft incorporates the December 1940 order to apply "ROYAL NAVY" in 4in high letters on the rear fuselage above the 4in high serial V4367.

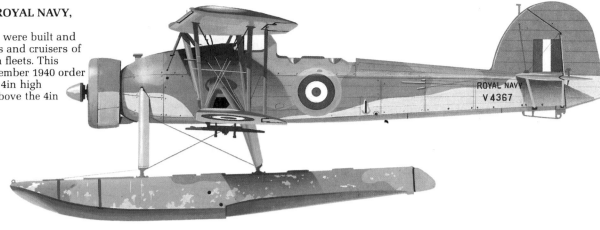

Mk II, 811 SQUADRON, FLEET AIR ARM, HMS *BITER*, LATE 1944
Dark Slate Gray and Dark Sea Gray with White undersurfaces extend over almost the whole fuselage. D-Day invasion stripes were applied to top and bottom of both wings and around the rear fuselage. Rocket-firing rails were fitted under lower wing for the anti-shipping/submarine role. Production of the Mk II totaled 1080 and all front-line Swordfish units flew this version from mid-1943 to June 1944.

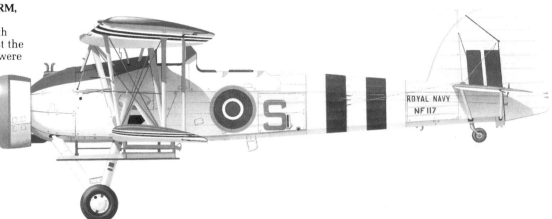

Mk III, 119 SQUADRON, RAF COASTAL COMMAND, KNOKKE-LE-ZOUTE, BELGIUM, 1945
In a sinister all-black finish, these Swordfish were assigned anti-E-boat and anti-midget submarine patrols along the supply lines between the UK and Belgian ports. They were fitted with ASV Mk X radar in place of the torpedo crutches and had aerials attached to the wing struts. This red-coded example (NF410) has a Donald Duck emblem on the fuselage.

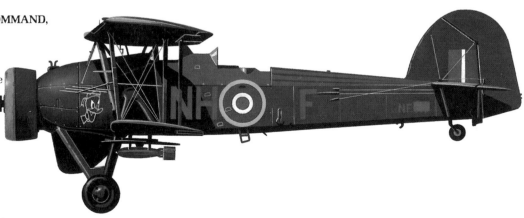

Mk II, 1 NAVAL AIR GUNNERY SCHOOL, CANADA, 1944
Sometimes erroneously referred to as a Mk IV, this is in fact a winterized Mk II fitted with a fully enclosed cockpit. The individual letter H in black on a yellow band ensured higher visibility.

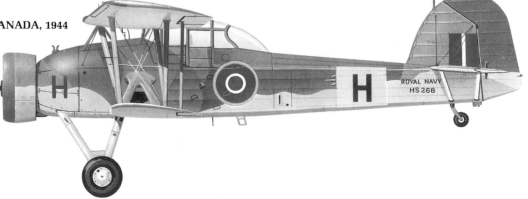

CURTISS HELLDIVER

The last of the US Navy's combat biplanes, the Helldiver was originally a monoplane with a parasol-wing, but the Navy's need for a carrier-based dive-bomber required the strength of a biplane layout. A year and a half after the prototype's first flight, deliveries began to Squadron VS-5 in July 1937. The first series model was the SBC-3, followed by the re-engined -4. Obsolete at the start of the war, the Helldiver remained well out of the way of the formidable Axis fighters, even though one Marine unit retained the type until 1943.

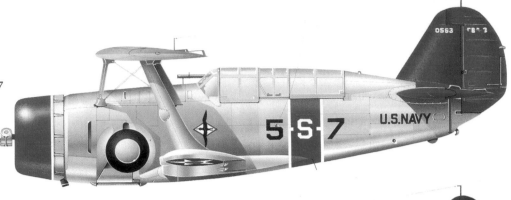

SBC-3, VS-5, US NAVY, USS _YORKTOWN_, 1937
These initial aircraft were delivered and operated in natural metal finish, apart from the chrome yellow on the upper wing surface and the red tail, the latter signifying the _Yorktown_. The blue areas denoted the 3rd section leader. Scouting Five's "Man O'War Bird" emblem is seen below the cockpit.

SBC-4 (CLEVELAND 1), RAF LITTLE RISSINGTON, UK, SEPTEMBER 1940
Five Helldivers found their way to the UK as a residue of 50 handed over to France by the USN. Sprayed Dark Green, Dark Earth with Sky undersides, the aircraft were used as ground instructional airframes.

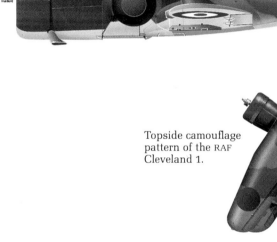

Topside camouflage pattern of the RAF Cleveland 1.

SBC-4, AERONAVALE, MARTINIQUE, 1940–1
Fifty of these obsolete carrier biplane bombers had been ordered by the French Navy, most ending up on Martinique. Camouflage was Green and Gray with Sky Blue undersides.

Plan view of the French Helldiver camouflage pattern.

GLOSTER GLADIATOR

Famous as the last of the RAF's biplane fighters, the Gladiator was the final refinement of the earlier Gauntlet and succeeded it in squadron service. Obsolete at the outbreak of World War II, the Gladiator fought with distinction and success against superior odds during the Norwegian campaign in 1940 and held its own against the Italian Regia Aeronautica in the Western Desert, Malta and Greece. Retired from RAF front-line use at the end of 1941, the type was retained as a fighter-reconnaissance aircraft by the Finnish Air Force, being finally withdrawn only in 1945.

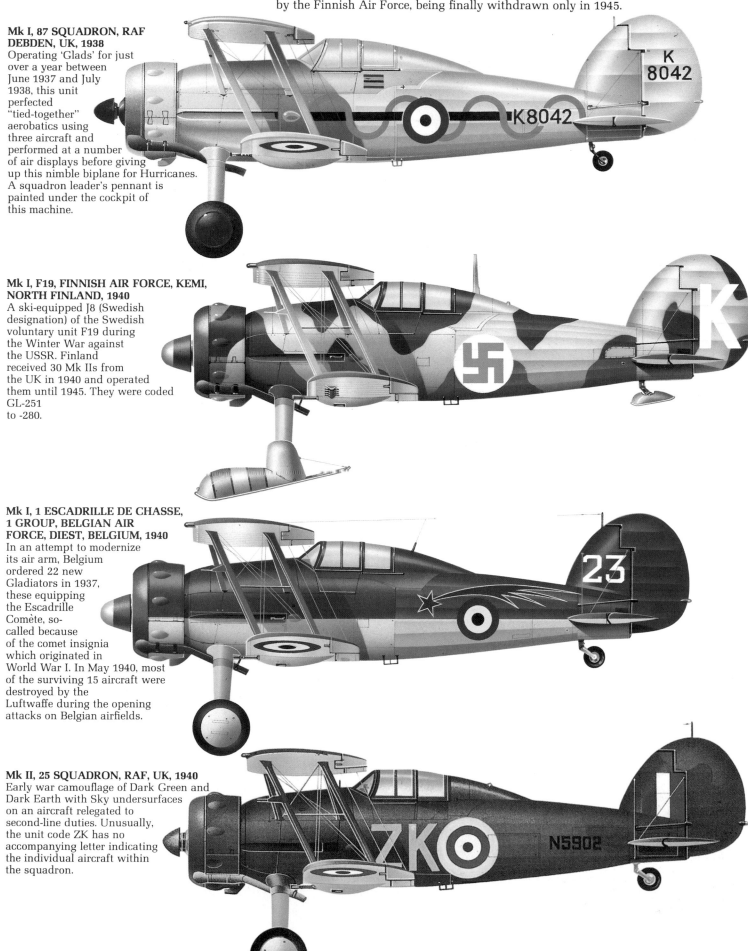

Mk I, 87 SQUADRON, RAF DEBDEN, UK, 1938
Operating 'Glads' for just over a year between June 1937 and July 1938, this unit perfected "tied-together" aerobatics using three aircraft and performed at a number of air displays before giving up this nimble biplane for Hurricanes. A squadron leader's pennant is painted under the cockpit of this machine.

Mk I, F19, FINNISH AIR FORCE, KEMI, NORTH FINLAND, 1940
A ski-equipped J8 (Swedish designation) of the Swedish voluntary unit F19 during the Winter War against the USSR. Finland received 30 Mk IIs from the UK in 1940 and operated them until 1945. They were coded GL-251 to -280.

Mk I, 1 ESCADRILLE DE CHASSE, 1 GROUP, BELGIAN AIR FORCE, DIEST, BELGIUM, 1940
In an attempt to modernize its air arm, Belgium ordered 22 new Gladiators in 1937, these equipping the Escadrille Comète, so-called because of the comet insignia which originated in World War I. In May 1940, most of the surviving 15 aircraft were destroyed by the Luftwaffe during the opening attacks on Belgian airfields.

Mk II, 25 SQUADRON, RAF, UK, 1940
Early war camouflage of Dark Green and Dark Earth with Sky undersurfaces on an aircraft relegated to second-line duties. Unusually, the unit code ZK has no accompanying letter indicating the individual aircraft within the squadron.

HAWKER HURRICANE

Rugged durability gave the Hurricane single-seat fighter an advantage over its main opponents during World War II and, although its top speed was less than that of the German Messerschmitt Bf 109, it could absorb considerable battle damage and still survive to return to the fray. The Hurricane fought in all war theaters, and at sea as the Sea Hurricane. It could carry bombs, rockets, tank-busting cannon and machine-guns. Including Canadian production, 14,231 were built.

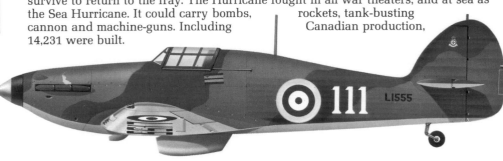

Mk I, 111 SQUADRON, RAF NORTHOLT, UK, 1938
This was Sqn Ldr J. Gillan's aircraft with rank pennant under cockpit, 8in-high unit crest on fin, 35in-diameter fuselage roundel and 6-in high serial number. The white 111 on the fuselage is of an unusual serif letter style.

Mk I, 56 SQUADRON, RAF NORTH WEALD, UK, 1939
The code letters in Medium Sea Gray, approximately 36in high, were changed to "US" from September 1939. There is no rudder flash.

Mk I, 85 SQUADRON, RAF DEBDEN, UK, 1940
This has the Battle of Britain finish, with Sky undersides and the unit badge under the cockpit. Note the rudder flash size and position.

Mk IIC, 1 SQUADRON, RAF TANGMERE, UK, 1942
This has standard day-fighter colors, with Sky spinner and a yellow wing leading edge. The black serial has been applied over the rear identification band.

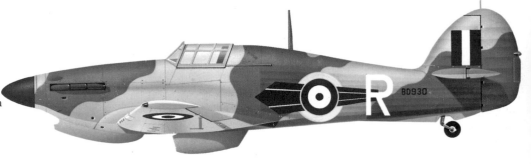

Mk IIB, 73 SQUADRON, RAF WESTERN DESERT, NORTH AFRICA, 1942
This was one of the very few units to display squadron insignia during wartime in the form of a prominent 'arrowhead' incorporated into the fuselage roundel.

Mk IC, No 2 & 3 COMMUNICATIONS FLIGHTS, ROYAL AUSTRALIAN AIR FORCE, 1944
This was the sole Australian example to survive the fall of Singapore. It retains the RAF serial number but in stenciled form.

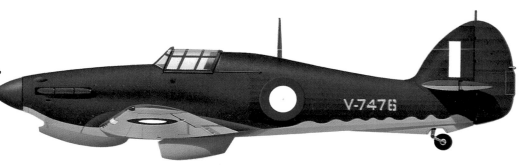

Mk IIC, INDIAN AIR FORCE, 1944
It is marked with the small SEAC (South East Asia Command) fuselage roundel and white identification bands on wings and tail.

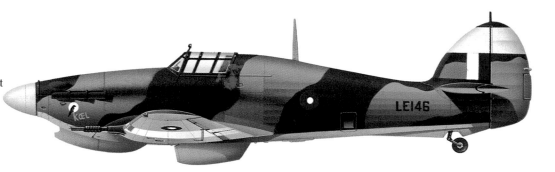

Mk IV 351 (YUGOSLAV) SQUADRON, PRKOS, YUGOSLAVIA, 1945
This was the second Yugoslav squadron formed within the RAF. The Red Star was marked on all roundels and on the fin stripes.

Mk I (?), LUFTWAFFE, MAGDEBURG, GERMANY, 1942
It carried the Luftwaffe test codes (DF-GC) and the standard trials yellow color on the undersides. It was possibly captured in France in 1940.

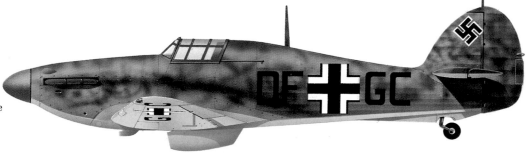

SEA HURRICANE (HURRICANE X), 440 SQUADRON, ROYAL CANADIAN AIR FORCE, 1942
Although built in Canada for the Royal Navy and finished in these colors, this aircraft was retained for use in Canada.

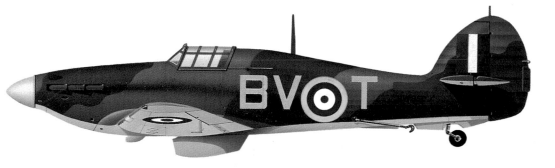

FOCKE-WULF Fw 200

Labeled the 'scourge of the Atlantic' by Winston Churchill, the German Condors posed a menace to the UK out of all proportion to their numbers. Originally designed as a 26-passenger airliner and making its first flight in July 1937, the Condor was developed into a long-range commerce raider and reconnaissance aircraft, entering service in the summer of 1940. The advent of longer-range Coastal Command aircraft and CAM (catapult-armed merchantman) fighters finally eliminated their threat and survivors of the 276 built reverted to a transport role.

Fw 200V1, PROTOTYPE, FOCKE-WULF GmbH, JULY 1937
Finished in the company colors with the National Socialist Swastika marking across the fin and rudder, the first Condor made an impressive flight from Berlin to New York on 10 August 1938, prompting Danish Airlines (DDL) to order two aircraft.

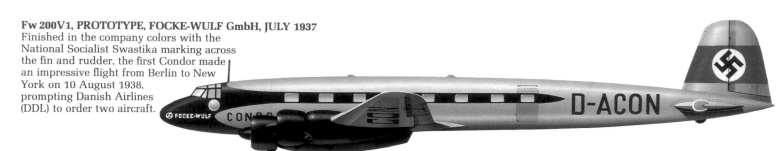

Fw 200V3, "IMMELMANN III", REGIERUNGSSTAFFEL, BERLIN, GERMANY, 1940
Hitler's personal transport received the standard bomber camouflage finish of Schwarzgrün and Dunkelgrün with Hellblau undersides. Hitler's compartment featured a large armored seat placed over an escape hatch and incorporated a parachute pack. The 26-00 code was previously used on the Führer's Ju 52s.

Fw 200A, DET DANSKE LUFTFARTSELSKAB (DDL), DENMARK, 1939
Two aircraft operated with DDL, *Dania* (OY-DAM) and *Jutlandia* (OY-DEM), both marked with the country name and the Danish flag on the fin and wings during the final months of peace. When Denmark was invaded, *Dania* flew to the UK and was impressed as G-AGAY, later receiving the RAF serial DX177.

Fw 200C-0, 1/KG 40, LUFTWAFFE, STALINGRAD, USSR, JANUARY 1943
Supply flights to the beleaguered 6th Army found large numbers of aircraft impressed into the operation, including this armed transport version which received a coat of "winter white" over the dark green upper surfaces. It was normally attached to the Reich Air Ministry Pool based at Berlin-Staaken.

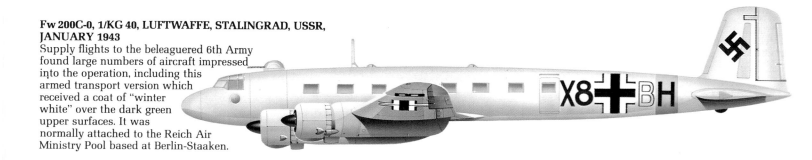

Fw 200C-8, III/KG 40, LUFTWAFFE, BORDEAUX-MARIGNAC, FRANCE, 1944
The last production variant was equipped with FuG 200 Hohentwiel search radar in the nose and a Henschel Hs293 anti-ship missile under each wing. Few successes were achieved by this combination and the type reverted to its original role – that of transportation.

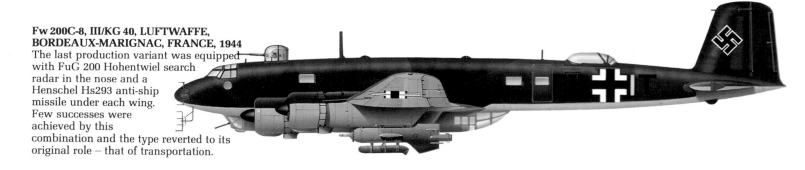

MORANE-SAULNIER M.S.406

Derived from a 1934 prototype, the M.S.406 was outclassed by the Luftwaffe's Bf 109s at the beginning of World War II. Although sturdy and highly maneuverable, it was too slow, had poor armament (one 20mm cannon and two 7.5mm machine guns) and an inferior engine (860hp Hispano-Suiza). It was, however, available, and 573 equipped 12 French Groupes de Chasse in September 1939. Finland used the type from 1940 to 1952; a development of the earlier M.S.405 gave rise to the Swiss D-3800 series.

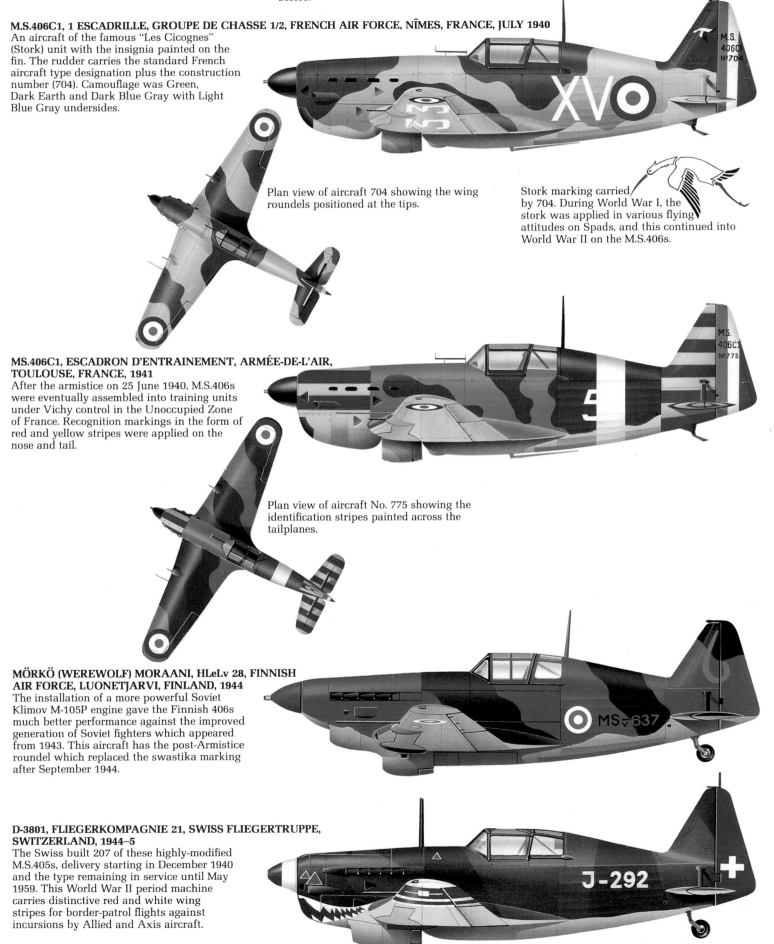

M.S.406C1, 1 ESCADRILLE, GROUPE DE CHASSE 1/2, FRENCH AIR FORCE, NÎMES, FRANCE, JULY 1940
An aircraft of the famous "Les Cicognes" (Stork) unit with the insignia painted on the fin. The rudder carries the standard French aircraft type designation plus the construction number (704). Camouflage was Green, Dark Earth and Dark Blue Gray with Light Blue Gray undersides.

Plan view of aircraft 704 showing the wing roundels positioned at the tips.

Stork marking carried by 704. During World War I, the stork was applied in various flying attitudes on Spads, and this continued into World War II on the M.S.406s.

MS.406C1, ESCADRON D'ENTRAINEMENT, ARMÉE-DE-L'AIR, TOULOUSE, FRANCE, 1941
After the armistice on 25 June 1940, M.S.406s were eventually assembled into training units under Vichy control in the Unoccupied Zone of France. Recognition markings in the form of red and yellow stripes were applied on the nose and tail.

Plan view of aircraft No. 775 showing the identification stripes painted across the tailplanes.

MÖRKÖ (WEREWOLF) MORAANI, HLeLv 28, FINNISH AIR FORCE, LUONETJARVI, FINLAND, 1944
The installation of a more powerful Soviet Klimov M-105P engine gave the Finnish 406s much better performance against the improved generation of Soviet fighters which appeared from 1943. This aircraft has the post-Armistice roundel which replaced the swastika marking after September 1944.

D-3801, FLIEGERKOMPAGNIE 21, SWISS FLIEGERTRUPPE, SWITZERLAND, 1944–5
The Swiss built 207 of these highly-modified M.S.405s, delivery starting in December 1940 and the type remaining in service until May 1959. This World War II period machine carries distinctive red and white wing stripes for border-patrol flights against incursions by Allied and Axis aircraft.

SUPERMARINE SPITFIRE

The best-known British fighter aircraft of all, the Spitfire was designed by R. J. Mitchell and the prototype made its first flight on 5 March 1936. Two years later, the first RAF squadron became operational (No 19 at Duxford). The Spitfire was developed through 24 marks, fought on every war front and finally retired from front-line service on 1 April 1954. A carrier-based version was called Seafire and this was developed through eight marks. Production was 20,351 plus 2556 Seafires.

Mk I, 19 SQUADRON, RAF DUXFORD, UK, OCTOBER 1938
One of the first RAF Spitfires delivered, carrying the soon-to-be-deleted unit number on the fin. The camouflage is Dark Green, Dark Earth disruptive pattern. The plane displays 56in upper-surface wing roundels, 35in Type A1 fuselage roundels and 50in underwing roundels.

Mk Vb, 133 "EAGLE" SQUADRON, RAF BIGGIN HILL, UK, MAY 1942
This US-manned squadron was operational on fighter sweeps and bomber escort over northern France and the Low Countries. The CO's aircraft has its rank badge under nose and on the mug, which has "Mild & Bitter" underneath. The unit was the third Eagle squadron of American volunteers formed within Fighter Command.

Mk IIb, 306 (POLISH) SQUADRON, RAF NORTHOLT, UK, AUGUST 1941
This was the month Fighter Command changed its colors from Dark Green, Dark Earth to Dark Green, Ocean Gray to reflect offensive operations which were getting underway at that time. Medium Sea Gray is now painted on the undersides. The badge on the nose is of the Polish Torunski unit.

Mk IIa, 41 SQUADRON, RAF HORNCHURCH, UK, DECEMBER 1941
A presentation aircraft from the Observer Corps and flown by Sqn Ldr D. O. Finlay, the unit's commanding officer. The spinner and fuselage band is in Sky, ordered to be applied in November 1940.

Mk Vb, 40 SQUADRON, SOUTH AFRICAN AIR FORCE, ITALY, AUGUST 1943
Dark Earth and Middle Stone with Azure Blue undersides was a scheme found to be ideal in the Middle East. This machine has an Aboukir tropical filter under the nose and a camera port in the rear fuselage.

Mk Vc, 308TH FIGHTER SQUADRON, 31st FG, USAAF, TUNISIA, 1943
Another variation of the ME scheme on an aircraft deployed for the Torch landings in North Africa. Note the different type of tropical sand filter under the nose compared with the previous machine.

Mk IX, 402 SQUADRON, ROYAL CANADIAN AIR FORCE, KENLEY, UK, 1943
Fighter Command's day fighter scheme for the mid-war years. For quick identification in combat, the Sky spinner and fuselage band were supplemented by yellow leading edges to the wings. Unit badge under cockpit.

Mk Vc, USS 'WASP', RAF, MALTA, MAY 1942
Equipped with a 90 gal slipper type drop-tank under the fuselage and a tropical filter under the engine, this aircraft was one of 61 Spitfires flown off Wasp and HMS Eagle to reinforce the defenses of Malta against increasing attacks by Axis bombers.

Mk 22, 603 (CITY OF EDINBURGH) SQUADRON, R AUX AF, TURNHOUSE, UK, 1950
Post-war the RAF promulgated an order for a return to the silver finish of pre-1939. This unit was initially allocated RAF codes, but these were later changed to XT when the unit transferred from Reserve status to Fighter Command; "Q" is the individual aircraft letter.

Mk 22, 607 (COUNTY OF DURHAM) SQUADRON, R AUX AF, OUSTON, UK, 1948
Retaining its wartime camouflage, this Spitfire carries the unit badge on the cowling, RAN codes denoting 607 Sqn and race numbers for participation in the Cooper Trophy race of 1948.

MESSERSCHMITT Bf 110

Seen by the Luftwaffe as the long-range element of its fighter arm, the elegant twin-engined Bf 110 proved unable to hold its own when confronted by modern fast single-seaters. Thus during the Battle of Britain, the Zerstörer (destroyer) units equipped with this type were badly mauled by the RAF's eight-gun fighters and required protection from the Bf 109s. However, it served with distinction in the night-fighter role and in a number of other tasks which better suited its performance. When production ended in March 1945, 6050 had been built.

Bf 110D-3, 1/NACHTJAGDGESCHWADER 3, LUFTWAFFE, CATANIA, SICILY, FEBRUARY 1941
This Mediterranean-based unit was formed from LG 1 and retained the L1 code on its black-painted night fighters. The unit emblem normally applied on the nose and obscured by the engine in this view consisted of an owl sitting on a moon.

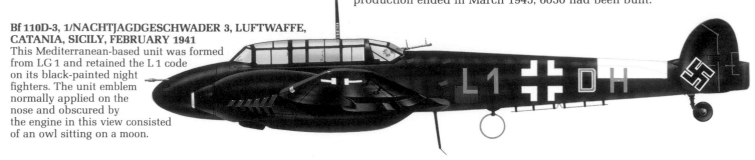

Bf 110C-4/B, 5/ZERSTÖRERGESCHWADER 1, LUFTWAFFE, CAUCASUS, USSR, 1942
Known as the Wespen (Wasp) Geschwader, the aircraft of this unit bore an elaborate wasp design on the nose and operated in the attack role against Russian targets. Other markings include the theater band around the fuselage and the aircraft's construction number just visible forward of the fin.

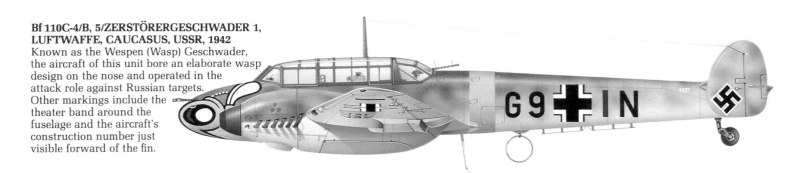

Bf 110E-1, OPERATIONAL CONVERSION UNIT, LUFTWAFFE, DĘBLIN-IRENA, POLAND, 1942
A large wolf's head painted on the nose and the unit code 4M have failed to identify the number of this OCU. The aircraft was a fighter-bomber version carrying standard Hellblau under-surface coloring with probably Schwarzgrün, Dunkelgrün over the top surfaces.

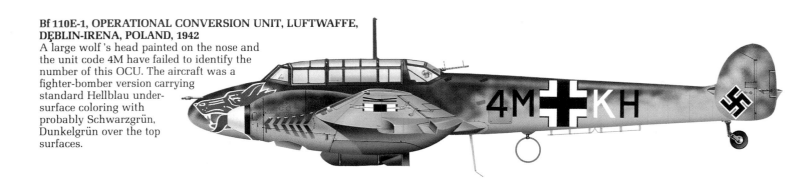

Bf 110 E-1/R4, 8./ZERSTÖRERGESCHWADER 26, LUFTWAFFE, BERCA, NORTH AFRICA, 1942
·Desert camouflage comprising Sandgelb (79) with a random spray of dark green over all upper and side surfaces. This was not an official scheme but one devised by the unit which best suited its type of low-level attack. The large cannon under the fuselage is a 37mm Flak gun for anti-tank use.

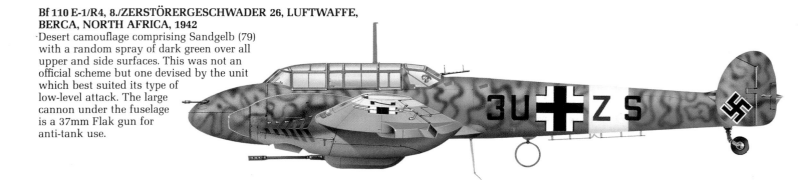

Bf 110G-2, 5./ZERSTÖRERGESCHWADER 76, LUFTWAFFE, WERTHEIM, GERMANY, 1943
Day fighter camouflage on a home defense aircraft employed to attack the heavy daylight raids by the USAAF B-17s and B-24s. Projecting from the nose are two 30mm cannon and under the wings are two unguided-rocket launchers. The black and white spiral spinner marking was intended to distract enemy gunners from their aim, but its effectiveness is unrecorded.

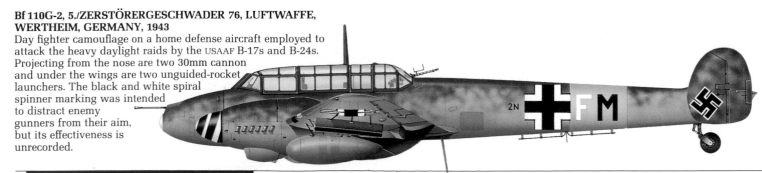

Bf 110C-4, 2./ZERSTORERGESCHWADER 26, LUFTWAFFE, ARGOS, GREECE, MAY 1941
The German assault on Crete involved attack operations against Allied positions by aircraft of this unit. Yellow engine cowlings were a visual identification marking.

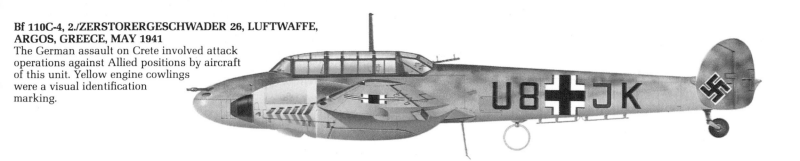

Bf 110C-2, STAB I/ZG 2, LUFTWAFFE, DARMSTADT-GRIESHEIM, GERMANY, APRIL 1940
Shown just before the May 1940 assault on France, this 'Zerstorer' has the early style fuselage cross over the dark green paint scheme. Two 'kill' markings appear on the fin and on the nose is the unit's blue lightning flash outlined in white.

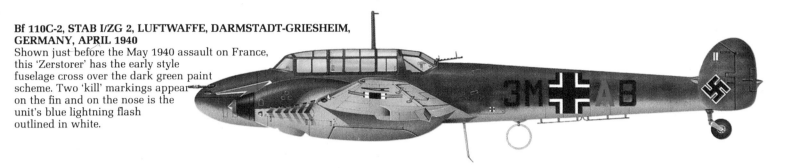

Bf 110D-3, 4./ZERSTORERGESCHWADER 76, LUFTWAFFE, IRAQ, MAY 1941
In support of the Iraqi uprising against the British, Germany sent aircraft like this example from ZG 76. The Iraqi national marking was applied over the fuselage code M8 + GM although the unit's shark-mouth insignia was retained.

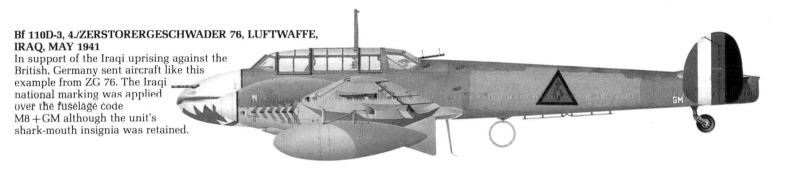

Bf 110G-4, 7./NACHTJAGDGESCHWADER 4, LUFTWAFFE, NORTH-WEST GERMANY, 1943–4
Night-fighter camouflage on an SN-2 radar-equipped aircraft. Note the flame-damping pipes on the engine exhausts.

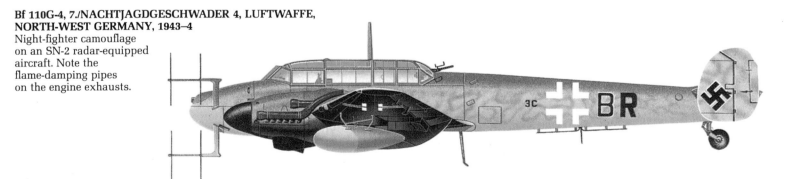

Bf 110G-2, 12./NJG 3, LUFTWAFFE, STAVANGER, NORWAY, EARLY 1945
No radar or matt black undersurfaces probably indicates a replacement aircraft rushed into service for free-ranging night fighting use.

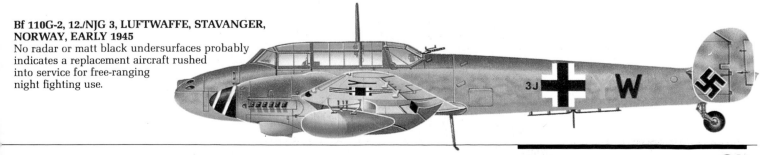

LOCKHEED HUDSON

Designed to an RAF Coastal Command requirement for a medium-range reconnaissance-bomber, Lockheed produced the Hudson from its Super-Electra airliner, adding a bomb-bay, gun turret, forward-firing guns in the nose and other military equipment. First flight was 10 December 1938 and the type entered RAF service with 224 Sqn at Gosport in mid 1939. Eight marks of Hudson were produced and 2584 were built. Hudsons also served with the RAAF, RNZAF and the US Navy (PBO-1) and USAAF (A-28, A-29, AT-18).

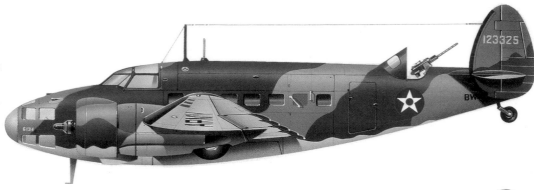

A-29, US ARMY AIR CORPS, EARLY 1942
Built for the RAF as a Hudson Mk IIIA but repossessed by USAAC for ASW patrols. British Dark Green, Dark Earth camouflage was retained. The Red in the star was removed from May 1942 after the US entered World War II. The RAF black serial was retained under the tail.

Mk V, 48 SQUADRON, RAF STORNOWAY, SCOTLAND, 1941
This Temperate Sea Scheme was ordered for all Hudsons and other RAF Coastal Command landplanes. Night (matt Black) undersides were carried for nocturnal bombing missions. Note the earlier roundels and rudder stripes compared with these on OS-T below.

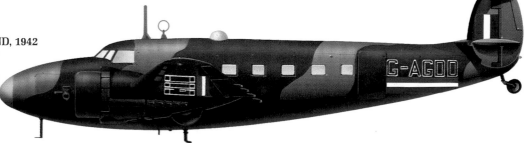

Mk VI, RAF, 1943
An uncoded Hudson armed with underwing rockets. This weapon was used successfully by aircraft of 608 Sqn against U-boats in the Mediterranean.

LODESTAR, BOAC, LEUCHARS, SCOTLAND, 1942
This civilian aircraft named *Loch Losna* was camouflaged Dark Green, Dark Earth and Night (Black) for courier service between the UK and Sweden. Registration G-A was painted above port wing and GDD above the starboard. Like the registration on the fuselage, both were underlined.

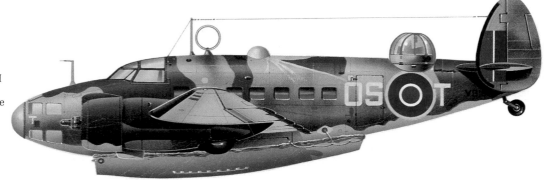

Mk III, 279 SQUADRON, RAF BIRCHAM NEWTON, UK, 1942
These aircraft were used for air-sea rescue duties and were fitted with an airborne lifeboat which could be dropped by parachute.

DOUGLAS A-20 BOSTON

The prototype of the DB-7 twin-engined attack bomber flew on 17 August 1939, with France as the type's first overseas customer. Neat in appearance with a then unusual tricycle undercarriage, the DB-7 had a respectable top speed of 314mph. Only a few were delivered to France before the collapse in 1940, the rest being assigned to the RAF as the Boston. For the night-intruder and fighter role, the aircraft was called Havoc, a name also adopted by the USAAF for its A-20 series. Production totaled 7385.

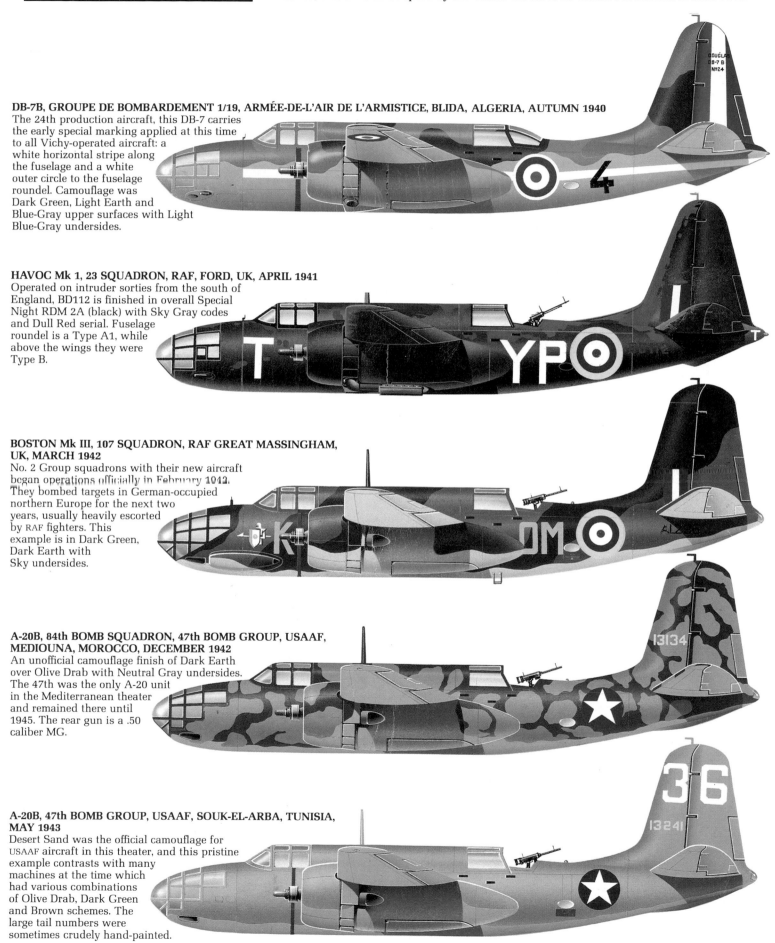

DB-7B, GROUPE DE BOMBARDEMENT 1/19, ARMÉE-DE-L'AIR DE L'ARMISTICE, BLIDA, ALGERIA, AUTUMN 1940
The 24th production aircraft, this DB-7 carries the early special marking applied at this time to all Vichy-operated aircraft: a white horizontal stripe along the fuselage and a white outer circle to the fuselage roundel. Camouflage was Dark Green, Light Earth and Blue-Gray upper surfaces with Light Blue-Gray undersides.

HAVOC Mk 1, 23 SQUADRON, RAF, FORD, UK, APRIL 1941
Operated on intruder sorties from the south of England, BD112 is finished in overall Special Night RDM 2A (black) with Sky Gray codes and Dull Red serial. Fuselage roundel is a Type A1, while above the wings they were Type B.

BOSTON Mk III, 107 SQUADRON, RAF GREAT MASSINGHAM, UK, MARCH 1942
No. 2 Group squadrons with their new aircraft began operations officially in February 1942. They bombed targets in German-occupied northern Europe for the next two years, usually heavily escorted by RAF fighters. This example is in Dark Green, Dark Earth with Sky undersides.

A-20B, 84th BOMB SQUADRON, 47th BOMB GROUP, USAAF, MEDIOUNA, MOROCCO, DECEMBER 1942
An unofficial camouflage finish of Dark Earth over Olive Drab with Neutral Gray undersides. The 47th was the only A-20 unit in the Mediterranean theater and remained there until 1945. The rear gun is a .50 caliber MG.

A-20B, 47th BOMB GROUP, USAAF, SOUK-EL-ARBA, TUNISIA, MAY 1943
Desert Sand was the official camouflage for USAAF aircraft in this theater, and this pristine example contrasts with many machines at the time which had various combinations of Olive Drab, Dark Green and Brown schemes. The large tail numbers were sometimes crudely hand-painted.

PBY CATALINA

Patrol-bomber squadrons of the US Navy introduced the twin-engined PBY-1 (later named Catalina by the RAF) into service in 1936. Long endurance was the main requirement which led to the design of this fine flying-boat and it served reliably throughout WWII in almost every theater. The main production versions were the PBY-5, -5A and -6, some being amphibious, and when production finally ended 2550 had been built in the USA, a further 731 in Canada (as the Canso) and an unknown quantity in the USSR as the GST.

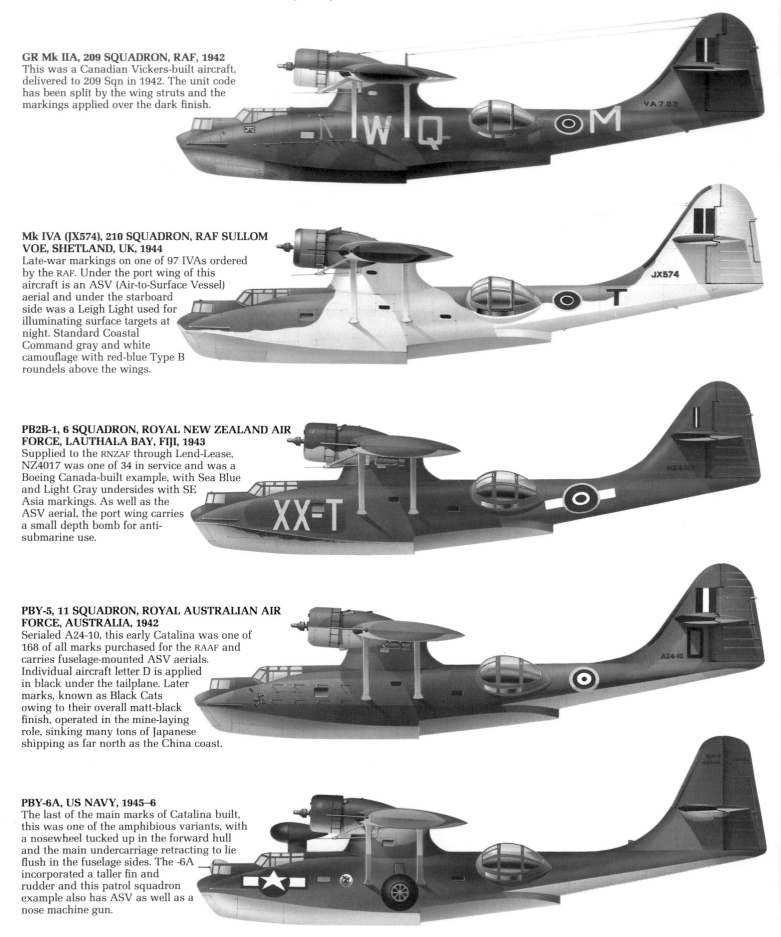

GR Mk IIA, 209 SQUADRON, RAF, 1942
This was a Canadian Vickers-built aircraft, delivered to 209 Sqn in 1942. The unit code has been split by the wing struts and the markings applied over the dark finish.

Mk IVA (JX574), 210 SQUADRON, RAF SULLOM VOE, SHETLAND, UK, 1944
Late-war markings on one of 97 IVAs ordered by the RAF. Under the port wing of this aircraft is an ASV (Air-to-Surface Vessel) aerial and under the starboard side was a Leigh Light used for illuminating surface targets at night. Standard Coastal Command gray and white camouflage with red-blue Type B roundels above the wings.

PB2B-1, 6 SQUADRON, ROYAL NEW ZEALAND AIR FORCE, LAUTHALA BAY, FIJI, 1943
Supplied to the RNZAF through Lend-Lease, NZ4017 was one of 34 in service and was a Boeing Canada-built example, with Sea Blue and Light Gray undersides with SE Asia markings. As well as the ASV aerial, the port wing carries a small depth bomb for anti-submarine use.

PBY-5, 11 SQUADRON, ROYAL AUSTRALIAN AIR FORCE, AUSTRALIA, 1942
Serialed A24-10, this early Catalina was one of 168 of all marks purchased for the RAAF and carries fuselage-mounted ASV aerials. Individual aircraft letter D is applied in black under the tailplane. Later marks, known as Black Cats owing to their overall matt-black finish, operated in the mine-laying role, sinking many tons of Japanese shipping as far north as the China coast.

PBY-6A, US NAVY, 1945–6
The last of the main marks of Catalina built, this was one of the amphibious variants, with a nosewheel tucked up in the forward hull and the main undercarriage retracting to lie flush in the fuselage sides. The -6A incorporated a taller fin and rudder and this patrol squadron example also has ASV as well as a nose machine gun.

BOULTON PAUL DEFIANT

The Defiant two-seat turreted fighter was conceived in 1935 and the prototype first flew on 11 August 1937. In May 1940 the RAF achieved some early successes with the type, but the Defiant's lack of forward armament proved to be a major weakness in daylight combat. High losses prompted its switch to the night fighting role, where it realized its true potential. The Defiant Mk I and II differed mainly in engine power, while the Mk III was used as a target tug. Production totaled 1060.

Mk I, 264 SQUADRON, RAF, KIRTON-IN-LINDSEY, UK, AUGUST 1940
Day fighter scheme of Dark Green and Dark Earth with Sky undersurfaces. This machine (N1535) was flown by the unit CO Sqn Ldr Philip Hunter who, with his gunner, Plt Off F.H. King, were killed on the 24th of August in an engagement with a Junkers Ju 88. Fuselage markings are 30in high, Medium Sea Gray Codes with 42in dia. roundels.

Mk II, 151 SQUADRON, RAF WITTERING, UK, 1942
Special Night Finish was the overall black color specified for application to RAF aircraft from the beginning of 1941. Codes were Dull Red and the Type C.1 roundel with 24in square fin flash date the scheme from mid 1942. Of the 14 squadrons with Defiant night fighters, four only were fully equipped with the Mk II version.

TT.II, TARGET FACILITIES UNIT, RAF, 1943
With the withdrawal of the Defiant from front-line units, the type was developed for secondary duties such as target towing. This example, operated by an unknown unit displays the standard black and yellow scheme for this role. The tropical filter under the nose indicates a Middle Eastern base.

TT.I, 286 SQUADRON, RAF, EXETER, UK, 1944
Built as a Mk III, this target tug is finished in a day fighter disruptive camouflage with yellow and black stripes on the undersides. The aircraft was operated over the Bristol Channel and the West Country.

JUNKERS
Ju 88

Probably the most versatile of all Germany's 1939–45 warplanes, the Ju 88 was developed through a series of different versions for tasks ranging from its originally designed role as a bomber, through ground-attack and night-fighting, to reconnaissance and high-speed courier aircraft. The Ju 88 V1 flew in December 1936 and production aircraft joined the first unit early in 1939. Nearly 15,000 had been built by the end of the war.

Ju 88A-5, III/LEHRGESCHWADER 1, X FLIEGERKORPS, LUFTWAFFE, SICILY, 1941
Standard finish for bombers of this period before improvization by the units took hold and more disruptive schemes appeared. LG 1 operated from Catania, mainly on anti-shipping operations around Malta between May 1941 and May 1942. White theater band around fuselage only.

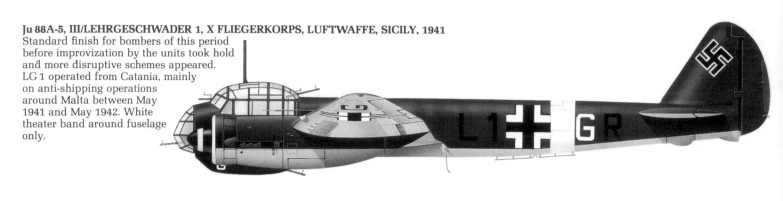

Ju 88A-10, II/LEHRGESCHWADER 1, LUFTWAFFE, CRETE, OCTOBER 1942
Hastily redeployed from North African operations to anti-shipping duties in Crete, this tropicalized version of the A-5 bomber retains its desert camouflage until an extended maintenance check is needed and a more appropriate color scheme can be applied.

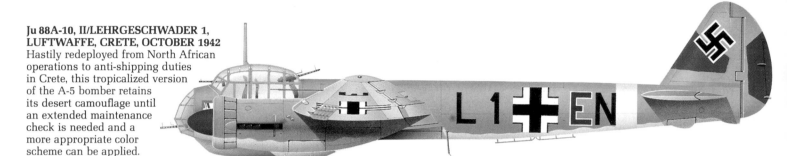

Ju 88A-4, III/KAMPFGESCHWADER 30, VII FLIEGERKORPS, LUFTWAFFE, MEDITERRANEAN, 1941
Known as the Adler Geschwader due to the unit's diving eagle badge applied to the nose, this aircraft has a confusing mixture of yellow Balkan markings on engines and rudder with white Mediterranean wing tips and fuselage band. The ship silhouettes on the fin indicate a number of successful anti-shipping missions.

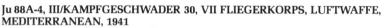

Ju 88 A-4, I/KAMPFGESCHWADER 54, LUFTWAFFE, ITALY, SEPTEMBER 1943
This unusual finish was dubbed Wellenmuster (wave pattern) camouflage and was sprayed over the existing color scheme. It was intended specifically for low-level over-water operations and this aircraft flew attacks against the Allied landings at Salerno.

Ju 88G-7a, IV/NACHTJAGDGESCHWADER 6, LUFTWAFFE, SCHWÄBISCH HALL, GERMANY, 1944–5
A light gray finish was adopted by Luftwaffe night fighters. Markings were usually black or dark gray and on this aircraft the tail has been painted to resemble that of the lower performance Ju 88C variant.

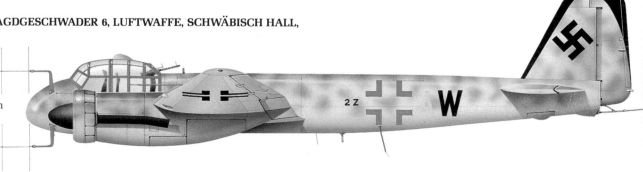

FIAT CR.42

At the end of the 1930s, while the main fighter design teams in the industrial countries were working on monoplane (and often stressed-skin) fighters, Italy's Fiat company was still perfecting the biplane and exporting the fruits of its designs. The CR.42 was the last of the breed and probably the best; but it was pitted against faster and more heavily armed opponents such as the Hurricane, against which it stood little chance of success. It was nevertheless ordered by Belgium, Hungary and Sweden as well as by the Regia Aeronautica. Production reached 1781 before the line closed in 1943.

CR.42, 97 SQUADRIGLIA, 9 GRUPPO, 4 STORMO, BENINA, LIBYA, 1940
Desert camouflage of Dark Green heavily mottled over the Yellow Ocher top-surface color. On the fin is the "Leg" emblem of the 97th and on the rear fuselage is the "Rampant Horse" of No 4 Stormo. This particular machine was abandoned to British troops during the Axis retreat.

CR.42, 83 SQUADRIGLIA, 18 GRUPPO, 3 STORMO, LIBYA, EARLY 1941
Dark Green and Red-Brown over the Yellow Ocher was another desert scheme used on Italian fighters, and it was retained by this unit during its brief series of operations in 1940 against the UK when based in Belgium. A Cmdte pennant is painted under the cockpit, and the dark stripe on the rear fuselage is an overpainted white marking used in Belgium.

CR.42, 377 SQUADRIGLIA AUTONOMA, REGIA AERONAUTICA, PALERMO, SICILY, MID 1942
Night-fighter operations to combat RAF raids were first attempted in Sicily in October 1941, but success was limited. Farther north, other aircraft achieved more against the attacks on Italy's industrial heartland. The unit insignia was an owl on a new moon.

CR.42, SEZIONE AUTONOMA COLLEGAMENTI, ROME, ITALY, WINTER 1945–6
At the time of the Italian armistice only 113 Falcos remained in use; this was one of the survivors that made it to the post-war air force. Some were used as training aircraft and painted silver.

CR.42, 1/4 SQUADRON, 1/11 GROUP, 1st FIGHTER REGIMENT, ROYAL HUNGARIAN AIR FORCE, BUDAPEST, HUNGARY, 1941
One of the 50 aircraft exported to Hungary and used in the Eastern Front War against the Russians, mainly in the ground-attack role. On the fuselage side is the Squadron's St George insignia.

MITSUBISHI ZERO-SEN

The most famous of all Japanese warplanes, the A6M series was the Navy's principal carrier-based fighter throughout the war. Under the Allied code-name system, the Reisen was called Zeke and when the clipped-wing A6M3 appeared it was allocated Hamp. However, to most people it was known as Zero. The prototype flew in April 1939, and early production aircraft first saw action in China. Four main variants were developed (A6M2, -3, -5 and -8) and by the end of the war some 10,450 had been built.

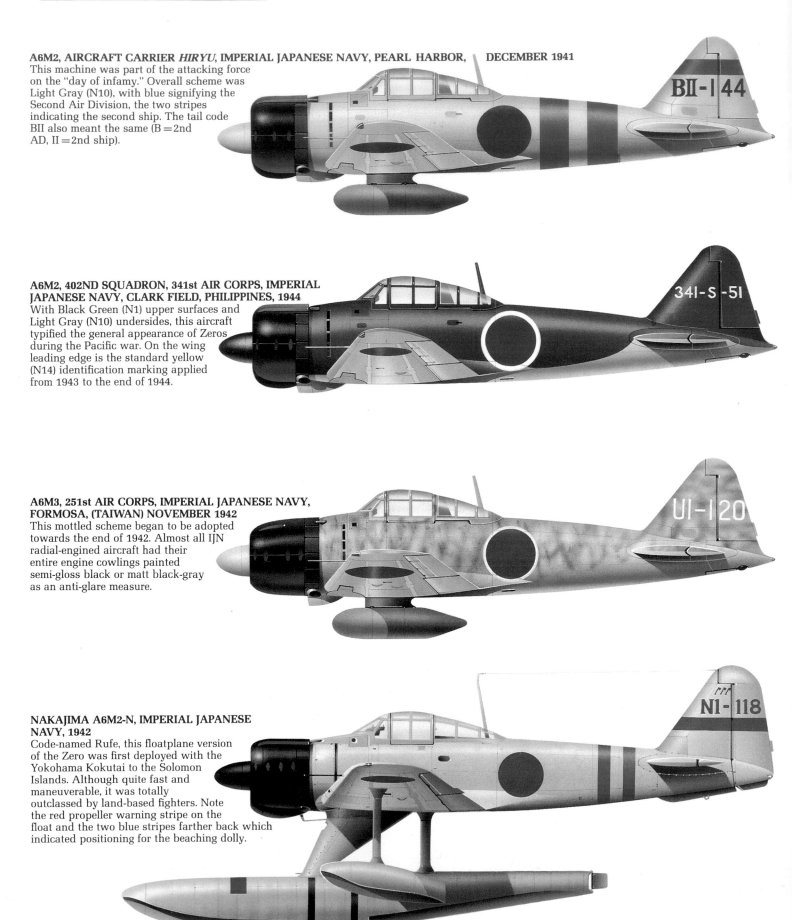

A6M2, AIRCRAFT CARRIER *HIRYU*, IMPERIAL JAPANESE NAVY, PEARL HARBOR, DECEMBER 1941
This machine was part of the attacking force on the "day of infamy." Overall scheme was Light Gray (N10), with blue signifying the Second Air Division, the two stripes indicating the second ship. The tail code BII also meant the same (B=2nd AD, II=2nd ship).

A6M2, 402ND SQUADRON, 341st AIR CORPS, IMPERIAL JAPANESE NAVY, CLARK FIELD, PHILIPPINES, 1944
With Black Green (N1) upper surfaces and Light Gray (N10) undersides, this aircraft typified the general appearance of Zeros during the Pacific war. On the wing leading edge is the standard yellow (N14) identification marking applied from 1943 to the end of 1944.

A6M3, 251st AIR CORPS, IMPERIAL JAPANESE NAVY, FORMOSA, (TAIWAN) NOVEMBER 1942
This mottled scheme began to be adopted towards the end of 1942. Almost all IJN radial-engined aircraft had their entire engine cowlings painted semi-gloss black or matt black-gray as an anti-glare measure.

NAKAJIMA A6M2-N, IMPERIAL JAPANESE NAVY, 1942
Code-named Rufe, this floatplane version of the Zero was first deployed with the Yokohama Kokutai to the Solomon Islands. Although quite fast and maneuverable, it was totally outclassed by land-based fighters. Note the red propeller warning stripe on the float and the two blue stripes farther back which indicated positioning for the beaching dolly.

BRISTOL BEAU- FIGHTER

A long-range heavy fighter, the Beaufighter used some 75 per cent of the components of the Beaufort bomber and incorporated a formidable armament of four 20mm cannon in the belly and six .303in machine-guns in the wings. It operated in most theaters in World War II and is best remembered for its night-fighter, coastal-strike and ground-attack roles. With a crew of two, it had a maximum speed of 321mph at 15,800ft.

Mk 1F, 25 SQUADRON, RAF NORTH WEALD, UK, 1940
This aircraft carries standard day fighter colors of Dark Green, Dark Earth and Sky undersurfaces. It has 35in diameter Type A1 fuselage roundels and 45in diameter Type A underwing roundels. 25 Sqn was, with 29 Sqn, the first unit to receive Beaufighters.

Mk II 307 (POLISH) SQUADRON, RAF EXETER, UK, 1941
It has overall Special Night (RDM2) matt black finish, dull Red codes, serial and badge, 24 × 27in fin flash and 35in diameter fuselage roundel.

Mk XXI, 22 SQUADRON, ROYAL AUSTRALIAN AIR FORCE, SANGA SANGA, PHILIPPINES, 1945
Red has been deleted from all markings to avoid any confusion with the Japanese red disc insignia.

Mk VIF, 416th NIGHT FIGHTER SQUADRON, USAAF, CORSICA, 1943–4
The color scheme is Medium Sea Gray overall with Dark Green upper surface shadow-shading. The star marking is found above the port wing only and on the sides of the fuselage.

Mk TT 10, 34 SQUADRON, RAF, 1950's
This final Beaufighter variant has a natural metal finish. It was employed on anti-aircraft co-operation duties, and the diagonal black and yellow stripes on the undersides of the wing denote its role as a target tug. The last example was withdrawn from service in 1960.

Despite losing five of the six aircraft despatched during its baptism of fire at the Battle of Midway in June 1942, the Avenger survived in service to become one of the outstanding torpedo bombers of World War II. Greatly modified, it continued in use until the 1960s. The prototype first flew on 7 August 1941. Grumman built 2291 TBF-1s before production switched to Eastern Aircraft, where 7543 TBM-1 and -3s were built. No less than 26 different models were in existence by 1946.

TBF-1, VT-8, US NAVY, MIDWAY, HAWAIIAN ISLANDS, USA, 4 JUNE 1942
One of the five aircraft shot down during the Avenger's first combat sortie. At this time the colors were Non-specular Blue Gray over all top surfaces and fuselage sides, with Non-specular Light Gray on the undersurfaces.

TBM-3, US NAVY, USS *RANDOLPH* (CV-15), TASK FORCE 58, EARLY 1944
Standard three-tone camouflage for the mid-war period (see the Hellcat for colors), with white stripes denoting the carrier and the aircraft number on the fuselage and nose. As an alternative to the single 22in torpedo, the Avenger's internal bomb-bay could carry up to 2000lb of bombs or mines.

AVENGER Mk II, ROYAL NAVY, RNAS DONIBRISTLE, UK MID 1944
Invasion bands circle the fuselage and wings of an aircraft with a fox head insignia under the cockpit, but there is little else to identify it apart from the partly obscured serial JZ490 on the dorsal fin. The RN received more than 950 Avengers, calling them Tarpons until January 1944.

TBM-3, ROYAL NETHERLANDS NAVAL AIR SERVICE, VALKENBURG, NETHERLANDS, 1954
One of 50 Avengers which equipped two squadrons of the Dutch Navy, one being shore-based and given the fin marking V, and the other flying off the aircraft carrier *Karel Doorman* (now *25 de Mayo* of the Argentine Navy). USN Glossy Sea Blue was retained.

TBM-3S2, JAPANESE MARITIME SELF-DEFENSE FORCE, SHIRAI, JAPAN, 1960
The Japanese began receiving ASW versions of the Avenger in 1955, but their use was relatively short-lived and most had been withdrawn by 1961. Ironic that an aircraft that helped defeat the Japanese should end up defending them! This particular example was used for crew training.

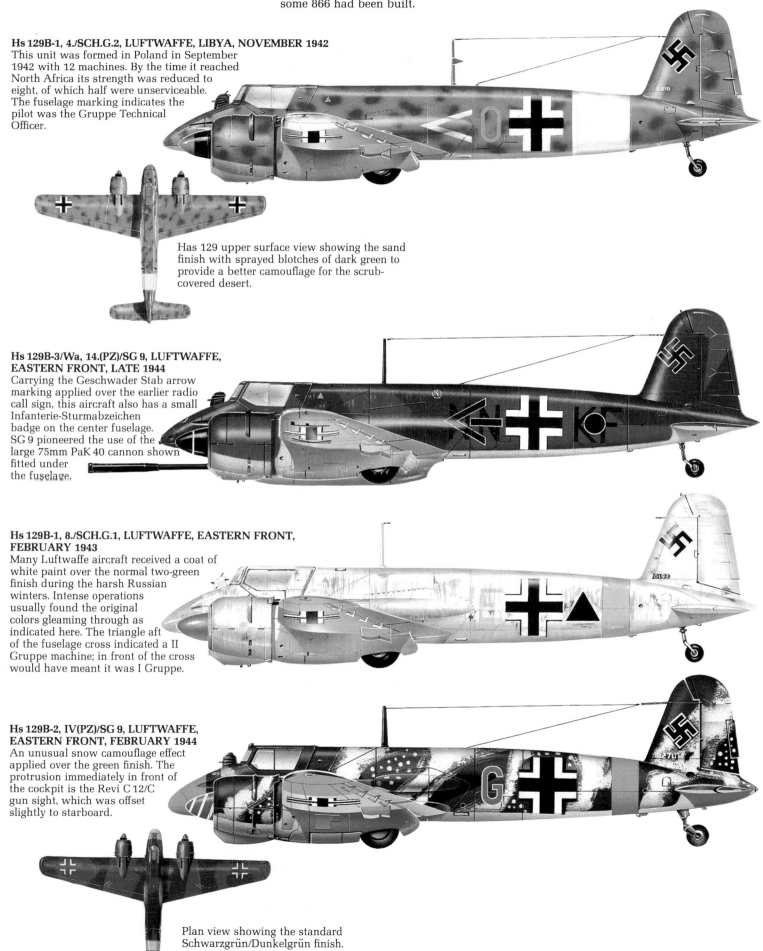

HENSCHEL Hs 129

Poor handling and plagued with serviceability problems, the Hs 129 struggled to achieve what it was designed to do, namely tank busting using heavy caliber cannon and light bombs. It was intended that this heavily armored attack aircraft would replace the Ju 87D Stuka, but it never gained the reliability of the older aircraft. The initial Hs 129A was powered by two Argus in-line engines, these being replaced in the B variant with unreliable Gnôme-Rhone 14Ms. Production terminated in 1944 after some 866 had been built.

Hs 129B-1, 4./SCH.G.2, LUFTWAFFE, LIBYA, NOVEMBER 1942
This unit was formed in Poland in September 1942 with 12 machines. By the time it reached North Africa its strength was reduced to eight, of which half were unserviceable. The fuselage marking indicates the pilot was the Gruppe Technical Officer.

Has 129 upper surface view showing the sand finish with sprayed blotches of dark green to provide a better camouflage for the scrub-covered desert.

Hs 129B-3/Wa, 14.(PZ)/SG 9, LUFTWAFFE, EASTERN FRONT, LATE 1944
Carrying the Geschwader Stab arrow marking applied over the earlier radio call sign, this aircraft also has a small Infanterie-Sturmabzeichen badge on the center fuselage. SG 9 pioneered the use of the large 75mm PaK 40 cannon shown fitted under the fuselage.

Hs 129B-1, 8./SCH.G.1, LUFTWAFFE, EASTERN FRONT, FEBRUARY 1943
Many Luftwaffe aircraft received a coat of white paint over the normal two-green finish during the harsh Russian winters. Intense operations usually found the original colors gleaming through as indicated here. The triangle aft of the fuselage cross indicated a II Gruppe machine; in front of the cross would have meant it was I Gruppe.

Hs 129B-2, IV(PZ)/SG 9, LUFTWAFFE, EASTERN FRONT, FEBRUARY 1944
An unusual snow camouflage effect applied over the green finish. The protrusion immediately in front of the cockpit is the Revi C 12/C gun sight, which was offset slightly to starboard.

Plan view showing the standard Schwarzgrün/Dunkelgrün finish.

CURTISS HAWK

Replacing the air-cooled radial engine of the Hawk 75 with a liquid-cooled powerplant produced the Hawk 81 series of famous P-40s and RAF-operated Tomahawks. The lack of performance of this racy-looking fighter was made up for by ruggedness which saw many aircraft gaining their bases badly damaged but still flying. As well as 524 delivered to the USAAF, 1280 went to the RAF and another 100 were supplied to the American Volunteer Group in China during 1941. The improved Warhawk/Kittyhawk followed and saw world-wide service; 11800 were built.

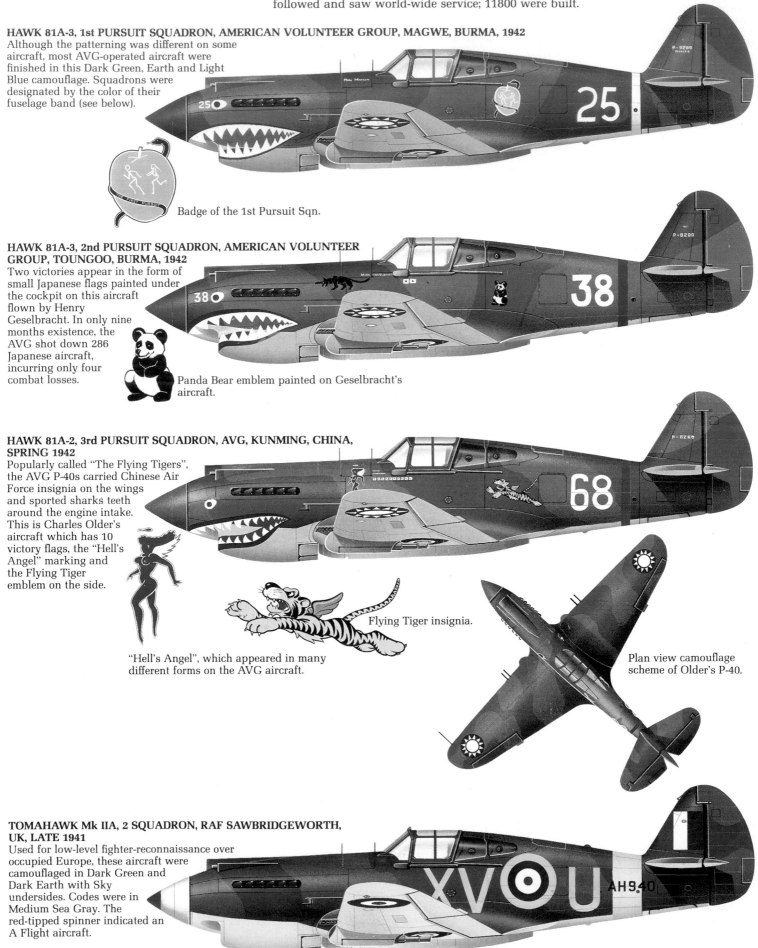

HAWK 81A-3, 1st PURSUIT SQUADRON, AMERICAN VOLUNTEER GROUP, MAGWE, BURMA, 1942
Although the patterning was different on some aircraft, most AVG-operated aircraft were finished in this Dark Green, Earth and Light Blue camouflage. Squadrons were designated by the color of their fuselage band (see below).

Badge of the 1st Pursuit Sqn.

HAWK 81A-3, 2nd PURSUIT SQUADRON, AMERICAN VOLUNTEER GROUP, TOUNGOO, BURMA, 1942
Two victories appear in the form of small Japanese flags painted under the cockpit on this aircraft flown by Henry Geselbracht. In only nine months existence, the AVG shot down 286 Japanese aircraft, incurring only four combat losses.

Panda Bear emblem painted on Geselbracht's aircraft.

HAWK 81A-2, 3rd PURSUIT SQUADRON, AVG, KUNMING, CHINA, SPRING 1942
Popularly called "The Flying Tigers", the AVG P-40s carried Chinese Air Force insignia on the wings and sported sharks teeth around the engine intake. This is Charles Older's aircraft which has 10 victory flags, the "Hell's Angel" marking and the Flying Tiger emblem on the side.

Flying Tiger insignia.

"Hell's Angel", which appeared in many different forms on the AVG aircraft.

Plan view camouflage scheme of Older's P-40.

TOMAHAWK Mk IIA, 2 SQUADRON, RAF SAWBRIDGEWORTH, UK, LATE 1941
Used for low-level fighter-reconnaissance over occupied Europe, these aircraft were camouflaged in Dark Green and Dark Earth with Sky undersides. Codes were in Medium Sea Gray. The red-tipped spinner indicated an A Flight aircraft.

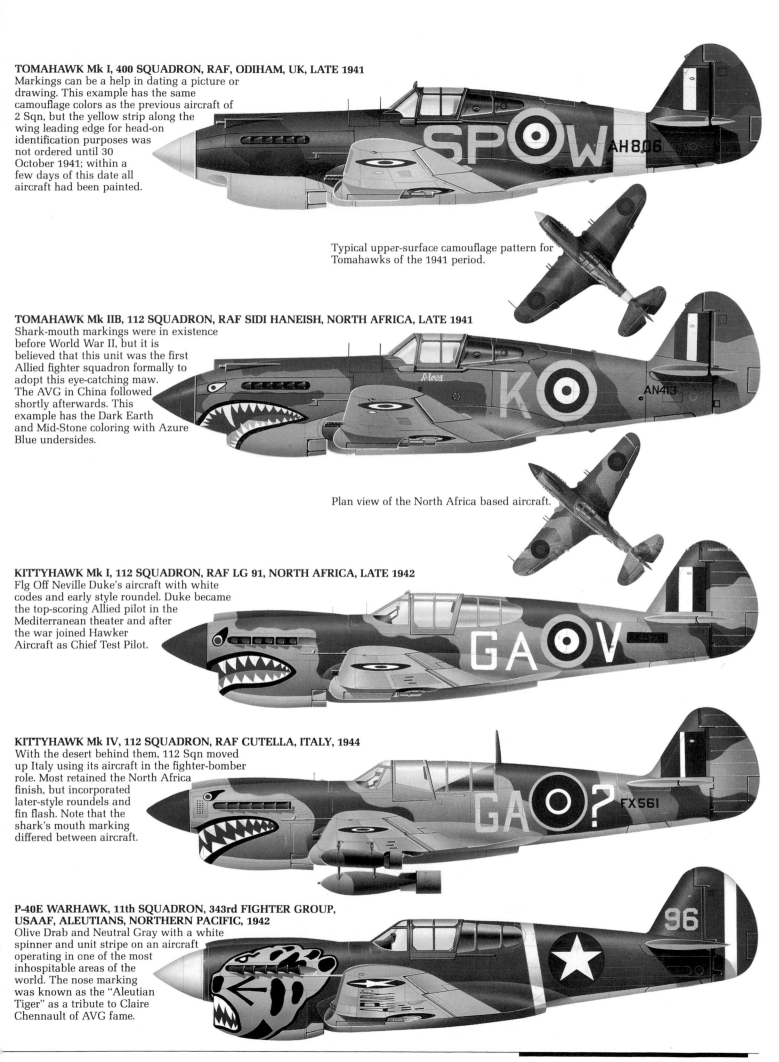

TOMAHAWK Mk I, 400 SQUADRON, RAF, ODIHAM, UK, LATE 1941
Markings can be a help in dating a picture or drawing. This example has the same camouflage colors as the previous aircraft of 2 Sqn, but the yellow strip along the wing leading edge for head-on identification purposes was not ordered until 30 October 1941; within a few days of this date all aircraft had been painted.

Typical upper-surface camouflage pattern for Tomahawks of the 1941 period.

TOMAHAWK Mk IIB, 112 SQUADRON, RAF SIDI HANEISH, NORTH AFRICA, LATE 1941
Shark-mouth markings were in existence before World War II, but it is believed that this unit was the first Allied fighter squadron formally to adopt this eye-catching maw. The AVG in China followed shortly afterwards. This example has the Dark Earth and Mid-Stone coloring with Azure Blue undersides.

Plan view of the North Africa based aircraft.

KITTYHAWK Mk I, 112 SQUADRON, RAF LG 91, NORTH AFRICA, LATE 1942
Flg Off Neville Duke's aircraft with white codes and early style roundel. Duke became the top-scoring Allied pilot in the Mediterranean theater and after the war joined Hawker Aircraft as Chief Test Pilot.

KITTYHAWK Mk IV, 112 SQUADRON, RAF CUTELLA, ITALY, 1944
With the desert behind them, 112 Sqn moved up Italy using its aircraft in the fighter-bomber role. Most retained the North Africa finish, but incorporated later-style roundels and fin flash. Note that the shark's mouth marking differed between aircraft.

P-40E WARHAWK, 11th SQUADRON, 343rd FIGHTER GROUP, USAAF, ALEUTIANS, NORTHERN PACIFIC, 1942
Olive Drab and Neutral Gray with a white spinner and unit stripe on an aircraft operating in one of the most inhospitable areas of the world. The nose marking was known as the "Aleutian Tiger" as a tribute to Claire Chennault of AVG fame.

Bv 138

Nicknamed by Luftwaffe personnel *Der Fliegende Holzschuh* (The Flying Clog) owing to the shape of its central hull, the unconventional 3-engined Bv 138 turned out to be a remarkably efficient flying-boat. Flown in prototype form in July 1937, production examples first saw service during the invasion of Norway in 1940. Following problems with the Bv 138A and B series, the C version appeared in 1941 and became the major production type. Reconnaissance, SAR, minesweeping and anti-shipping duties were its main roles. Production totaled 279.

C-1, 2./KÜSTENFLIEGERGRUPPEN 406, LUFTWAFFE, NORWAY, 1942
The standard finish on flying-boats reflected the general Luftwaffe color scheme, that of Dunkelgrün (dark green), Schwartzgrün (black-green) with Hellblau (clear blue) undersides. This example was employed against the Arctic Convoy PQ 13 taking war supplies to the Soviet Union.

Emblem of 2./Kü.Fl.Gr.406. This Iron Hand marking was previously used on the unit's Do 18s prior to re-equipment with Bv 138s.

C-1/U1, 1.(F)/SAGr 130, LUFTWAFFE, TRONDHEIM AREA, NORWAY, APRIL 1944
During operations in the Arctic Ocean aircraft were often given a random application of white paint to enable them to merge better with the ice floes on reconnaissance missions. The aircraft were refuelled from U-boats to extend their range.

"Telescope-equipped Penguin" badge of 1.(F)/SAGr 130.

MS (MINENSUCHE), 6./MSGr.1, LUFTWAFFE, GROSSENBRODE, BALTIC SEA, 1944–5
Dubbed the *Mouse-catching aircraft* owing to the circular de-gaussing ring for mine sweeping, these modified machines had the auxiliary motor for energizing the ring mounted in place of the front turret.

Plan view of the Bv 138 MS. Armament was removed from this version.

C-1, 3./SAGr 125, LUFTWAFFE, MAMAIA/CONSTANTA, ROMANIA, APRIL 1943
The yellow theater colors indicate an Eastern Front aircraft. The front and rear turrets contained a single 20mm cannon, and the position behind the center engine had one 13mm MG. Unusually, the center Jumo engine on the C series drove a four-bladed propeller, the other two engines powering three-bladed props.

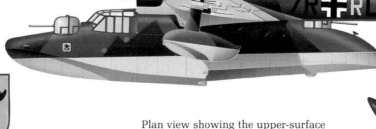

Bomb-carrying Penguin emblem of 3./SAGr 125 – an allusion to the type's ability to carry weapons under the wing center-section.

Plan view showing the upper-surface camouflage pattern applied to the 3./SAGr 125 aircraft.

SHORT SUNDERLAND

Dubbed by the Germans who fought it, the "Flying Porcupine", the Sunderland long-range flying boat bristled with defensive armament and at one time carried up to 12 MGs in addition to bombs and depth charges. It entered service with RAF Coastal Command in 1938 and finally retired in 1960 when the last French-operated example was withdrawn. Mks I, II and III were powered by Bristol Pegasus engines; the Mk V switched to Pratt & Whitney Twin Wasps. Production totaled 721 plus 31 Mk IVs, which became the Seaford.

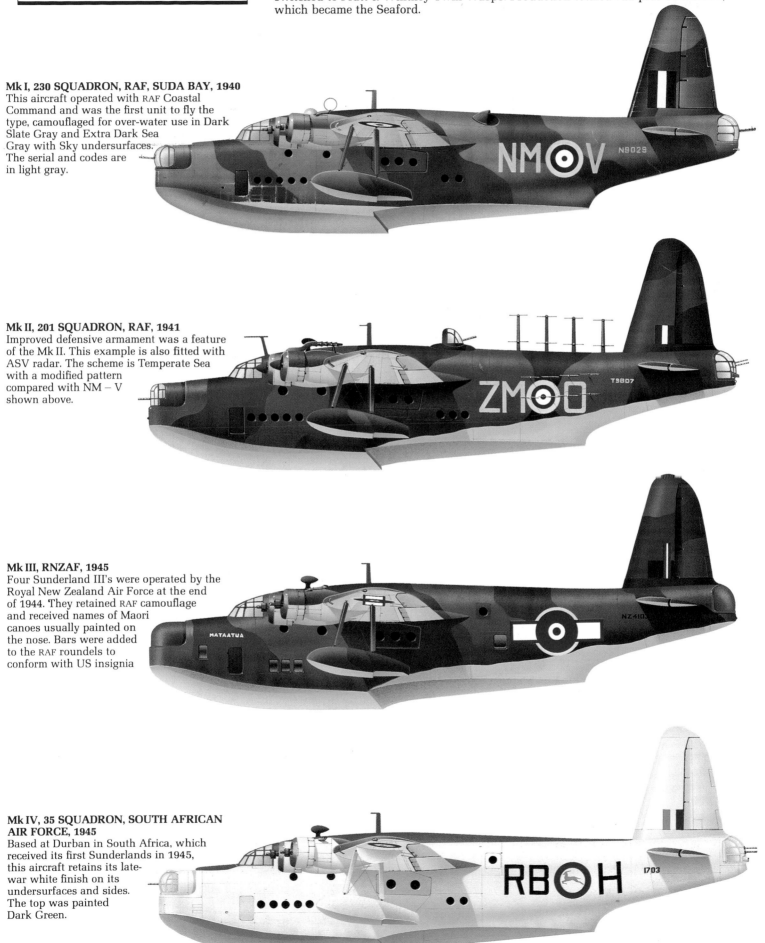

Mk I, 230 SQUADRON, RAF, SUDA BAY, 1940
This aircraft operated with RAF Coastal Command and was the first unit to fly the type, camouflaged for over-water use in Dark Slate Gray and Extra Dark Sea Gray with Sky undersurfaces. The serial and codes are in light gray.

Mk II, 201 SQUADRON, RAF, 1941
Improved defensive armament was a feature of the Mk II. This example is also fitted with ASV radar. The scheme is Temperate Sea with a modified pattern compared with NM – V shown above.

Mk III, RNZAF, 1945
Four Sunderland III's were operated by the Royal New Zealand Air Force at the end of 1944. They retained RAF camouflage and received names of Maori canoes usually painted on the nose. Bars were added to the RAF roundels to conform with US insignia

Mk IV, 35 SQUADRON, SOUTH AFRICAN AIR FORCE, 1945
Based at Durban in South Africa, which received its first Sunderlands in 1945, this aircraft retains its late-war white finish on its undersurfaces and sides. The top was painted Dark Green.

DOUGLAS DAUNTLESS

Developed in the mid 1930s as a carrier-based dive-bomber for the US Navy, the Dauntless was relatively slow and technically outmoded when it began its combat career in 1942. However, it was a rugged dependable aircraft and by the time it gave way to the Helldiver it had gained the distinction of sinking more Japanese shipping than any other Allied aircraft. The first prototype, known as the XBT-1, flew in July 1935 and production SBD-1s began reaching units in mid 1940. As well as the SBD-1 to -6 series, the USAAF operated a variant designed A-24. Production of all types totaled 5936.

SBD-1, VMSB-232 (EX-VMB-2), US MARINE CORPS AIR GROUP 21, HAWAIIAN ISLANDS, DECEMBER 1941
When the Japanese struck Oahu on 7 December 1941 they caught the Dauntlesses of Marine Air Group 21 on the ground and badly battered them. At the time these early SBD-1s were finished in the Non-Specular Light Gray as directed by a 30 December 1940 order.

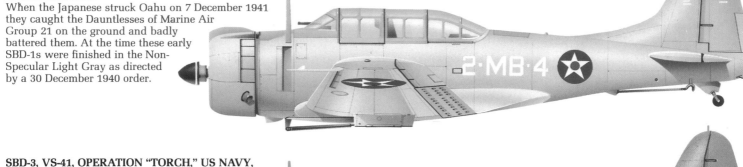

SBD-3, VS-41, OPERATION "TORCH," US NAVY, USS *"RANGER"*, NOVEMBER 1942
A specially enlarged and crudely applied national insignia on an aircraft used in the invasion of French North Africa. The Light Gray was overpainted on the top surfaces by Non-Specular Blue Gray. On the side of the fuselage is the unit number (41), the role letter (S =Scout) and the aircraft within the unit (9).

SBD-4, VMSB-243, 1st MARINE AIR WING, MUNDA, NEW GEORGIA, SOLOMON ISLANDS, AUGUST 1943
Radio navigation aids, a Hamilton Standard constant-speed prop and an electric fuel pump were improvements on the 780 -4s delivered. Wearing the short-lived red-bordered insignia, this Marine aircraft carries a 500lb "calling card" under the fuselage.

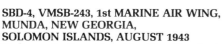

SBD-5, 25 SQUADRON, ROYAL NEW ZEALAND AIR FORCE, PIVA, BOUGAINVILLE, SOLOMON ISLANDS, APRIL 1944
Two months of operations by the RNZAF against the Japanese, using borrowed USMC -5s, resulted in the loss of six of the 23 aircraft on 32 missions. The RNZAF retained the US color-scheme with the addition of modified roundels and fin flashes.

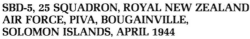

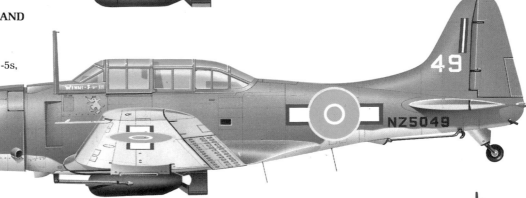

A-24B, GROUPE DE CHASSE-BOMBARDEMENT (GCB) 1/18 "VENDÉE," VANNES, FRANCE, NOVEMBER 1944
The USAAF ordered 953 of this Dauntless version for attack duties. Some 50 examples were passed on to the French Air Force, which used them near the end of the war to attack and harass the Germans retreating from the south of France. Olive Drab and Neutral Gray colors were overpainted with invasion stripes and in this case, a large Free French Cross of Lorraine.

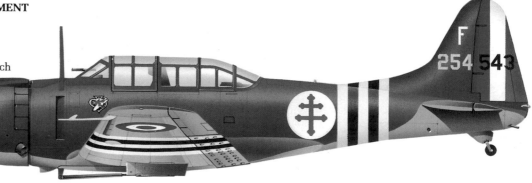

NAKAJIMA Ki-49 DONRYU

Named by the Japanese, Donryu (Storm Dragon) and code-named "Helen" by the Allies, the eight-seat Ki 49 was a heavy, underpowered bomber operated by the Army Air Force. The prototype flew in August 1938 and production aircraft made their first combat sortie on a raid against Port Darwin, Australia, on 19 February 1942. Defensive armament in later versions comprised 12.7mm MGs in nose, tail, ventral and beam positions, plus a single 20mm manually aimed cannon in the dorsal position. More than 800 were built, the type ending its career with the *kamikaze* pilots.

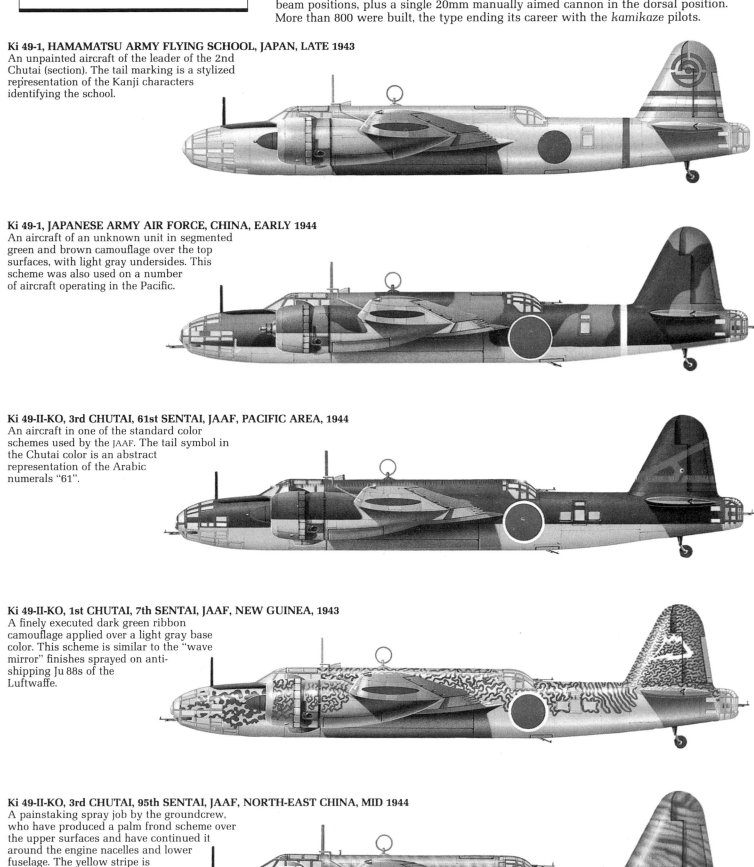

Ki 49-1, HAMAMATSU ARMY FLYING SCHOOL, JAPAN, LATE 1943
An unpainted aircraft of the leader of the 2nd Chutai (section). The tail marking is a stylized representation of the Kanji characters identifying the school.

Ki 49-1, JAPANESE ARMY AIR FORCE, CHINA, EARLY 1944
An aircraft of an unknown unit in segmented green and brown camouflage over the top surfaces, with light gray undersides. This scheme was also used on a number of aircraft operating in the Pacific.

Ki 49-II-KO, 3rd CHUTAI, 61st SENTAI, JAAF, PACIFIC AREA, 1944
An aircraft in one of the standard color schemes used by the JAAF. The tail symbol in the Chutai color is an abstract representation of the Arabic numerals "61".

Ki 49-II-KO, 1st CHUTAI, 7th SENTAI, JAAF, NEW GUINEA, 1943
A finely executed dark green ribbon camouflage applied over a light gray base color. This scheme is similar to the "wave mirror" finishes sprayed on anti-shipping Ju 88s of the Luftwaffe.

Ki 49-II-KO, 3rd CHUTAI, 95th SENTAI, JAAF, NORTH-EAST CHINA, MID 1944
A painstaking spray job by the groundcrew, who have produced a palm frond scheme over the upper surfaces and have continued it around the engine nacelles and lower fuselage. The yellow stripe is in the Chutai color and the white band is a combat stripe.

MACCHI M.C.205

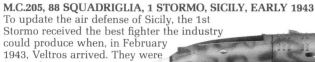

Based on the earlier M.C.200 Saetta, the M.C.202 Folgore (Lightning) was a major advance in fighter performance for the Regia Aeronautica. The German DB601 in-line engine gave the Italian pilots an aircraft capable of outperforming Allied fighters such as the Hurricane and P-40. About 1500 were built before production switched to the higher-powered Veltro (Greyhound) which represented the peak of Italian World War II fighter design. Poor industrial effort, however, resulted in only 262 being built before the end of hostilities.

M.C.205, 88 SQUADRIGLIA, 1 STORMO, SICILY, EARLY 1943
To update the air defense of Sicily, the 1st Stormo received the best fighter the industry could produce when, in February 1943, Veltros arrived. They were finished in a scheme of green mottle on Sand with Gray undersides and the standard white theater fuselage band and white spinner.

M.C.205 III SERIES, 2 SQUADRIGLIA, 1 GRUPPO, AERONAUTICA NAZIONALE REPUBLICANA, CAMPOFORMIDO, ITALY, 1944
Operating on the side of the Germans following the September 1943 armistice, ANR aircraft initially retained their original finish as shown on this Veltro which has the Dark Green "ringlet" pattern over a Yellow Ocher base with a Light Gray underside. The black nose spiral shows a definite German influence.

M.C.205 III SERIES, 1 SQUADRIGLIA, 1 GRUPPO, ANR, REGGIO NELL' EMILIA, ITALY, 1944
Aircraft 16 of the unit carries a mottled finish similar to that used on the Luftwaffe fighters towards the end of the war, namely Brown Violet (81), Blue Green (83) over Light Gray. On the nose is the Ace of Clubs badge and the spinner is segmented white and black.

M.C.205 III SERIES, 155 GRUPPO, 51 STORMO, CO-BELLIGERENT AIR FORCE, LECCE-GALATINA, ITALY, 1944
A roundel in the Italian national colours was the obvious choice for aircraft flown with the Allies. Existing camouflage was retained, as were the famous unit badges such as the Cat and Mouse marking on the fin.

M.C.205 III SERIES, II/JAGDGESCHWADER 77, LUFTWAFFE, LONATE POZZOLO, ITALY, 1943
Having requisitioned all Italian war material following the armistice, the Germans gave a number of Veltros hastily applied Luftwaffe markings and pressed them into service. With the formation of the Repubblica Sociale Italiana (RSI), the aircraft were returned to Italian units.

B-24 LIBERATOR

Although overshadowed by the B-17 Flying Fortress, the B-24 had a number of virtues which made it a much more sought-after bomber: it was fast (300mph at 30,000ft), capable of carrying 8000lb of bombs, and had a range of more than 2000 miles. The prototype XB-24 flew in December 1939 and first deliveries were made in 1941 to the RAF. The worth of this big aircraft was soon realized and production took the design through nine major variants to peak at 18,482, a run greater than any other US World War II combat aircraft.

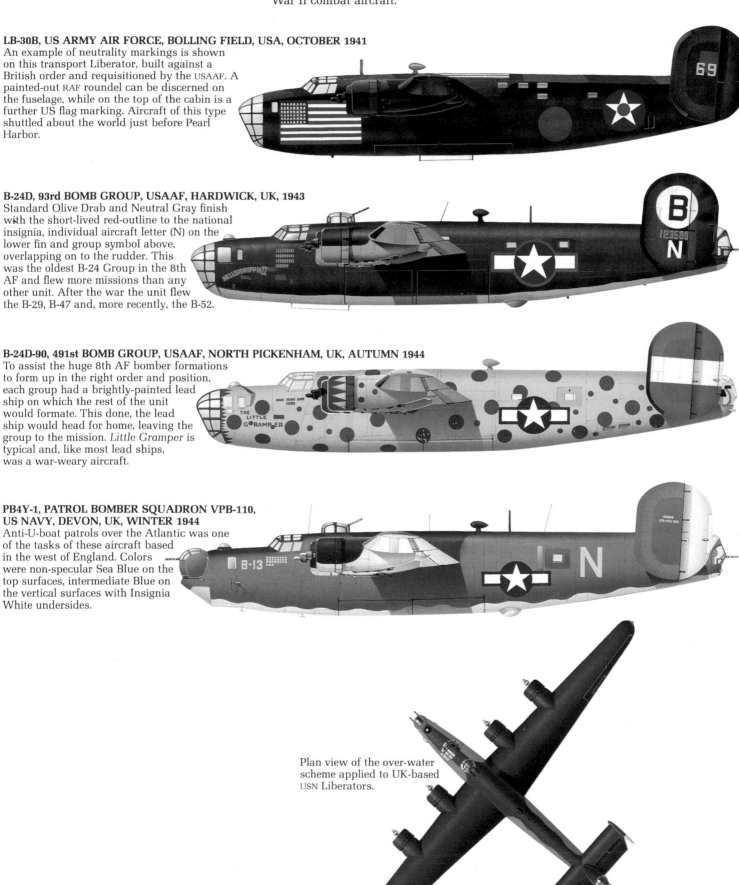

LB-30B, US ARMY AIR FORCE, BOLLING FIELD, USA, OCTOBER 1941
An example of neutrality markings is shown on this transport Liberator, built against a British order and requisitioned by the USAAF. A painted-out RAF roundel can be discerned on the fuselage, while on the top of the cabin is a further US flag marking. Aircraft of this type shuttled about the world just before Pearl Harbor.

B-24D, 93rd BOMB GROUP, USAAF, HARDWICK, UK, 1943
Standard Olive Drab and Neutral Gray finish with the short-lived red-outline to the national insignia, individual aircraft letter (N) on the lower fin and group symbol above, overlapping on to the rudder. This was the oldest B-24 Group in the 8th AF and flew more missions than any other unit. After the war the unit flew the B-29, B-47 and, more recently, the B-52.

B-24D-90, 491st BOMB GROUP, USAAF, NORTH PICKENHAM, UK, AUTUMN 1944
To assist the huge 8th AF bomber formations to form up in the right order and position, each group had a brightly-painted lead ship on which the rest of the unit would formate. This done, the lead ship would head for home, leaving the group to the mission. *Little Gramper* is typical and, like most lead ships, was a war-weary aircraft.

PB4Y-1, PATROL BOMBER SQUADRON VPB-110, US NAVY, DEVON, UK, WINTER 1944
Anti-U-boat patrols over the Atlantic was one of the tasks of these aircraft based in the west of England. Colors were non-specular Sea Blue on the top surfaces, intermediate Blue on the vertical surfaces with Insignia White undersides.

Plan view of the over-water scheme applied to UK-based USN Liberators.

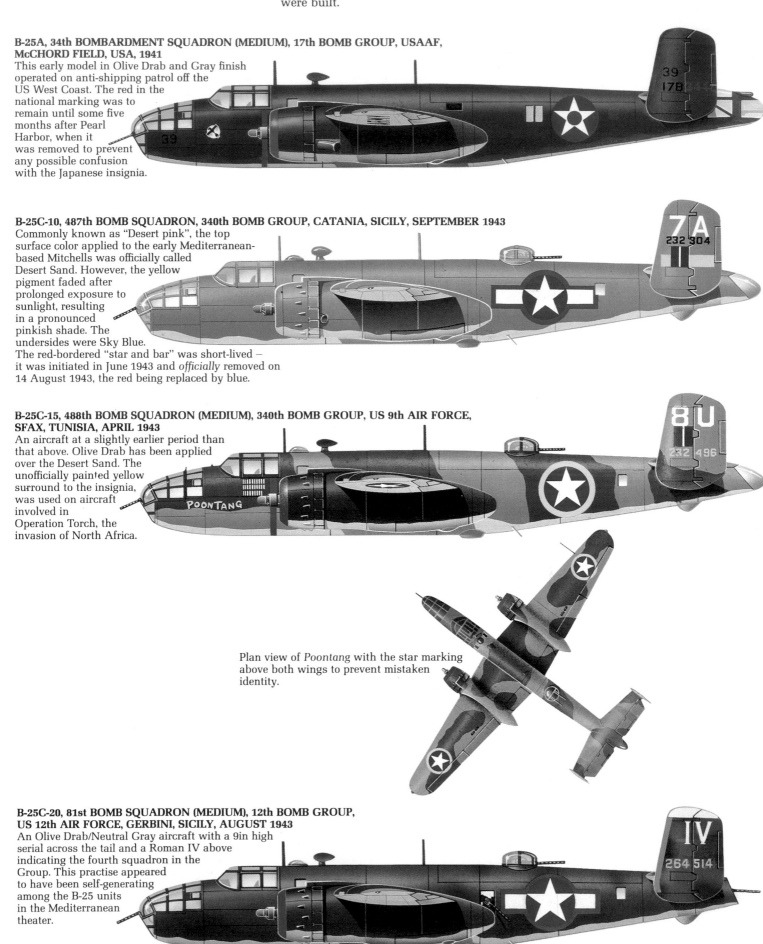

NORTH AMERICAN B-25

"A pilot's airplane" best describes the docile and adaptable Mitchell. Operating mainly in the daylight bombing role, it fought on all fronts and as well as equipping the US Air Forces, hundreds were supplied to Allied nations. A production contract was awarded to NA before the first aircraft had flown, an event which took place on 19 August 1940. As the war progressed, so too did development of the B-25, including solid-nose versions and one with a 75mm cannon for anti-shipping use. Nearly 11,000 were built.

B-25A, 34th BOMBARDMENT SQUADRON (MEDIUM), 17th BOMB GROUP, USAAF, McCHORD FIELD, USA, 1941
This early model in Olive Drab and Gray finish operated on anti-shipping patrol off the US West Coast. The red in the national marking was to remain until some five months after Pearl Harbor, when it was removed to prevent any possible confusion with the Japanese insignia.

B-25C-10, 487th BOMB SQUADRON, 340th BOMB GROUP, CATANIA, SICILY, SEPTEMBER 1943
Commonly known as "Desert pink", the top surface color applied to the early Mediterranean-based Mitchells was officially called Desert Sand. However, the yellow pigment faded after prolonged exposure to sunlight, resulting in a pronounced pinkish shade. The undersides were Sky Blue. The red-bordered "star and bar" was short-lived – it was initiated in June 1943 and *officially* removed on 14 August 1943, the red being replaced by blue.

B-25C-15, 488th BOMB SQUADRON (MEDIUM), 340th BOMB GROUP, US 9th AIR FORCE, SFAX, TUNISIA, APRIL 1943
An aircraft at a slightly earlier period than that above. Olive Drab has been applied over the Desert Sand. The unofficially painted yellow surround to the insignia, was used on aircraft involved in Operation Torch, the invasion of North Africa.

Plan view of *Poontang* with the star marking above both wings to prevent mistaken identity.

B-25C-20, 81st BOMB SQUADRON (MEDIUM), 12th BOMB GROUP, US 12th AIR FORCE, GERBINI, SICILY, AUGUST 1943
An Olive Drab/Neutral Gray aircraft with a 9in high serial across the tail and a Roman IV above indicating the fourth squadron in the Group. This practise appeared to have been self-generating among the B-25 units in the Mediterranean theater.

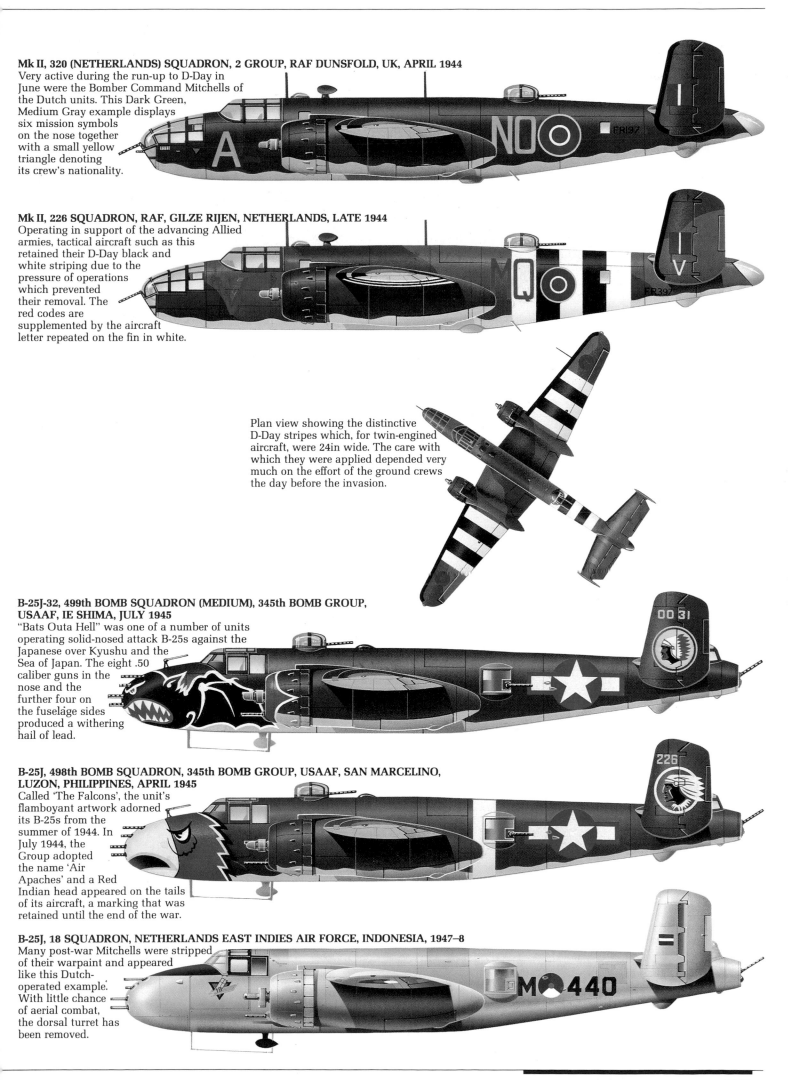

Mk II, 320 (NETHERLANDS) SQUADRON, 2 GROUP, RAF DUNSFOLD, UK, APRIL 1944
Very active during the run-up to D-Day in June were the Bomber Command Mitchells of the Dutch units. This Dark Green, Medium Gray example displays six mission symbols on the nose together with a small yellow triangle denoting its crew's nationality.

Mk II, 226 SQUADRON, RAF, GILZE RIJEN, NETHERLANDS, LATE 1944
Operating in support of the advancing Allied armies, tactical aircraft such as this retained their D-Day black and white striping due to the pressure of operations which prevented their removal. The red codes are supplemented by the aircraft letter repeated on the fin in white.

Plan view showing the distinctive D-Day stripes which, for twin-engined aircraft, were 24in wide. The care with which they were applied depended very much on the effort of the ground crews the day before the invasion.

B-25J-32, 499th BOMB SQUADRON (MEDIUM), 345th BOMB GROUP, USAAF, IE SHIMA, JULY 1945
"Bats Outa Hell" was one of a number of units operating solid-nosed attack B-25s against the Japanese over Kyushu and the Sea of Japan. The eight .50 caliber guns in the nose and the further four on the fuselage sides produced a withering hail of lead.

B-25J, 498th BOMB SQUADRON, 345th BOMB GROUP, USAAF, SAN MARCELINO, LUZON, PHILIPPINES, APRIL 1945
Called 'The Falcons', the unit's flamboyant artwork adorned its B-25s from the summer of 1944. In July 1944, the Group adopted the name 'Air Apaches' and a Red Indian head appeared on the tails of its aircraft, a marking that was retained until the end of the war.

B-25J, 18 SQUADRON, NETHERLANDS EAST INDIES AIR FORCE, INDONESIA, 1947–8
Many post-war Mitchells were stripped of their warpaint and appeared like this Dutch-operated example. With little chance of aerial combat, the dorsal turret has been removed.

MITSUBISHI G4M 'BETTY'

Of all the Japanese bombers produced during World War II, Betty was probably the best known. Naval-operated, it had a considerable range (in excess of 3700 miles) achieved by structural lightness and a total disregard for armor protection, the latter proving to be the type's weakness when Allied opposition increased later in the war. First flight of the prototype was in October 1939 and production extended through three main variants – G4M1, G4M2 and G4M3 – until the end of the war when the last of 2446 aircraft was completed.

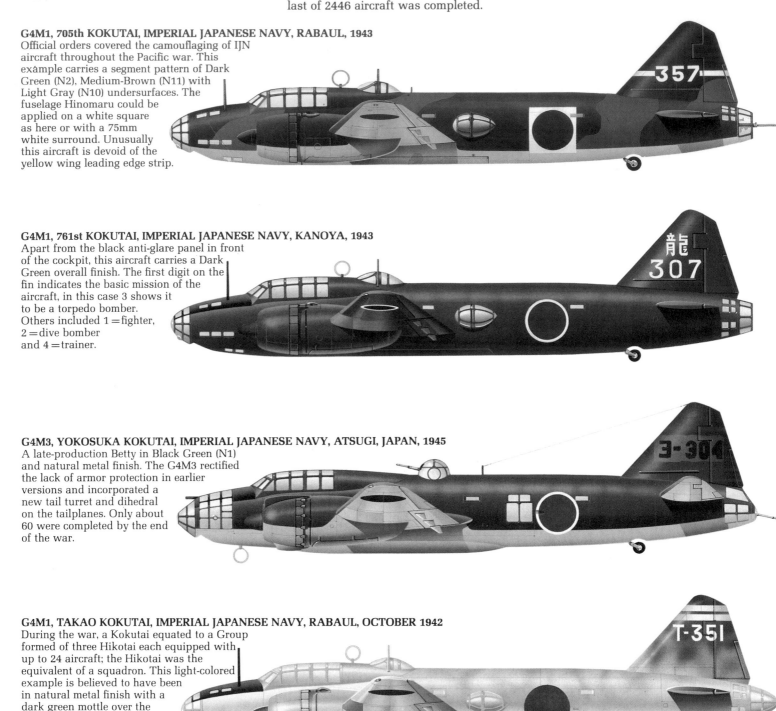

G4M1, 705th KOKUTAI, IMPERIAL JAPANESE NAVY, RABAUL, 1943
Official orders covered the camouflaging of IJN aircraft throughout the Pacific war. This example carries a segment pattern of Dark Green (N2), Medium-Brown (N11) with Light Gray (N10) undersurfaces. The fuselage Hinomaru could be applied on a white square as here or with a 75mm white surround. Unusually this aircraft is devoid of the yellow wing leading edge strip.

G4M1, 761st KOKUTAI, IMPERIAL JAPANESE NAVY, KANOYA, 1943
Apart from the black anti-glare panel in front of the cockpit, this aircraft carries a Dark Green overall finish. The first digit on the fin indicates the basic mission of the aircraft, in this case 3 shows it to be a torpedo bomber. Others included 1=fighter, 2=dive bomber and 4=trainer.

G4M3, YOKOSUKA KOKUTAI, IMPERIAL JAPANESE NAVY, ATSUGI, JAPAN, 1945
A late-production Betty in Black Green (N1) and natural metal finish. The G4M3 rectified the lack of armor protection in earlier versions and incorporated a new tail turret and dihedral on the tailplanes. Only about 60 were completed by the end of the war.

G4M1, TAKAO KOKUTAI, IMPERIAL JAPANESE NAVY, RABAUL, OCTOBER 1942
During the war, a Kokutai equated to a Group formed of three Hikotai each equipped with up to 24 aircraft; the Hikotai was the equivalent of a squadron. This light-colored example is believed to have been in natural metal finish with a dark green mottle over the top surfaces.

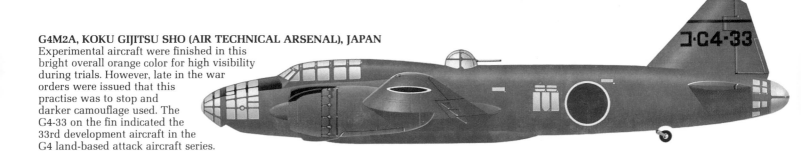

G4M2A, KOKU GIJITSU SHO (AIR TECHNICAL ARSENAL), JAPAN
Experimental aircraft were finished in this bright overall orange color for high visibility during trials. However, late in the war orders were issued that this practise was to stop and darker camouflage used. The G4-33 on the fin indicated the 33rd development aircraft in the G4 land-based attack aircraft series.

LOCKHEED VENTURA

A heavier and more powerful development of the Hudson, the Ventura made its first flight on 31 July 1941 and deliveries to the RAF began a year later. Despite improvements and having an additional gun position under the rear fuselage, the Ventura was unsuccessful as a daylight bomber and with 394 delivered, the RAF withdrew the type in mid-1943. It operated in the reconnaissance role with some Commonwealth air arms and as the B-34 with the USAAF and PV-1 with the US Navy.

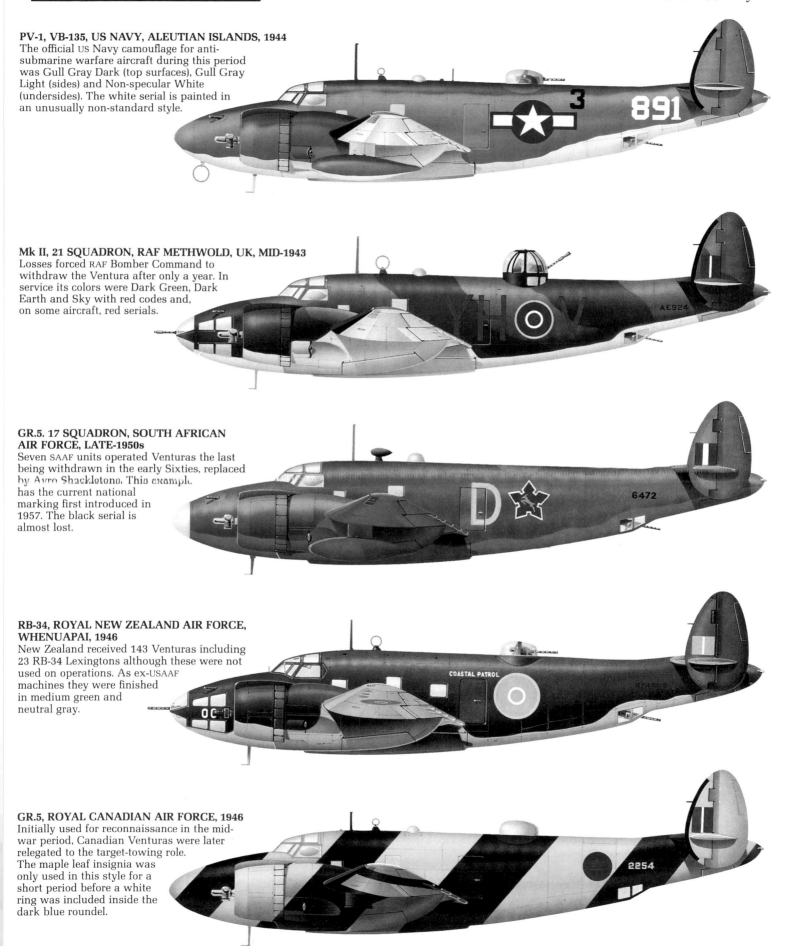

PV-1, VB-135, US NAVY, ALEUTIAN ISLANDS, 1944
The official US Navy camouflage for anti-submarine warfare aircraft during this period was Gull Gray Dark (top surfaces), Gull Gray Light (sides) and Non-specular White (undersides). The white serial is painted in an unusually non-standard style.

Mk II, 21 SQUADRON, RAF METHWOLD, UK, MID-1943
Losses forced RAF Bomber Command to withdraw the Ventura after only a year. In service its colors were Dark Green, Dark Earth and Sky with red codes and, on some aircraft, red serials.

GR.5. 17 SQUADRON, SOUTH AFRICAN AIR FORCE, LATE-1950s
Seven SAAF units operated Venturas the last being withdrawn in the early Sixties, replaced by Avro Shackletons. This example has the current national marking first introduced in 1957. The black serial is almost lost.

RB-34, ROYAL NEW ZEALAND AIR FORCE, WHENUAPAI, 1946
New Zealand received 143 Venturas including 23 RB-34 Lexingtons although these were not used on operations. As ex-USAAF machines they were finished in medium green and neutral gray.

GR.5, ROYAL CANADIAN AIR FORCE, 1946
Initially used for reconnaissance in the mid-war period, Canadian Venturas were later relegated to the target-towing role. The maple leaf insignia was only used in this style for a short period before a white ring was included inside the dark blue roundel.

Nicknamed the "Wooden Wonder" because of its method of construction, the Mosquito was developed initially as a fast, twin-engined, unarmed bomber, but the enormous potential of the design encouraged the development of fighter, reconnaissance and high-speed transport versions. Two Rolls-Royce Merlin engines provided the power and gave the later Mk IX a top speed of 397mph at 26,000ft. The armament of the fighter version included four 20mm cannon and four .303 machine-guns. As a bomber, it could carry up to 5,000lb of bombs. Total production was 7781 aircraft.

B Mk IV, 105 SQUADRON, RAF, HORSHAM ST FAITH, UK, 1942
It has Dark Green, Ocean Gray, Medium Sea Gray (undersurfaces) camouflage with Sky spinners and fuselage band. The wing leading edges are yellow for head-on identification.

FB Mk VI, 4 SQUADRON, RAF, CELLE, WEST GERMANY, 1949
The aircraft has postwar markings, its black undersurfaces indicating a night bomber role. The underwing serials are white.

The 4 Squadron fin badge which shows the sun divided by a flash of lightning, indicating day and night operations. The lightning flash alludes to the Squadron's early wireless use.

Standard factory camouflage scheme applicable to the 4 Squadron, FB Mk VI above. The D wing roundel was introduced in June 1947.

Mk I, NO. 1 PHOTOGRAPHIC RECONNAISSANCE UNIT, RAF, 1941
The sixth production aircraft, W4055 operated with No. 1 PRU until lost on 4 December 1941. It has the PRU Blue overall with Pale Gray codes and Type B roundels.

PR Mk XVI, 653rd BOMB SQUADRON (LIGHT), USAAF, WATTON, UK, 1944
This aircraft was used for weather recce and visual coverage of target strikes. The D-Day stripes were each 24in wide.

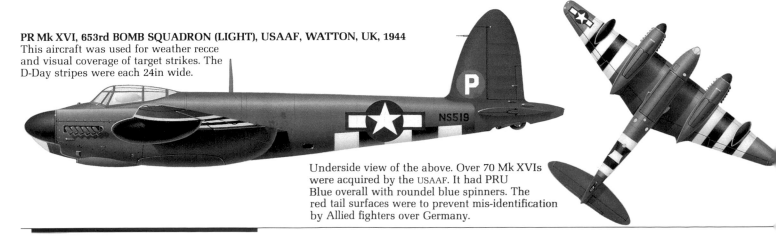

Underside view of the above. Over 70 Mk XVIs were acquired by the USAAF. It had PRU Blue overall with roundel blue spinners. The red tail surfaces were to prevent mis-identification by Allied fighters over Germany.

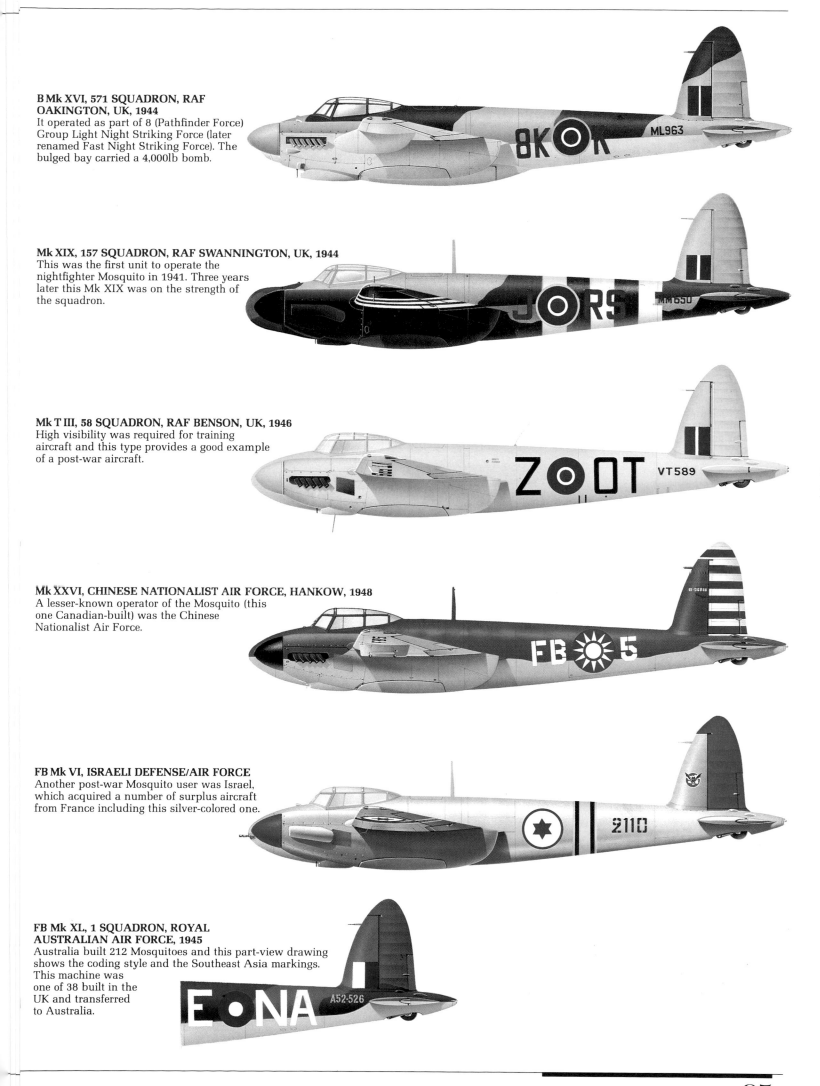

B Mk XVI, 571 SQUADRON, RAF OAKINGTON, UK, 1944
It operated as part of 8 (Pathfinder Force) Group Light Night Striking Force (later renamed Fast Night Striking Force). The bulged bay carried a 4,000lb bomb.

Mk XIX, 157 SQUADRON, RAF SWANNINGTON, UK, 1944
This was the first unit to operate the nightfighter Mosquito in 1941. Three years later this Mk XIX was on the strength of the squadron.

Mk T III, 58 SQUADRON, RAF BENSON, UK, 1946
High visibility was required for training aircraft and this type provides a good example of a post-war aircraft.

Mk XXVI, CHINESE NATIONALIST AIR FORCE, HANKOW, 1948
A lesser-known operator of the Mosquito (this one Canadian-built) was the Chinese Nationalist Air Force.

FB Mk VI, ISRAELI DEFENSE/AIR FORCE
Another post-war Mosquito user was Israel, which acquired a number of surplus aircraft from France including this silver-colored one.

FB Mk XL, 1 SQUADRON, ROYAL AUSTRALIAN AIR FORCE, 1945
Australia built 212 Mosquitoes and this part-view drawing shows the coding style and the Southeast Asia markings. This machine was one of 38 built in the UK and transferred to Australia.

AVRO LANCASTER

Undoubtedly the most successful heavy bomber to serve with any of the combatants in World War II, the Lancaster was developed from the less than capable twin-engined Avro Manchester. Four Rolls-Royce Merlins (a few had Hercules radial engines) enabled the Lancaster to lift bomb loads of up to 22,000lb. The basic aircraft had a crew of seven and was armed with three gun turrets. Production totaled 7374.

AVRO MANCHESTER I, 207 SQUADRON, RAF WADDINGTON, UK, 1941
Painted in Dark Green, Dark Earth, Black camouflage with gray codes and fuselage roundels 63in in diameter. The Manchester was deployed in late 1940 to 207 Sqn.

PROTOTYPE LANCASTER, AEROPLANE AND ARMAMENT EXPERIMENTAL ESTABLISHMENT, UK, 1941
This aircraft, which first flew on 9 January 1941, has a Type A1 fuselage roundel, a black serial and yellow undersurfaces denoting its non-operational function.

"PICCADILLY PRINCESS", B Mk I, 424 (TIGER) SQUADRON, ROYAL CANADIAN AIR FORCE, SKIPTON-ON-SWALE, UK, 1945
It has, rather unusually, light blue codes with the Type C1 roundel. Nose art was a particular feature of Canadian-operated aircraft.

B Mk III, 617 SQUADRON, RAF CONINGSBY, UK, 1943
This aircraft is specially modified for the attack of the Mohner, Eder and Sorpe Dams. It has the standard Dark Red codes and serial (note G = Guard suffix). The mid-upper turret has been deleted and the bomb-bay cut away.

B Mk I, 149 (EAST INDIA) SQUADRON, RAF METHWOLD, UK, 1945
The yellow fin bars denote the G-H radar-equipped C Flight leader in 3 Group.

B Mk VI, 635 SQUADRON, RAF, DOWNHAM MARKET, UK, 1944
This late Lancaster version had increased performance for Pathfinder duties and carried radar jamming devices. Note the absense of nose and mid-upper turrets.

B Mk I (SPECIAL), 617 SQUADRON, RAF WOODHALL SPA, UK, 1945
Shown here camouflaged for daylight operations with Type C roundels above and below the wings. It is shown carrying a "Grand Slam" bomb.

B Mk VIII, 9 SQUADRON, RAF, INDIA, 1946
White upper surfaces were ordered in February 1945 for "Tiger Force" aircraft destined for the war against Japan. The surrender took place before the aircraft began operations.

B Mk I, FLOTILLE 24F, AERONAVALE, FRANCE, 1953
Formerly PA432, WU40 was one of 54 delivered and used for maritime reconnaissance. The color was royal blue overall.

GR Mk III, SCHOOL OF MARITIME RECONNAISSANCE, RAF ST MAWGAN, UK
Finished in glossy Dark Sea Gray overall of Coastal Command, RF 325 was the last Lancaster in RAF service when retired in 1956.

Unusual formation-keeping markings experimented with by 166 Squadron when based at Kirmington as part of No 1 Group in 1944. The scheme was not widely adopted.

Note the Type B style upper wing roundel.

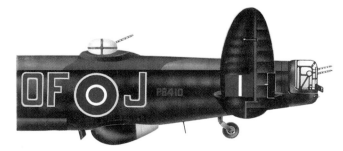

This shows a late war coding presentation used by a BIII of 166 Squadron. This location was by no means standard for codes.

ILYUSHIN Il-2

Built in greater numbers than any other combat aircraft, the Soviet Il-2 was the outstanding all-purpose ground-attack aircraft of World War II. Armored in all the right places – mainly around the engine and cockpit – it was capable of surviving considerable damage, and was large enough to carry and deliver 1300lb of bombs and rockets. The early aircraft were single-seaters, a gunner's position being added on the Il-2m3. An improved model, the Il-10, appeared in 1944, and production of both types is believed to have reached some 40,000.

Il-2m3, V-VS (SOVIET AIR FORCE), EASTERN FRONT, 1944–5
Inscriptions were often applied to Soviet-operated aircraft during WWII, some relating to individuals, some hailing the virtues of the Motherland, while many were just propaganda slogans crudely painted on the fuselage. This is "The Avenger." The white fin and rudder markings denote the unit, which is unknown.

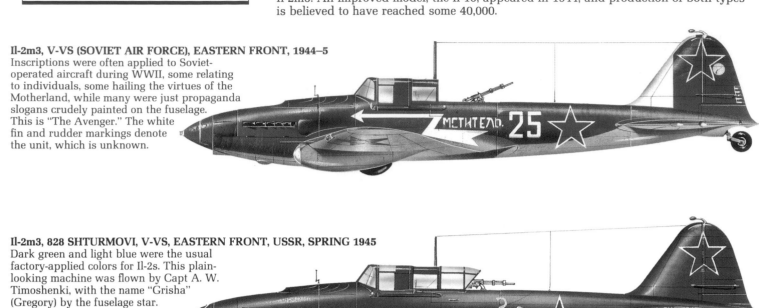

Il-2m3, 828 SHTURMOVI, V-VS, EASTERN FRONT, USSR, SPRING 1945
Dark green and light blue were the usual factory-applied colors for Il-2s. This plain-looking machine was flown by Capt A. W. Timoshenki, with the name "Grisha" (Gregory) by the fuselage star. Wrapped around the spinner is a painted star marking.

Il-2m3, V-VS (SOVIET AIR FORCE), EASTERN FRONT, USSR, 1944–5
The significance of the three white fuselage bands and the yellow rudder is unkown, although they probably related to the Regiment to which the machine was attached. Such was the protection afforded by the armored "bath" surrounding the engine and cockpit that even 20mm cannon shells often failed to penetrate it.

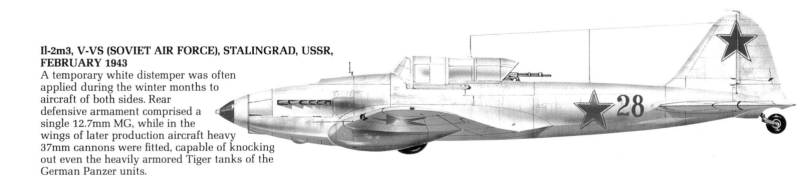

Il-2m3, V-VS (SOVIET AIR FORCE), STALINGRAD, USSR, FEBRUARY 1943
A temporary white distemper was often applied during the winter months to aircraft of both sides. Rear defensive armament comprised a single 12.7mm MG, while in the wings of later production aircraft heavy 37mm cannons were fitted, capable of knocking out even the heavily armored Tiger tanks of the German Panzer units.

Il-2B (B-31), CZECHOSLOVAK AIR FORCE, 1948–9
Having operated the type with the 1st Czech Mixed Air Division's 3rd Assault Regiment in 1944–5, the Czech AF retained the Il-2 as one of its post-war front-line combat aircraft. On the nose is the coat of arms of Ostrava, a city near the Polish frontier.

NORTH AMERICAN HARVARD

Derived from the original fixed undercarriage NA-16 of 1935, the Harvard was by far the most important Allied training aircraft in World War II. In American service it was known under a variety of designations including BC-1, AT-6 and T-6 Texan, while in British and Commonwealth use it was known as Harvard. Between 1935 and 1954, more than 20,000 were built, license-production being undertaken in Canada, Australia, Japan and Sweden.

Mk I, No 2 FLYING TRAINING SCHOOL, ROYAL AIR FORCE, 1939–40
The standard trainer scheme used from 1938 through the opening stages of World War II. Markings include the 2 FTS badge below the cockpit and the gas patch applied over the rear fuselage (designed to change color should the aircraft fly through a gas cloud).

Mk IIA, 1832 SQN, ROYAL NAVAL VOLUNTEER RESERVE, RNAS STRETTON, LATE 1940s
Wartime trainer markings are retained on this RN-operated Harvard which was in service during the post-war period, JA on the fin was the station code.

AT-6A, ROYAL SWEDISH AIR FORCE, EARLY 1950s
Sweden bought a number of surplus ex-USAAF Texans after WWII, giving them the designation Sk 14A. These remained in service until the early 1970s. Dayglo patches ensured a higher degree of visibility for training use.

Mk IIA, ROYAL NEW ZEALAND AIR FORCE, WIGRAM, NEW ZEALAND, MID 1960s
After 36 years, the Harvard was finally retired from RNZAF service on 24 June 1977. It not only operated in the flying training role, but also as a Forward Air Control aircraft.

Mk II, No. 2 WIRELESS SCHOOL, ROYAL CANADIAN AIR FORCE, 1942
The serial number indicates that this aircraft was originally destined for the RAF, but was diverted to Canada for training use.

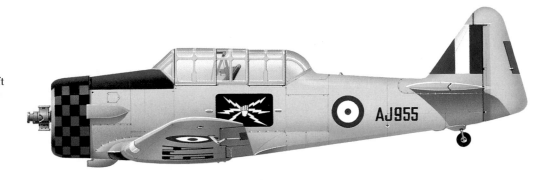

When the first P-47s arrived in England, pilots transitioning from the streamlined Spitfire could hardly believe that such a large aircraft as the "Jug" could protect itself, let alone fight! They were soon proved wrong and this massive fighter established itself as a fine example of American engineering design. From first flight in May 1941 through to final delivery in September 1945, a total of 15,660 Thunderbolts were built and the type lingered on into the 1960s with some Latin American air arms.

P-47D, EX-358th FIGHTER SQUADRON, 355th FG, SOND, AUFKLARUNGSSTAFFEL 103, LUFTWAFFE, ORLY, FRANCE, 1944
Flown by Second Lt William Roach, USAAF, "Beetle" ran out of fuel and force-landed in France. Salvaged by the Germans, it was given Luftwaffe markings although the 8th AF code (YF) and nose art were retained. It is believed to have been used to work out tactics and also to monitor US bomber formations.

P-47D-20-RA, 19th FIGHTER SQUADRON, 318th FIGHTER GROUP, USAAF, SAIPAN, MARIANAS, JULY 1944
The personal aircraft of Maj Henry McAfee, "Miss Mary Lou" carries four victory marks in the form of Japanese flags under the cockpit. The unit had natural metal cowlings and tails to distinguish its aircraft, the white letter C being the identity letter of this particular machine.

P-47D-25-RE, 352nd FIGHTER SQUADRON, 353rd FIGHTER GROUP, USAAF, RAYDON, UK, JULY 1944
To answer complaints of a lack of rearward vision, a bubble canopy was fitted to aircraft from the D-25 series. "Butch II" has invasion bands and a disruptive camouflage of Dark Green and Ocean Gray with natural metal undersides. Serial number was 42-26459.

P-47D-25-RE, 1 GRUPO DE CACA, BRAZILIAN AIR FORCE, TARQUINIA, ITALY, NOVEMBER 1944
This unit formed the fourth squadron attached to the 350th FG, the last of the 12th AF "Jug" (short for Juggernaut) units to form in the Mediterranean theater. Manned by Brazilians, it used Olive Drab/Neutral Gray-finished aircraft with the national star marking applied over the US version, unit badge and 30in high recognition code on the engine cowling.

P-47D-30-RA, 366th FIGHTER SQUADRON, 358th FIGHTER GROUP, USAAF, TOUL, FRANCE, 1944
Shown following its transfer to the 1st Tactical Air Force, this aircraft has the letter/number code (1A), the 1st TAF 18in red cowl and the orange tail unit. The dorsal fin fillet (introduced on the D-40 version and retrofitted) reduced a tail flutter problem associated with the loss of the original "razorback" fuselage.

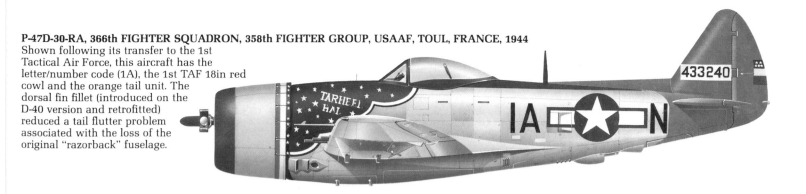

P-47D, 86th FIGHTER SQUADRON, 79th FIGHTER GROUP, USAAF, FANO, ITALY, FEBRUARY 1945
Receiving its first P-47s in March 1944, this unit adopted the coding system used previously on its P-40s. Sometimes as a prefix, as here, or as a suffix, the letter X and a number provided quick identification of the unit in the air, enhanced by the lightning insignia on the tail and the red base to the engine cowling. The anti-glare panel fore and aft of the canopy was in Olive Drab.

P-47M-1, 63rd FIGHTER SQUADRON, 56th FIGHTER GROUP, USAAF, BOXTED, UK, SPRING 1945
The fastest production "Jug" of all was the M with a top speed of 473mph at 32,000ft. The 56th was the last P-47-equipped unit in the 8th AF and received Ms in early 1945. Colors used by the 63rd FS were dark and light blue shadow shading with natural metal undersides and code letters. A medium blue was used for the serial number and rudder.

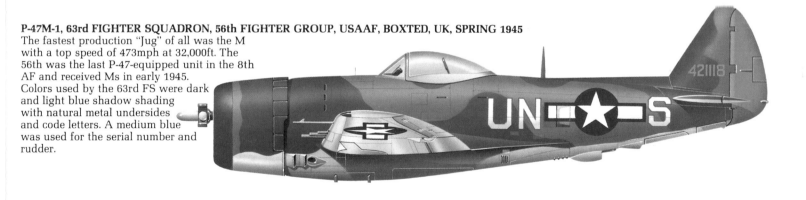

P-47D-30-RA, 512th FIGHTER SQUADRON, 406th FIGHTER GROUP, USAAF, NORD-HOLZ, GERMANY, SUMMER 1945
A natural metal-finished aircraft depicted after cessation of hostilities, when the Group was assigned to the occupation air forces and carried that organization's red-yellow-red fuselage band.

B-29 SUPER-FORTRESS

Best remembered as the aircraft that dropped the atomic bombs on Hiroshima and Nagasaki in 1945, the B-29 first flew on 21 September 1942 and became America's major weapon in the war against Japan's war industry. Bomb-load was a respectable 10 tons, while defensive armament in remote-controled positions totaled 10 .50in and one 20mm cannon. Four factories had produced 3974 B-29s by the time the last was delivered in June 1946. Some flew with the RAF as the Washington, and both China and Russia produced pirated copies.

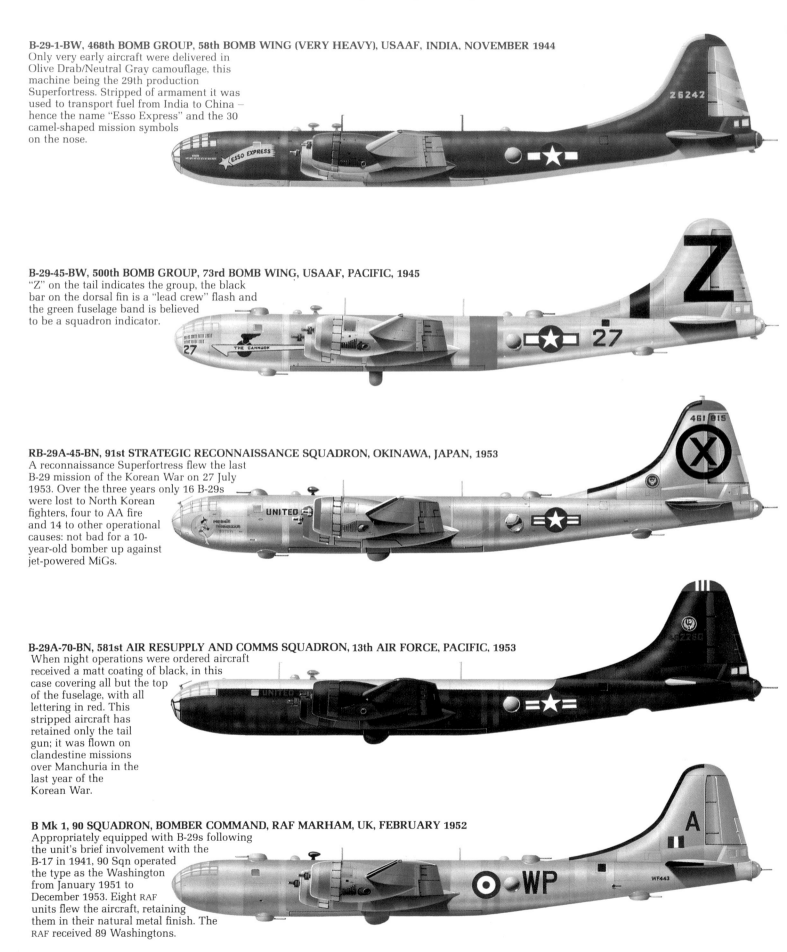

B-29-1-BW, 468th BOMB GROUP, 58th BOMB WING (VERY HEAVY), USAAF, INDIA, NOVEMBER 1944
Only very early aircraft were delivered in Olive Drab/Neutral Gray camouflage, this machine being the 29th production Superfortress. Stripped of armament it was used to transport fuel from India to China – hence the name "Esso Express" and the 30 camel-shaped mission symbols on the nose.

B-29-45-BW, 500th BOMB GROUP, 73rd BOMB WING, USAAF, PACIFIC, 1945
"Z" on the tail indicates the group, the black bar on the dorsal fin is a "lead crew" flash and the green fuselage band is believed to be a squadron indicator.

RB-29A-45-BN, 91st STRATEGIC RECONNAISSANCE SQUADRON, OKINAWA, JAPAN, 1953
A reconnaissance Superfortress flew the last B-29 mission of the Korean War on 27 July 1953. Over the three years only 16 B-29s were lost to North Korean fighters, four to AA fire and 14 to other operational causes: not bad for a 10-year-old bomber up against jet-powered MiGs.

B-29A-70-BN, 581st AIR RESUPPLY AND COMMS SQUADRON, 13th AIR FORCE, PACIFIC, 1953
When night operations were ordered aircraft received a matt coating of black, in this case covering all but the top of the fuselage, with all lettering in red. This stripped aircraft has retained only the tail gun; it was flown on clandestine missions over Manchuria in the last year of the Korean War.

B Mk 1, 90 SQUADRON, BOMBER COMMAND, RAF MARHAM, UK, FEBRUARY 1952
Appropriately equipped with B-29s following the unit's brief involvement with the B-17 in 1941, 90 Sqn operated the type as the Washington from January 1951 to December 1953. Eight RAF units flew the aircraft, retaining them in their natural metal finish. The RAF received 89 Washingtons.

LOCKHEED NEPTUNE

A refined turboprop version of the Neptune is still operational with the Japanese Maritime air arm, more than 40 years after the prototype's first flight in May 1945. There were seven major variants with production reaching 1051, 838 for the US Navy and the rest for Allied and friendly countries. Early P2V designation gave way to P-2 series from 1962. Late production aircraft had their piston engines supplemented by underwing jet pods. The RAF designation was Neptune MR Mk 1.

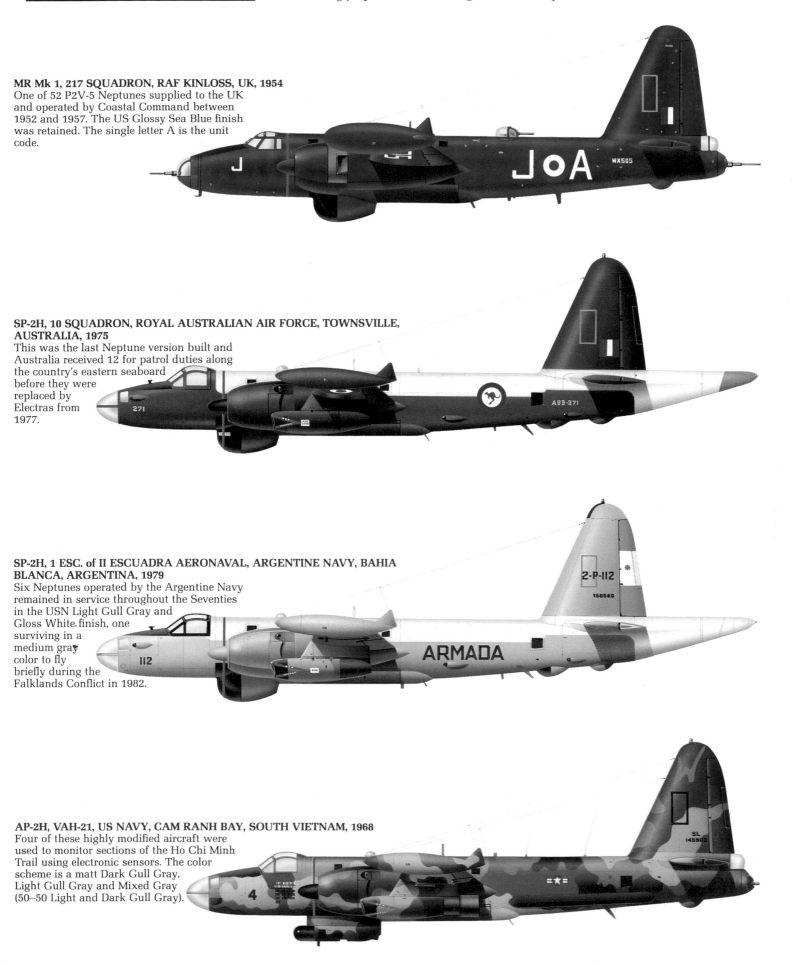

MR Mk 1, 217 SQUADRON, RAF KINLOSS, UK, 1954
One of 52 P2V-5 Neptunes supplied to the UK and operated by Coastal Command between 1952 and 1957. The US Glossy Sea Blue finish was retained. The single letter A is the unit code.

SP-2H, 10 SQUADRON, ROYAL AUSTRALIAN AIR FORCE, TOWNSVILLE, AUSTRALIA, 1975
This was the last Neptune version built and Australia received 12 for patrol duties along the country's eastern seaboard before they were replaced by Electras from 1977.

SP-2H, 1 ESC. of II ESCUADRA AERONAVAL, ARGENTINE NAVY, BAHIA BLANCA, ARGENTINA, 1979
Six Neptunes operated by the Argentine Navy remained in service throughout the Seventies in the USN Light Gull Gray and Gloss White finish, one surviving in a medium gray color to fly briefly during the Falklands Conflict in 1982.

AP-2H, VAH-21, US NAVY, CAM RANH BAY, SOUTH VIETNAM, 1968
Four of these highly modified aircraft were used to monitor sections of the Ho Chi Minh Trail using electronic sensors. The color scheme is a matt Dark Gull Gray, Light Gull Gray and Mixed Gray (50–50 Light and Dark Gull Gray).

LOCKHEED P-80

The first practical jet combat aircraft accepted into USAAF service, the P-80 (later F-80) Shooting Star saw action in Korea, operating with considerable success in the fighter-bomber role. The prototype took less than 20 weeks to build and flew on 8 January 1944, powered by a British de Havilland H-1 turbojet. From the P-80 stemmed the reconnaissance RF-80, T-33 two-seat trainer, F-94 Starfire and T2V Seastar deck-landing carrier trainer. P-80 production totaled 1718.

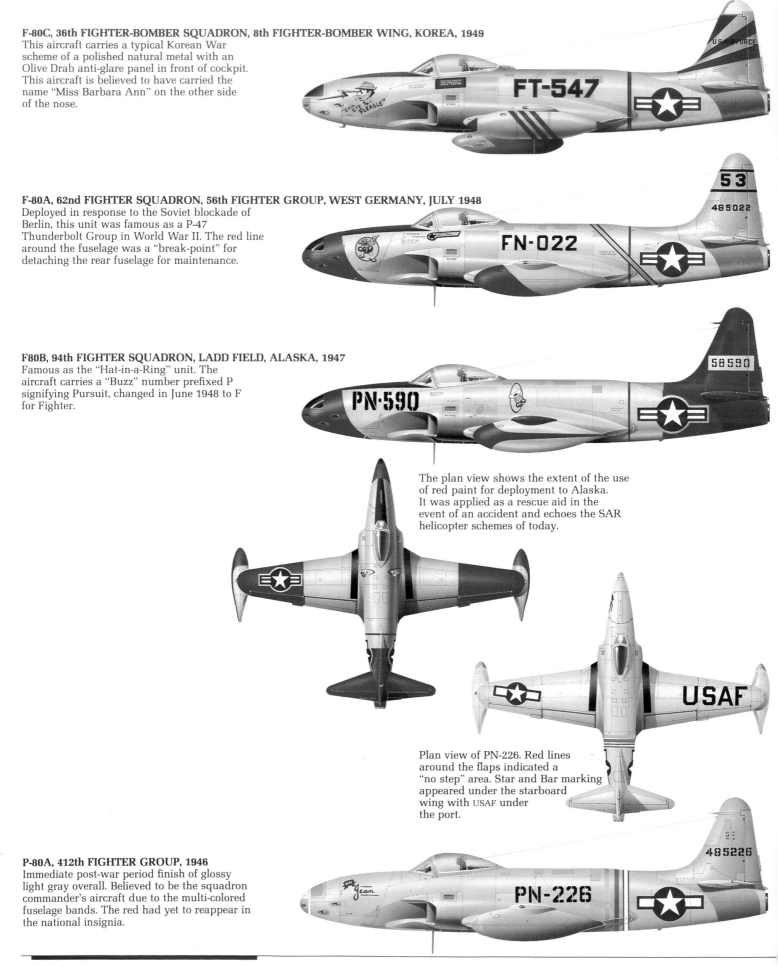

F-80C, 36th FIGHTER-BOMBER SQUADRON, 8th FIGHTER-BOMBER WING, KOREA, 1949
This aircraft carries a typical Korean War scheme of a polished natural metal with an Olive Drab anti-glare panel in front of cockpit. This aircraft is believed to have carried the name "Miss Barbara Ann" on the other side of the nose.

F-80A, 62nd FIGHTER SQUADRON, 56th FIGHTER GROUP, WEST GERMANY, JULY 1948
Deployed in response to the Soviet blockade of Berlin, this unit was famous as a P-47 Thunderbolt Group in World War II. The red line around the fuselage was a "break-point" for detaching the rear fuselage for maintenance.

F80B, 94th FIGHTER SQUADRON, LADD FIELD, ALASKA, 1947
Famous as the "Hat-in-a-Ring" unit. The aircraft carries a "Buzz" number prefixed P signifying Pursuit, changed in June 1948 to F for Fighter.

The plan view shows the extent of the use of red paint for deployment to Alaska. It was applied as a rescue aid in the event of an accident and echoes the SAR helicopter schemes of today.

Plan view of PN-226. Red lines around the flaps indicated a "no step" area. Star and Bar marking appeared under the starboard wing with USAF under the port.

P-80A, 412th FIGHTER GROUP, 1946
Immediate post-war period finish of glossy light gray overall. Believed to be the squadron commander's aircraft due to the multi-colored fuselage bands. The red had yet to reappear in the national insignia.

114

HAWKER FURY

Developed during World War II for the RAF and Royal Navy, the Centaurus-powered Fury and Sea Fury single-seat fighters suffered under post-war cut-backs and only the latter type entered UK service. Korea provided the proving-ground for this fighter (Mk X) turned fighter-bomber (FB.II) and it acquitted itself well – even against North Korean MiG-15 jets. The Fury was exported to a number of countries and a 2-seat T. 20 was also produced. Total production was 864.

FB Mk II, 805 SQUADRON, ROYAL NAVY FLEET AIR ARM, 1948
The FAA aircraft is painted Extra Dark Sea Gray with Sky undersurfaces and an individual aircraft number (103) and two-letter station code (JR Eglinton). The rear fuselage serial and ROYAL NAVY were 4in high.

Mk 50, ROYAL NETHERLANDS NAVY, 1951
47 aircraft received from the UK and Fokker production and operated with 1, 3 and 860 Squadrons. The final aircraft was struck off charge in January 1959. Overall finish was the same as for Royal Navy operated aircraft.

FB Mk 11, CUBAN REVOLUTIONARY AIR FORCE, 1960
Fifteen ex-Royal Navy aircraft were delivered to the Castro Government in 1959 including two 2-seaters. All the markings and camouflage was applied locally. FAR on the fin refers to *Fuerza Aerea Revolucionaria*.

"BAGHDAD" FURY, IRAQI AIR FORCE, 1948
All painted in desert camouflage of sand and stone with Arabic style number behind the national marking (254 in this case), a total of 55 single seat and five two-seater aircraft was delivered between 1948 and 1953.

Mk 60, PAKISTAN AIR FORCE, 1950
The largest export order for Furies was for 93 Mk 60s and five Mk 61 trainers for Pakistan, delivered between 1949 and 1954. The unit badge and squadron leader's pennant can be seen under the cockpit.

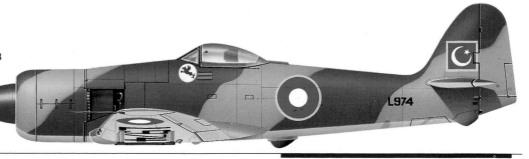

The Cold War Years
1945-1961

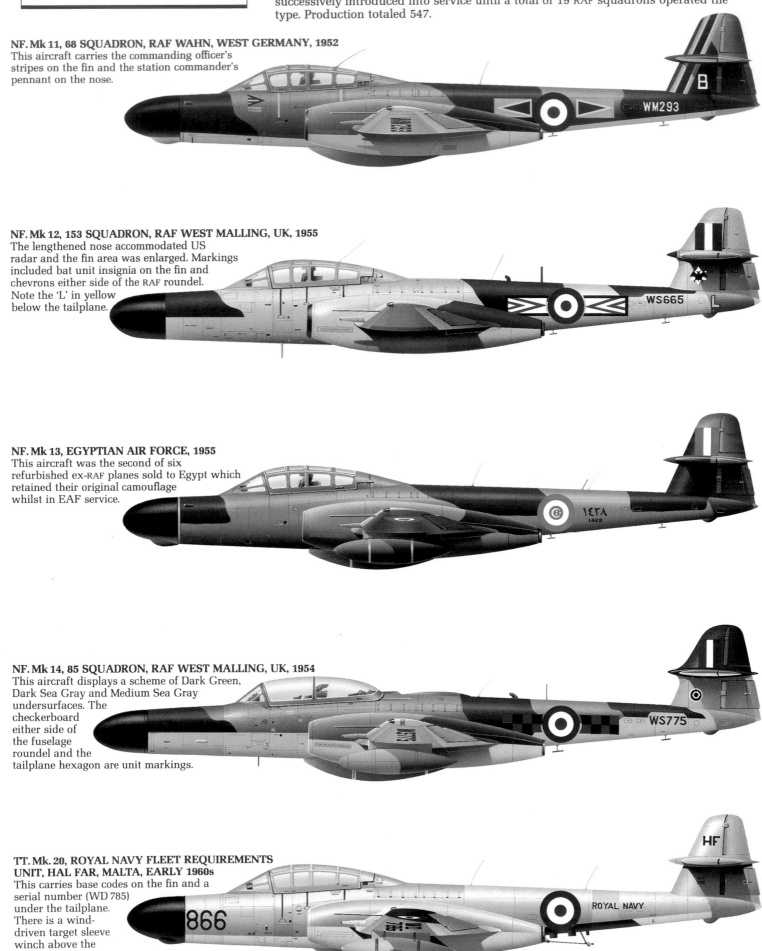

A.W. METEOR

Using the Meteor T.7 trainer as the basis of the design, Armstrong Whitworth produced a night fighting version of the single-seat Meteor day fighter, designated NF.11. Armament was moved to the wings and the extended nose housed radar and a second seat for the radar operator. The first flight was on 23 December 1948, with initial deliveries to 29 Squadron at Tangmere in 1950. The NF.12, 13 and 14 were successively introduced into service until a total of 19 RAF squadrons operated the type. Production totaled 547.

NF. Mk 11, 68 SQUADRON, RAF WAHN, WEST GERMANY, 1952
This aircraft carries the commanding officer's stripes on the fin and the station commander's pennant on the nose.

WM293

NF. Mk 12, 153 SQUADRON, RAF WEST MALLING, UK, 1955
The lengthened nose accommodated US radar and the fin area was enlarged. Markings included bat unit insignia on the fin and chevrons either side of the RAF roundel. Note the 'L' in yellow below the tailplane.

WS665

NF. Mk 13, EGYPTIAN AIR FORCE, 1955
This aircraft was the second of six refurbished ex-RAF planes sold to Egypt which retained their original camouflage whilst in EAF service.

١٤٢٨

NF. Mk 14, 85 SQUADRON, RAF WEST MALLING, UK, 1954
This aircraft displays a scheme of Dark Green, Dark Sea Gray and Medium Sea Gray undersurfaces. The checkerboard either side of the fuselage roundel and the tailplane hexagon are unit markings.

WS775

TT. Mk. 20, ROYAL NAVY FLEET REQUIREMENTS UNIT, HAL FAR, MALTA, EARLY 1960s
This carries base codes on the fin and a serial number (WD 785) under the tailplane. There is a wind-driven target sleeve winch above the starboard wing.

866 ROYAL NAVY HF

DOUGLAS AD-SKYRAIDER

Just too late for World War II, the Skyraider or "Spad" came from the drawing board of that great designer Ed Heinemann, chief engineer of Douglas El Segundo. Initially called the AD-1 and later A-1, this robust machine, which had a 10-hour endurance and seven weapon pylons each side, was the largest single seat production aircraft when it entered service in 1947. Such was its flexibility that the later AD-5 (A-1E) incorporated a larger cockpit for two crew. Total production was 3180.

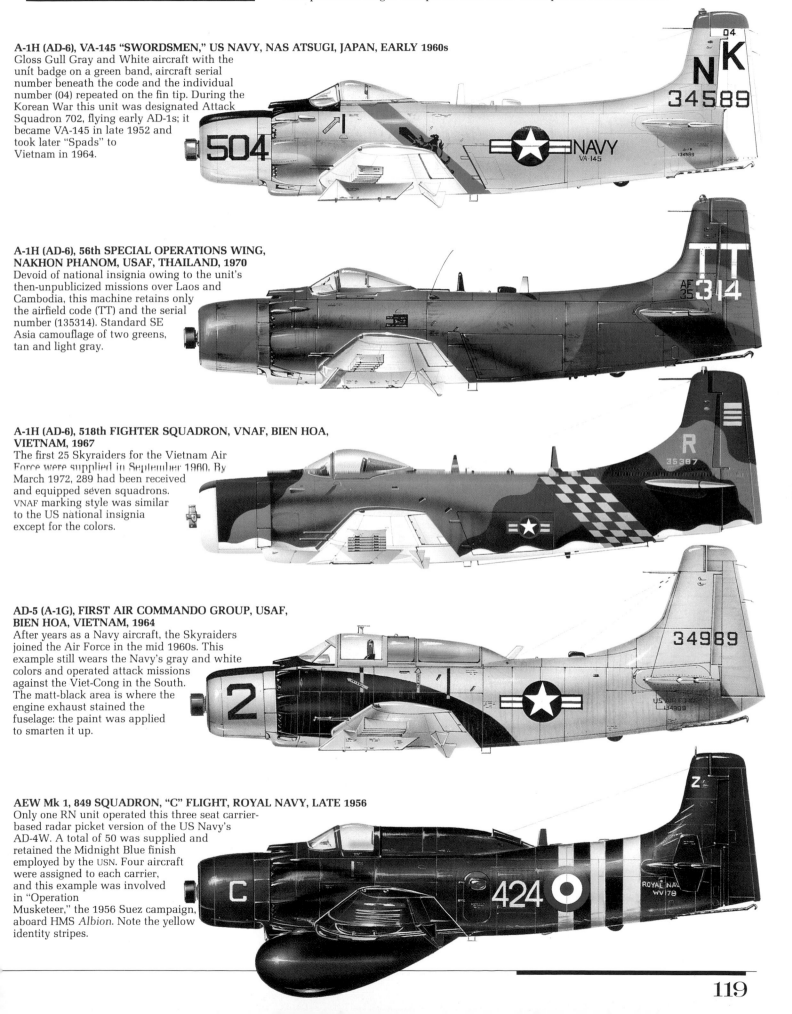

A-1H (AD-6), VA-145 "SWORDSMEN," US NAVY, NAS ATSUGI, JAPAN, EARLY 1960s
Gloss Gull Gray and White aircraft with the unit badge on a green band, aircraft serial number beneath the code and the individual number (04) repeated on the fin tip. During the Korean War this unit was designated Attack Squadron 702, flying early AD-1s; it became VA-145 in late 1952 and took later "Spads" to Vietnam in 1964.

A-1H (AD-6), 56th SPECIAL OPERATIONS WING, NAKHON PHANOM, USAF, THAILAND, 1970
Devoid of national insignia owing to the unit's then-unpublicized missions over Laos and Cambodia, this machine retains only the airfield code (TT) and the serial number (135314). Standard SE Asia camouflage of two greens, tan and light gray.

A-1H (AD-6), 518th FIGHTER SQUADRON, VNAF, BIEN HOA, VIETNAM, 1967
The first 25 Skyraiders for the Vietnam Air Force were supplied in September 1960. By March 1972, 289 had been received and equipped seven squadrons. VNAF marking style was similar to the US national insignia except for the colors.

AD-5 (A-1G), FIRST AIR COMMANDO GROUP, USAF, BIEN HOA, VIETNAM, 1964
After years as a Navy aircraft, the Skyraiders joined the Air Force in the mid 1960s. This example still wears the Navy's gray and white colors and operated attack missions against the Viet-Cong in the South. The matt-black area is where the engine exhaust stained the fuselage: the paint was applied to smarten it up.

AEW Mk 1, 849 SQUADRON, "C" FLIGHT, ROYAL NAVY, LATE 1956
Only one RN unit operated this three seat carrier-based radar picket version of the US Navy's AD-4W. A total of 50 was supplied and retained the Midnight Blue finish employed by the USN. Four aircraft were assigned to each carrier, and this example was involved in "Operation Musketeer," the 1956 Suez campaign, aboard HMS Albion. Note the yellow identity stripes.

119

D. H. VAMPIRE

The Vampire single-seat fighter-bomber entered RAF service in 1946, just too late to see action in World War II. With tapering wings and a tail supported on slim booms, the Vampire had an unmistakable shape and at one time the RAF had some 40 squadrons equipped with the type. The original F.1 was succeeded by the F. 3, the FB. 5 and the tropicalized FB. 9. The aircraft was widely exported and total production of all Vampires reached 4206.

FB. Mk 5, 112 SQUADRON, RAF BRUGGEN, WEST GERMANY, 1953
It has Dark Green, Dark Sea Gray and PR Blue undersides. There is an 18in diameter roundel on the boom.

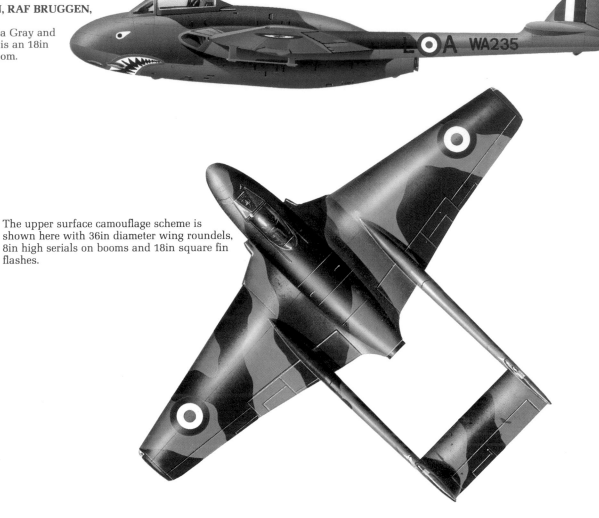

The upper surface camouflage scheme is shown here with 36in diameter wing roundels, 8in high serials on booms and 18in square fin flashes.

FB. Mk 6, SWISS AIR FORCE, MID-1950s
This was the fifth Swiss Vampire built under license out of 100 produced by F + W, Emmen, from 1951. The finish is silver overall.

FB. Mk 5, 2 SQUADRON, RHODESIAN AIR FORCE, THORNHILL, RHODESIA, 1971
It has dark green and brown upper surface camouflage with national markings adopted on declaration of UDI in 1970.

FB. Mk 5, FRENCH AIR FORCE, 1950
Known as the Mistral to the French Air Force, 247 were built under license in France.

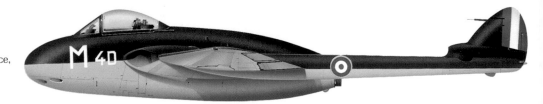

NORTH AMERICAN F-86 SABRE

Victor in the skies over Korea, the Sabre was the successful outcome of American engineering genius combined with the fruits of German wartime research on swept wings. The prototype XP-86 flew in October 1947 and the USAF deployed the F-86A to Korea three years later where its qualities outfought the Chinese-flown MiG-15 jets. Through the Fifties, the Sabre was updated and re-engined until US, Canadian, Australian and Japanese production resulted in 9502 being completed.

F MK 4, 92 SQUADRON, RAF FIGHTER COMMAND, LINTON-ON-OUSE, UK, 1954
US Mutual Aid funds were used to provide 430 Canadair-built Sabres to the RAF in the mid-1950s. Finish was Dark Green, Dark Sea Gray and Light Gray undersides. On the nose is a small squadron badge.

Mk 6, 439 SQUADRON, ROYAL CANADIAN AIR FORCE, MARVILLE, FRANCE, 1957
Canada's No 1 Air Division consisted of 12 squadrons of Sabres based in France and West Germany. Bright tail markings were a hallmark of these units.

Mk 6, JG 71 "RICHTHOFEN", WEST GERMAN AIR FORCE, WITTMUNDHAFEN, 1963
Three Luftwaffe day fighter Wings operated 225 of the Canadair-built Sabre's. The bright unit markings on JG 71 aircraft are a variation of a scheme carried on the unit's Messerschmitt 109s during WWII. The Richthofen association goes back to World War I.

F-86F, 2 SQUADRON, SOUTH AFRICAN AIR FORCE, KOREA, 1953
Between March and October 1952, the SAAF's "Flying Cheetah" squadron operated 20 or so Sabres in this natural metal scheme over Korea. The broad yellow band was an identification marking and the over-large fin stripes were also applied to assist with visual recognition.

Mk 6, 1 SQUADRON, SOUTH AFRICAN AIR FORCE, PIETERSBURG, SOUTH AFRICA, 1973
This unit was the last SAAF squadron to operate the type in a front-line role. The extremely effective camouflage comprised Olive Drab, Deep Buff with Light Admiralty Gray undersides.

CONVAIR B-36

"Six turning – four burning" was the quip most often associated with this largest of all front-line bombers, the 10-engined B-36. Intended to attack German targets from the USA, low priority and the end of the war slowed development so that the XB-36 first flew on 8 August 1946, with entry into service of the B-36A with Strategic Air Command a year later. Severe technical problems dogged the aircraft throughout its career and the last of 385 was delivered in August 1954. It was withdrawn from service in 1959.

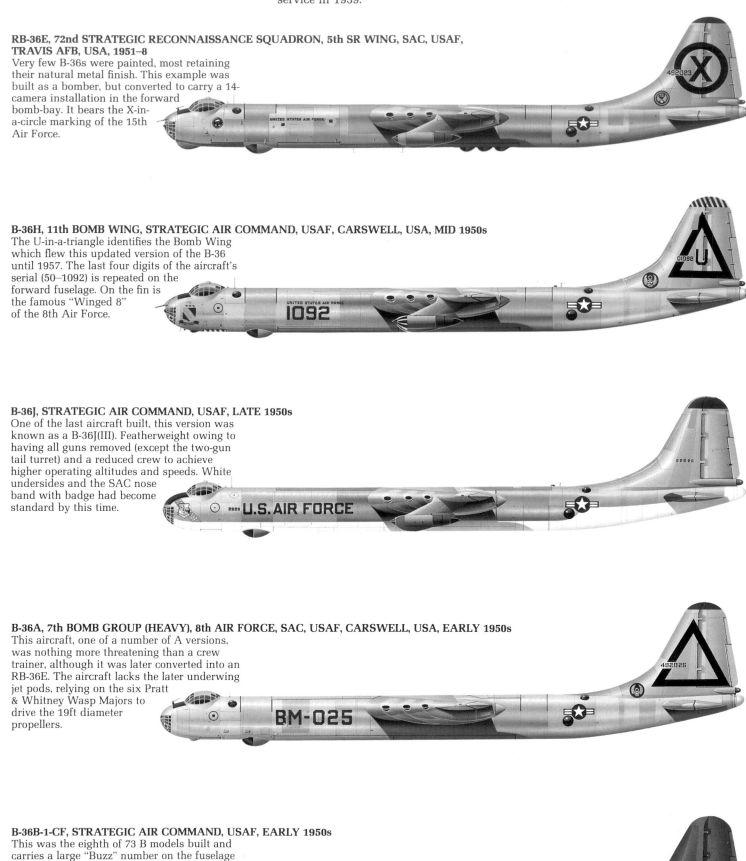

RB-36E, 72nd STRATEGIC RECONNAISSANCE SQUADRON, 5th SR WING, SAC, USAF, TRAVIS AFB, USA, 1951–8
Very few B-36s were painted, most retaining their natural metal finish. This example was built as a bomber, but converted to carry a 14-camera installation in the forward bomb-bay. It bears the X-in-a-circle marking of the 15th Air Force.

B-36H, 11th BOMB WING, STRATEGIC AIR COMMAND, USAF, CARSWELL, USA, MID 1950s
The U-in-a-triangle identifies the Bomb Wing which flew this updated version of the B-36 until 1957. The last four digits of the aircraft's serial (50–1092) is repeated on the forward fuselage. On the fin is the famous "Winged 8" of the 8th Air Force.

B-36J, STRATEGIC AIR COMMAND, USAF, LATE 1950s
One of the last aircraft built, this version was known as a B-36J(III). Featherweight owing to having all guns removed (except the two-gun tail turret) and a reduced crew to achieve higher operating altitudes and speeds. White undersides and the SAC nose band with badge had become standard by this time.

B-36A, 7th BOMB GROUP (HEAVY), 8th AIR FORCE, SAC, USAF, CARSWELL, USA, EARLY 1950s
This aircraft, one of a number of A versions, was nothing more threatening than a crew trainer, although it was later converted into an RB-36E. The aircraft lacks the later underwing jet pods, relying on the six Pratt & Whitney Wasp Majors to drive the 19ft diameter propellers.

B-36B-1-CF, STRATEGIC AIR COMMAND, USAF, EARLY 1950s
This was the eighth of 73 B models built and carries a large "Buzz" number on the fuselage for identification purposes. Arctic markings were applied to many aircraft during this period, when the Cold War appeared likely to erupt into a full-scale conflict requiring "over the Pole" operations.

MIKOYAN-GUREVICH MiG-15

Basing their design on captured German material on swept wing research, the Russian MiG Bureau's famous MiG-15 first flew on the power of a British Nene jet engine, a number of which had been exported to the USSR in 1947. Production aircraft actually entered service before the USAF's F-86 Sabre, but both met in the skies over Korea for the first true jet fighter combats. The two aircraft had their good points and the high score achieved by the Americans was probably due to superior pilot training. The name Fagot in the heading is the NATO code name for the MiG-15.

MiG-15bis, SOVIET AIR FORCE, CZECHOSLOVAKIA, 1955
Unpainted airframes were standard for Soviet-operated fighters during the Fifties and Sixties. This aircraft made a navigational error and force-landed in West Germany. On the fin is the construction number and on the nose is the regiment aircraft number.

SHENYANG J-2, AIR FORCE OF THE PEOPLE'S LIBERATION ARMY, CHINA, LATE-1950s
Camouflage patterns applied to Chinese-operated fighters usually differed from aircraft to aircraft. The national star and bar marking incorporates the Chinese characters 8 over 1.

MiG-15bis, MOSKOVSKY OKRUG PVO (SOVIET AIR FORCE), 1954
Appropriately named the Red Falcons, the Soviet Air Force aerobatic display team used a number of these brightly-painted aircraft. No national insignia was carried on the upper wing surface

MiG-15bis, PÉCS MILITARY DISTRICT, HUNGARIAN AIR FORCE, 1960
A disruptive green and brown scheme over the upper surfaces contrasted with many eastern Bloc fighters at this time which were often left in natural metal.

MiG-15 bis, AEROBATIC TEAM, CZECHOSLOVAK AIR FORCE, LATE 1950s.
Comparatively plain by today's standards of international aerobatic teams, the early aircraft of the Czechoslovak team only allowed themselves a red lightning flash and arrowhead for decoration. The team used aircraft numbered 3213 to 3233 inclusive.

BOEING B-47

As was the case with the F-86 Sabre jet fighter, wartime German research into the use of swept wings to improve performance inspired Boeing to incorporate this type of wing into its first multi-engined turbojet bomber, the B-47. Although the prototype XB-47 first flew in December 1947, the advanced nature of the design slowed the program: it was 1952 before the first B-47Bs began re-equipping SAC medium-bomber units in any numbers. Over 1800 eventually equipped 81 squadrons before its withdrawal in the mid 1960s.

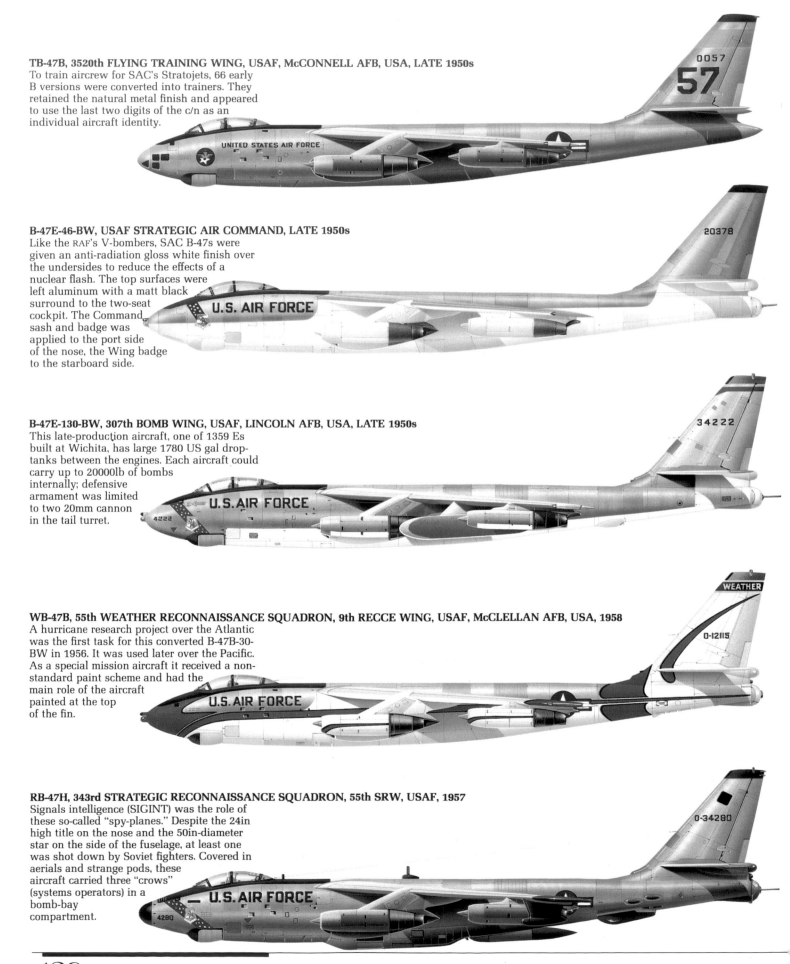

TB-47B, 3520th FLYING TRAINING WING, USAF, McCONNELL AFB, USA, LATE 1950s
To train aircrew for SAC's Stratojets, 66 early B versions were converted into trainers. They retained the natural metal finish and appeared to use the last two digits of the c/n as an individual aircraft identity.

B-47E-46-BW, USAF STRATEGIC AIR COMMAND, LATE 1950s
Like the RAF's V-bombers, SAC B-47s were given an anti-radiation gloss white finish over the undersides to reduce the effects of a nuclear flash. The top surfaces were left aluminum with a matt black surround to the two-seat cockpit. The Command sash and badge was applied to the port side of the nose, the Wing badge to the starboard side.

B-47E-130-BW, 307th BOMB WING, USAF, LINCOLN AFB, USA, LATE 1950s
This late-production aircraft, one of 1359 Es built at Wichita, has large 1780 US gal drop-tanks between the engines. Each aircraft could carry up to 20000lb of bombs internally; defensive armament was limited to two 20mm cannon in the tail turret.

WB-47B, 55th WEATHER RECONNAISSANCE SQUADRON, 9th RECCE WING, USAF, McCLELLAN AFB, USA, 1958
A hurricane research project over the Atlantic was the first task for this converted B-47B-30-BW in 1956. It was used later over the Pacific. As a special mission aircraft it received a nonstandard paint scheme and had the main role of the aircraft painted at the top of the fin.

RB-47H, 343rd STRATEGIC RECONNAISSANCE SQUADRON, 55th SRW, USAF, 1957
Signals intelligence (SIGINT) was the role of these so-called "spy-planes." Despite the 24in high title on the nose and the 50in-diameter star on the side of the fuselage, at least one was shot down by Soviet fighters. Covered in aerials and strange pods, these aircraft carried three "crows" (systems operators) in a bomb-bay compartment.

BOEING B-52

When the eight-engined B-52 entered service with Strategic Air Command in 1955, few can have predicted that it would still be operational in 1990. Some 261 remain in the USAF inventory, their main roles being as air-launched cruise missile carriers and anti-surface warfare aircraft armed with sea-skimming Harpoon missiles. Each with a crew of six, these remaining aircraft of 744 built between 1954 and 1962 will continue flying for some time to come.

B-52D, 367th BOMB SQUADRON, 306th BOMB WING, McCOY AFB, USA, 1971
The tall pointed tail identified the early variants. It was the D version, painted in the scheme shown here, that pounded North Vietnam. The SE Asia colors were Tan (34201), Green (34079), Green (34159) and Black (17038). The nose markings include a SAC badge and the legend "ORLANDO ... where the action is". On the fin is the symbol of the 2nd Air Force.

B-52G, STRATEGIC AIR COMMAND, US AIR FORCE, 1980
Devoid of any markings other than the standard serial in black on the fin tip (repeated on the nose) and the national insignia, which is hidden by the wing in this view, on the fuselage side, this G variant has the latest electro-optical viewing system blisters under the nose. White undersides replaced the black of the Vietnam era.

B-52G, STRATEGIC AIR COMMAND, US AIR FORCE, 1986
Another G version, this time sporting the SAC badge on the nose. The emblem was the result of a competition staged in 1951 for an appropriate Command crest. The winning insignia was submitted by SSgt R. T. Barnes of the 92nd Bomb Wing at Fairchild AFB, Washington, and approved by the USAF in January 1952.

B-52G, STRATEGIC AIR COMMAND, US AIR FORCE, 1988
The latest color combination consists of two dark grays and a green which SAC chose in 1985 to conceal B-52s better in their low-level attack role. The result is a particularly sombre finish; but it is non-reflective, which reduces its visibility when viewed from above against the ground.

B-52H, 319th BOMB WING, US AIR FORCE, GRAND FORKS AFB, USA, 1986
The H version differs from the G in having eight TF33 turbofan engines in place of the J57 turbojets, and a single 20mm cannon in the tail instead of four .50 caliber MGs; both types of tail turret are remotely controlled. Ninety-five B-52Hs will be cruise missile carriers, each having 12 missiles externally mounted and eight on a rotary launcher in the bomb-bay.

MCDONNELL DOUGLAS A-4

Nicknamed the Bantam Bomber when it first went to sea in 1954, the A-4 was a superb design, lightweight and simple. The wing was small enough not to require folding for carrier stowage, yet contained enough fuel to give a respectable combat range. More than 17 different configurations and a run of 2960 aircraft over 25 years are worthy achievements. Current operators include Argentina, Malaysia, New Zealand and Singapore.

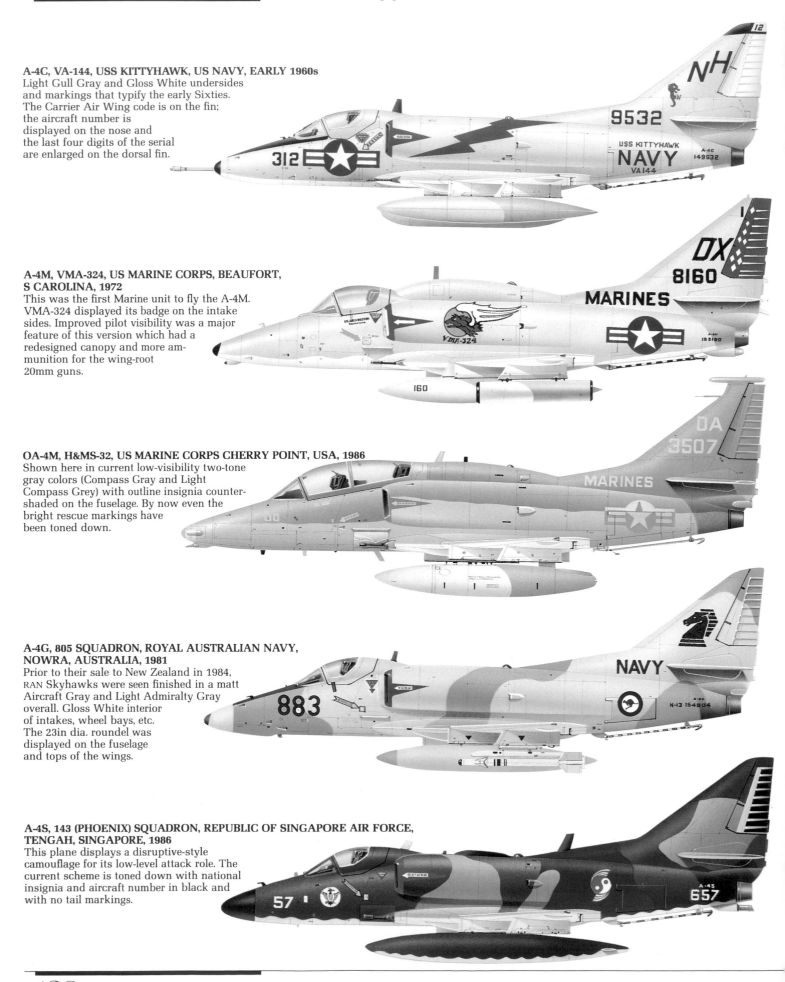

A-4C, VA-144, USS KITTYHAWK, US NAVY, EARLY 1960s
Light Gull Gray and Gloss White undersides and markings that typify the early Sixties. The Carrier Air Wing code is on the fin; the aircraft number is displayed on the nose and the last four digits of the serial are enlarged on the dorsal fin.

A-4M, VMA-324, US MARINE CORPS, BEAUFORT, S CAROLINA, 1972
This was the first Marine unit to fly the A-4M. VMA-324 displayed its badge on the intake sides. Improved pilot visibility was a major feature of this version which had a redesigned canopy and more ammunition for the wing-root 20mm guns.

OA-4M, H&MS-32, US MARINE CORPS CHERRY POINT, USA, 1986
Shown here in current low-visibility two-tone gray colors (Compass Gray and Light Compass Grey) with outline insignia countershaded on the fuselage. By now even the bright rescue markings have been toned down.

A-4G, 805 SQUADRON, ROYAL AUSTRALIAN NAVY, NOWRA, AUSTRALIA, 1981
Prior to their sale to New Zealand in 1984, RAN Skyhawks were seen finished in a matt Aircraft Gray and Light Admiralty Gray overall. Gloss White interior of intakes, wheel bays, etc. The 23in dia. roundel was displayed on the fuselage and tops of the wings.

A-4S, 143 (PHOENIX) SQUADRON, REPUBLIC OF SINGAPORE AIR FORCE, TENGAH, SINGAPORE, 1986
This plane displays a disruptive-style camouflage for its low-level attack role. The current scheme is toned down with national insignia and aircraft number in black and with no tail markings.

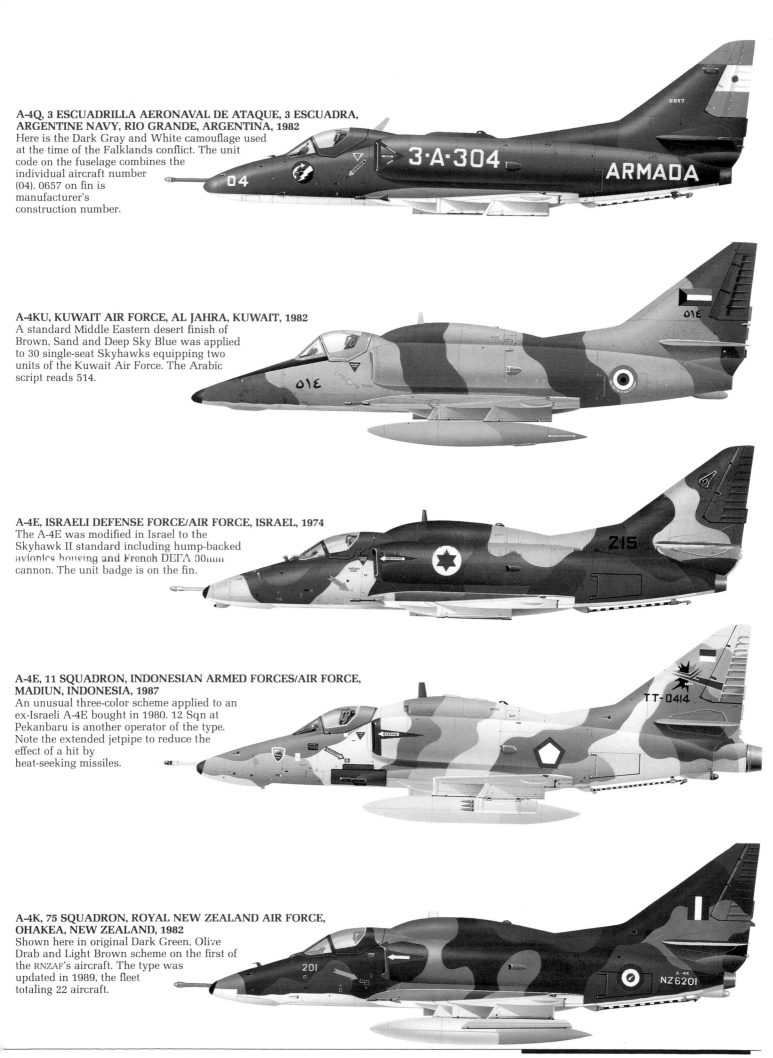

A-4Q, 3 ESCUADRILLA AERONAVAL DE ATAQUE, 3 ESCUADRA, ARGENTINE NAVY, RIO GRANDE, ARGENTINA, 1982
Here is the Dark Gray and White camouflage used at the time of the Falklands conflict. The unit code on the fuselage combines the individual aircraft number (04). 0657 on fin is manufacturer's construction number.

A-4KU, KUWAIT AIR FORCE, AL JAHRA, KUWAIT, 1982
A standard Middle Eastern desert finish of Brown, Sand and Deep Sky Blue was applied to 30 single-seat Skyhawks equipping two units of the Kuwait Air Force. The Arabic script reads 514.

A-4E, ISRAELI DEFENSE FORCE/AIR FORCE, ISRAEL, 1974
The A-4E was modified in Israel to the Skyhawk II standard including hump-backed avionics housing and French DEFA 00mm cannon. The unit badge is on the fin.

A-4E, 11 SQUADRON, INDONESIAN ARMED FORCES/AIR FORCE, MADIUN, INDONESIA, 1987
An unusual three-color scheme applied to an ex-Israeli A-4E bought in 1980. 12 Sqn at Pekanbaru is another operator of the type. Note the extended jetpipe to reduce the effect of a hit by heat-seeking missiles.

A-4K, 75 SQUADRON, ROYAL NEW ZEALAND AIR FORCE, OHAKEA, NEW ZEALAND, 1982
Shown here in original Dark Green, Olive Drab and Light Brown scheme on the first of the RNZAF's aircraft. The type was updated in 1989, the fleet totaling 22 aircraft.

REPUBLIC F-84

The F-84 series began as a straight-wing jet-powered fighter-bomber which, although outclassed in Korea by the MiG-15, achieved a measure of success in the tactical role. Redesigned with swept wings, the F-84F version emerged as the main nuclear weapon-carrying fighter-bomber with NATO's air arms from 1954. The same year, the RF-84F Thunderflash reconnaissance version entered production, cameras being positioned in a lengthened nose with engine intakes at the wing roots. F-84F/RF-84F production totaled 3428.

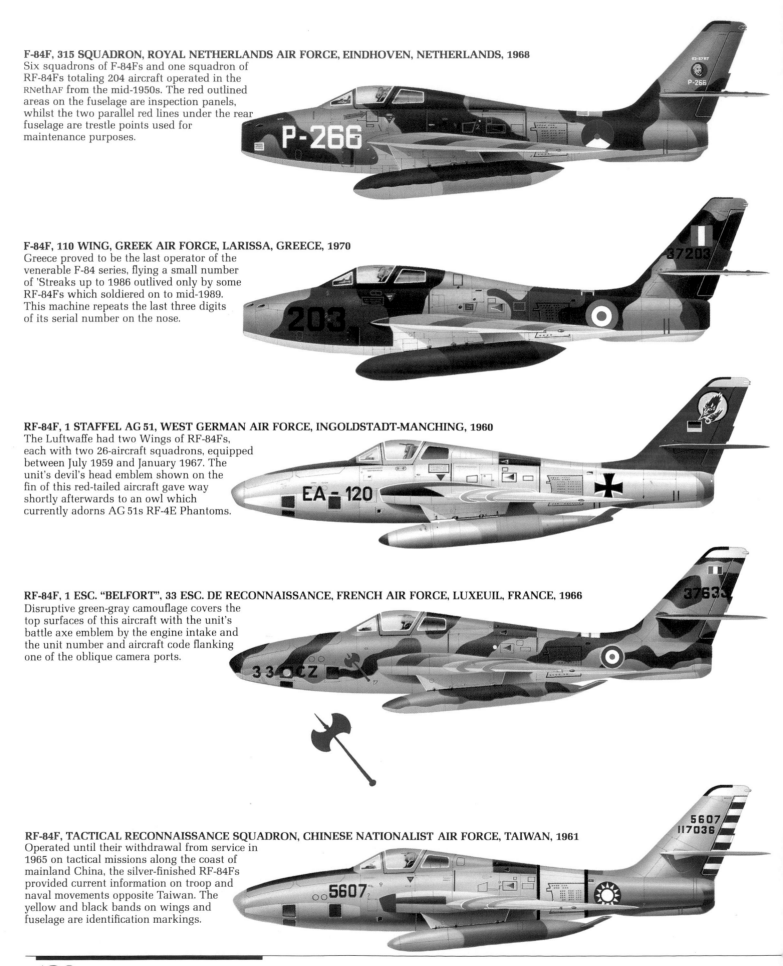

F-84F, 315 SQUADRON, ROYAL NETHERLANDS AIR FORCE, EINDHOVEN, NETHERLANDS, 1968
Six squadrons of F-84Fs and one squadron of RF-84Fs totaling 204 aircraft operated in the RNethAF from the mid-1950s. The red outlined areas on the fuselage are inspection panels, whilst the two parallel red lines under the rear fuselage are trestle points used for maintenance purposes.

F-84F, 110 WING, GREEK AIR FORCE, LARISSA, GREECE, 1970
Greece proved to be the last operator of the venerable F-84 series, flying a small number of 'Streaks up to 1986 outlived only by some RF-84Fs which soldiered on to mid-1989. This machine repeats the last three digits of its serial number on the nose.

RF-84F, 1 STAFFEL AG 51, WEST GERMAN AIR FORCE, INGOLDSTADT-MANCHING, 1960
The Luftwaffe had two Wings of RF-84Fs, each with two 26-aircraft squadrons, equipped between July 1959 and January 1967. The unit's devil's head emblem shown on the fin of this red-tailed aircraft gave way shortly afterwards to an owl which currently adorns AG 51s RF-4E Phantoms.

RF-84F, 1 ESC. "BELFORT", 33 ESC. DE RECONNAISSANCE, FRENCH AIR FORCE, LUXEUIL, FRANCE, 1966
Disruptive green-gray camouflage covers the top surfaces of this aircraft with the unit's battle axe emblem by the engine intake and the unit number and aircraft code flanking one of the oblique camera ports.

RF-84F, TACTICAL RECONNAISSANCE SQUADRON, CHINESE NATIONALIST AIR FORCE, TAIWAN, 1961
Operated until their withdrawal from service in 1965 on tactical missions along the coast of mainland China, the silver-finished RF-84Fs provided current information on troop and naval movements opposite Taiwan. The yellow and black bands on wings and fuselage are identification markings.

HAWKER HUNTER

A good-looking and highly successful fighter, the Hunter was once the backbone of RAF Fighter Command, and the type served in 21 air arms. The principal engine was the Rolls-Royce Avon and weapons comprised four 30mm Aden cannon and underwing pylons for bombs, rockets and/or drop tanks. A special reconnaissance nose could be fitted to the standard airframe, while for training, two-seater versions were produced. Production totaled 1972.

F-100C, 127
In SE Asia
stationed in
received an
marking.

F. Mk 6, 43 SQUADRON, RAF LEUCHARS, UK, LATE 1950s
An aircraft of the famous "Fighting Cocks" squadron, camouflaged in gloss Dark Green and Dark Sea Gray with Aluminum (silver) undersides.

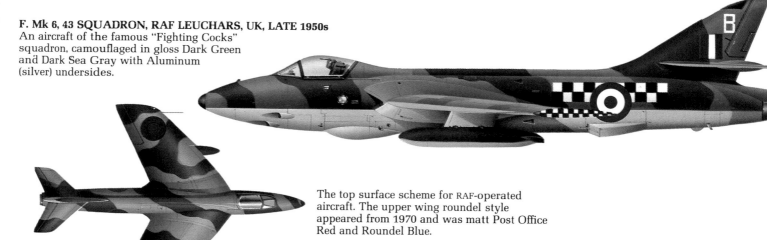

F-100D, ES
Denmark re
seaters beg
more than
Olive Drab
withdrawn

The top surface scheme for RAF-operated aircraft. The upper wing roundel style appeared from 1970 and was matt Post Office Red and Roundel Blue.

FR. Mk 71A, FUERZA AEREA DE CHILE, EARLY 1980s
This converted, ex-RAF F.4 (XF317) retains UK day fighter finish, but with Light Aircraft Gray undersides.

Mk 12, RAE FARNBOROUGH, UK, 1964
Operated on equipment trials, the aircraft had a high gloss finish which made it easier to maintain. This plan view shows the roundel position. The aircraft was subsequently withdrawn from use and employed for fire-fighting practice.

F-100D, RC
Three squa
Karup and
Aircraft we
natural me
low visibili
adopted. T
crashed in

F-100D, ES
France init
aircraft to
Mk 43 one
Seventies t
convention
being base
final withd
December

T. Mk 75A, 141 SQUADRON, REPUBLIC OF SINGAPORE AIR FORCE, TENGAH, SINGAPORE, EARLY 1980s
This is a trainer version displaying bright markings before high visibility colors were deleted.

F-100C, 11
More than
Turkey, in
late-1950s.
lost it arou
due to hea
early C va

T. Mk 7, 4 FLYING TRAINING SCHOOL, RAF VALLEY, UK, LATE 1970s
A high-visibility scheme was applied to the aircraft of this training unit for safety reasons. The unit badge (palm tree and pyramid) is on the fin.

F-100D,
The silve
squadro
to reside
Fifties. A
and alon

F-100F,
First of
SAM (S
convers
over No
external
aircraft
version
addition
the fin.

F-100D,
An exan
operatec
Viet Co
aircraft'
radio an

Vietnam and Beyond
1961-the present day

MCDONNELL DOUGLAS F-4 PHANTOM II

Designed initially for carrier-based operation with the US Navy, the Phantom was subsequently adopted by both the Marine Corps and the US Air Force. The prototype F4H-1 first flew in May 1958 and 23 years later, the 5201st and last new-build Phantom rolled off the production line. Armed with cannon and missiles, the type still serves with at least ten air forces and the various update programs now under consideration should ensure the Phantom will be around into the 21st century.

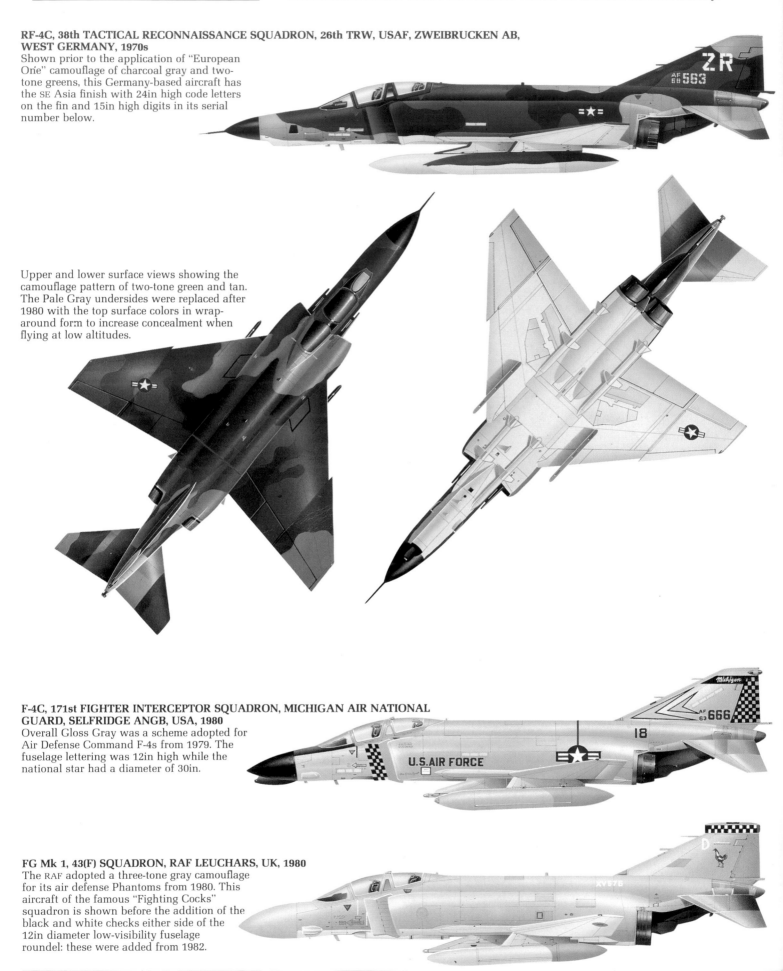

RF-4C, 38th TACTICAL RECONNAISSANCE SQUADRON, 26th TRW, USAF, ZWEIBRUCKEN AB, WEST GERMANY, 1970s
Shown prior to the application of "European One" camouflage of charcoal gray and two-tone greens, this Germany-based aircraft has the SE Asia finish with 24in high code letters on the fin and 15in high digits in its serial number below.

Upper and lower surface views showing the camouflage pattern of two-tone green and tan. The Pale Gray undersides were replaced after 1980 with the top surface colors in wrap-around form to increase concealment when flying at low altitudes.

F-4C, 171st FIGHTER INTERCEPTOR SQUADRON, MICHIGAN AIR NATIONAL GUARD, SELFRIDGE ANGB, USA, 1980
Overall Gloss Gray was a scheme adopted for Air Defense Command F-4s from 1979. The fuselage lettering was 12in high while the national star had a diameter of 30in.

FG Mk 1, 43(F) SQUADRON, RAF LEUCHARS, UK, 1980
The RAF adopted a three-tone gray camouflage for its air defense Phantoms from 1980. This aircraft of the famous "Fighting Cocks" squadron is shown before the addition of the black and white checks either side of the 12in diameter low-visibility fuselage roundel: these were added from 1982.

FGR Mk 2, 23 SQUADRON, RAF WATTISHAM, UK, 1980
Before the introduction of the grey low-visibility scheme, RAF-operated aircraft looked like this. An RWR (radar warning receiver) pod was subsequently fitted to the fin tip, many units preferring to apply their traditional marking to that instead of the fin, as in this case.

RF-4B, VMFP-3 SQUADRON, US MARINE CORPS, EL TORO, USA, 1980
Low-visibility markings with just a hint of the old flamboyance which characterized American military aircraft of previous years. 46 of these reconnaissance Phantoms were delivered to the USMC.

F-4EJ, 301 HIKOTAI, 7th KOKUDAN, JAPANESE AIR SELF-DEFENSE FORCE, HYAKURI, JAPAN, 1980
140 Phantoms were built for the JASDF, all but the first two by Mitsubishi. This green-gray camouflaged example bears the frog emblem of the unit, seven stars on the yellow muffler indicating the 7th Kokudan.

F-4F, JAGDGESCHWADER (JG) 71 "RICHTHOFEN," WEST GERMAN AIR FORCE, WITTMUNDHAFEN, 1981
Medium and light gray camouflage known as "Norm 81," was applied to aircraft of this unit and those of JG74 "Molders" in the early 1980s. On the engine intake is a small unit emblem. The Luftwaffe received 175 F-4Fs and 88 RF-4E recce versions.

F-4E, ISRAELI DEFENSE FORCE/AIR FORCE, ISRAEL, 1987
The Green, Brown and Sand disruptive scheme has proved an acceptable camouflage for operations over the desert, this typical Israeli Phantom also carrying the IAF badge at the top of the fin. Like most F-4s, the aircraft has luminous strips on the nose, fuselage and fin for night formation flying.

AEROSPATIALE ALOUETTE III

The Alouette (Lark) II was the original design from which was to come the more powerful Alouette III. This was to establish Aérospatiale (formerly Sud Aviation) as Europe's leading helicopter company. Deliveries of 1455 machines to 75 countries is no mean feat, and although French production has now ceased, the type continues to appear in much modified form from other countries, notably Romania with the Airfox gunship and South Africa with another combat version.

CHETAK, INDIAN AIR FORCE, 1984
The IAF operates both French-built and Hindustan Aeronautics-built Alouettes with an estimated 175 in service. Duties include SAR, liaison, training, etc.

ALOUETTE III, NO 1 SUPPORT WING, IRISH AIR CORPS, BALDONNEL, EIRE, 1984
Marked with a prominent tricolor behind the segmented IAC insignia, the Irish machines operate on a variety of tasks including SAR, liaison and border patrol. The prominent tail guard prevents damage to the rotor.

SA. 361B, TUNISIAN AIR FORCE, EL AOUINA, TUNISIA, 1984
Eight were originally supplied, but numbers have probably dropped to less than five. The exposed Artouste turboshaft engine incorporates an all important sand filter over the bell-mouth intake, with the exhaust projecting behind and over the tail boom.

SA 316B, 7 SQUADRON, ROYAL JORDANIAN AIR FORCE, AMMAN, JORDAN, 1981
Before their withdrawal from use, 16 machines were operated by the RJAF, including this example, numbered 318, which had a special communications 'fit' on board. The national roundel incorporates the seven-pointed star representing the first seven verses of the Koran.

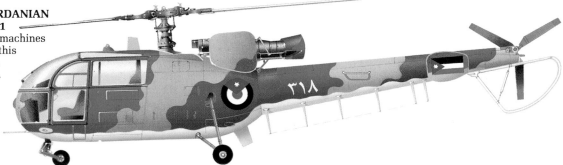

SA.316B, ESCUADRON 552, GRUPO 31, FORÇA AEREA PORTUGUESA, TANCÓS, PORTUGAL, 1986
Semi-matt dark green has been standard for the 25 or so machines operating in the liaison role. Helicopters in the Portuguese Air Force have numbers prefixed with 9.

BLACKBURN BUCCANEER

Recognized as one of the world's finest low-level attack aircraft, the Buccaneer was originally designed by Blackburn as the B.103 to meet a Royal Navy specification NA39 (by which it was known before being named). The prototype flew in April 1958 and the slightly underpowered S1 joined HMS *Ark Royal* in early 1963. Two years later the longer-ranged S2 entered RN service. These were carrier-based until transferred to the RAF in 1979. In updated form, Buccaneers continue in RAF service in the maritime strike role. The survivors of 16 sold to South Africa as S.50s are also in use. Total built was 189.

S Mk 2, 801 NAVAL AIR SQUADRON, HMS *VICTORIOUS*, ROYAL NAVY, 1965

Gloss-finished in Extra Dark Sea Gray and White, RN-operated aircraft were fitted with a "rhino horn" refueling probe to extend their range. Weapons were carried in the ventral rotating bomb bay.

S Mk 2, 809 NAVAL AIR SQUADRON, RNAS LOSSIEMOUTH, UK, 1969

A change in coloring for Buccaneers, to render them less visible in their low-level role, produced this overall gloss Extra Dark Sea Gray finish. On the fin is the unit badge, repeated in heraldic form on the engine intake.

S Mk 2B, 16 SQUADRON, RAF LAARBRUCH, WEST GERMANY, 1974

Replacing Canberras in the strike role as part of RAF Germany, Buccaneers were given a scheme of matt Dark Green, Dark Sea Gray and Light Aircraft Gray, then the RAF's standard disruptive finish. A bulged bomb bay fuel tank was fitted to increase the range; the nose probe was removed.

S Mk 2A, 208 SQUADRON, ROYAL AIR FORCE, NELLIS AIR FORCE BASE, USA, 1977

For participation in American Red Flag exercises, aircraft were given a Light Stone and Dark Earth camouflage which proved remarkably effective in merging their shape into the desert background. The rear fuselage area retained the European green/gray colors, as did the nose radome. The probe was retained on UK-based Bucs for the maritime strike role.

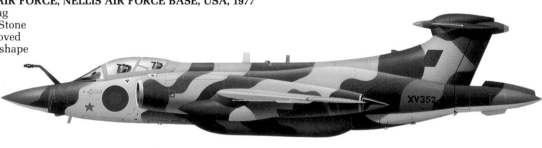

S Mk 50, 24 SQUADRON, SOUTH AFRICAN AIR FORCE, WATERKLOOF, SA, 1981

Only six aircraft of 16 ordered continue in SAAF use. A miniaturized national insignia has replaced the larger type originally applied. Gloss colors are Dark Sea Gray and PRU Blue undersides.

NORTHROP F-5

First flown on 30 July 1959, the N-156F was designed as a low-cost supersonic fighter. It carried about 485 gallons of fuel, two 20mm cannon and two Sidewinder missiles. Three years later the type entered production as the F-5 and over the next 20 years some 30 countries either bought, were given, or acquired examples of this small American combat aircraft. The early F-5A and two-seat F-5B gave way to the improved F-5E and F-5F from 1972 and there were also reconnaissance versions with nose-mounted cameras and sensors. Total production was 2610 of all versions.

CF-5A/D, 434 "BLUENOSE" SQUADRON, CANADIAN ARMED FORCES, CHATHAM CFB, CANADA, 1980
Canadair-built CF-5As have a speed and climb rate superior to the basic F-5A. This example has the standard bi-lingual titling either side of the national marking on the nose and prominent squadron insignia on the fin and engine intakes. The refuelling probe is an optional fitting and is used for long-range deployments.

F-5A, 1 SQUADRON, ROYAL JORDANIAN AIR FORCE, KING HUSSEIN AB, MAFRAQ, JORDAN, 1978
Supplied by Iran from 1974, 30 F-5As were operational with two units of the RJAF until replaced by F-5Es from the mid 1980s. Desert camouflage of sand, brown and dark green with blue undersides forms the standard scheme for this country's fighters. The nose number is 605.

F-5E, 64th FITS, 57th FIGHTER WEAPONS WING, USAF, NELLIS AFB, USA, 1977
For Dissimilar Air Combat Training (DACT) the USAF painted their F5Es in camouflage schemes similar to those used by Soviet fighters. This is the "snake" scheme using green, brown and tan colors with the last two digits of the serial number painted on the nose. The unit badge is on the intake with the TAC badge on the fin.

F-5E, 57th FIGHTER WEAPONS WING, USAF, NELLIS AFB, USA, 1978
American artist Keith Ferris devised a number of color schemes to break up the outline of an aircraft using blues and grays with sharp edges to the colors. This is one of the experimental schemes used by an "aggressor" training unit.

F-5E, US NAVY FIGHTER WEAPONS SCHOOL, MIRAMAR NAS, USA, 1978
Made famous by the film "Top Gun," the USN aggressor training unit at Miramar is established along the same lines as that of the USAF's units. The F-5E "drivers" duplicate Soviet tactics, wear Soviet insignia and learn Soviet doctrine. The School badge is located on the fin.

F-5E, 527th TFTAS, RAF ALCONBURY, UK, 1978
One of the five different "aggressor" schemes used by the 527th, this one was called "gray ghost." During mock combat training, opposing pilots found the aggressor F-5s very difficult to see.

F-5E, 64th FITS, 57th FIGHTER WEAPONS WING, NELLIS AFB, USA, 1978
This brown and tan scheme was known as "lizard" and particularly suited the Nevada desert training grounds situated around Nellis. The wingtip pylons carried dummy AIM-9 Sidewinder missiles instrumented to record imaginary air-to-air kills.

RF-5E TIGEREYE, 17 SQUADRON, ROYAL SAUDI AIR FORCE, TABUK, SAUDI ARABIA, 1988
Tactical reconnaissance is the main task of the ten specialized Tigereye versions in Saudi service. Disruptive desert camouflage colors appear to be standard on RSAF Tornados, F-5s, Strikemasters and Hawks.

F-5E, NO 1 SQUADRON, NO 1 FIGHTER GROUP, BRAZILIAN AIR FORCE, SANTA CRUZ AFB, BRAZIL, 1980
Brazilian F-5s differ from some other operator's aircraft in having a VHF dorsal antenna in place of the standard UHF type and also a dorsal fin extension. The jungle camouflage owes much to the USAF's Vietnam scheme.

F-5E, MOROCCAN ROYAL AIR FORCE, 1987
Twenty aircraft were acquired by the Moroccan AF in 1981 and about 13 survive following combat operations against the Polisario guerrillas. The tail flash is a pentagram, or Soloman's Seal emblem, repeated with the addition of a crown in the circular marking.

F-5E, 2nd FIGHTER WING, REPUBLIC OF CHINA AIR FORCE, TAIWAN, 1978
Another variation on the American SE Asia three-color camouflage which has been adopted by a number of air arms. This particular aircraft (74-00959) called 'Chung Chang' was one of an initial batch supplied by Northrop; subsequent machines were assembled at Taichung.

BELL IROQUOIS

Dubbed Huey, the UH-1 was the US forces' workhorse of the Vietnam War. It was the "cornerstone of airmobility" thoughout the campaign, moving troops into battle, lifting them out, giving them fire-support, food and ammunition, and emitting that distinctive rotor beat which was music to the ears of the wounded GIs awaiting evacuation. The Huey also "made" the Bell company, which produced more than 20,000 from the first example delivered in 1959. Although the Sikorsky UH-60 is intended as its replacement, the ubiquitous UH-1 will be around until well into the 21st century.

UH-1A, UTILITY TACTICAL TRANSPORT HELICOPTER COMPANY, US ARMY, OKINAWA, 1961
The Platoon Leader of Red Platoon operated this early model Huey. Color was Olive Drab overall, with clearly marked hand-hold accesses on the rear cabin and a red line around the engine where the turbine is located.

UH-1B, 121st ASSAULT HELICOPTER CO, 13th COMBAT AVN BATTALION, US ARMY, SOC TRANG, VIETNAM, 1967
"BLITZ-KRIEG" of the "Vikings" armed (gunship) platoon. The national insignia had been removed from US Army UH-1s by this time, leaving them dark and dull apart from crew embellishments or the tactical marks as shown on this example.

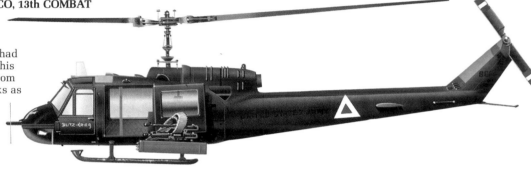

UH-1B, 2/20th ARA, 1st CAVALRY DIVISION, US ARMY, VIETNAM, 1967
Armed with a Nord SS11 (US M22) anti-tank missile and carrying the famous Air Cavalry badge on the tail, this is a B Battalion machine. Inboard of the missiles is an XM-3 24 or 36-tube rocket-launcher pack.

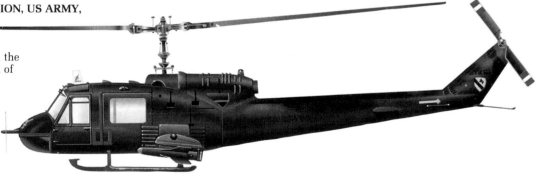

UH-1B, 1st AVIATION BATTALION, 1st INF. DIV, US ARMY, VIETNAM, 1967
One of a number of experimental camouflage schemes applied to Hueys in Vietnam. Being a troop carrier it was known as a "slick"; although it was officially capable of accommodating seven passengers, the B version regularly carried considerably more.

UH-1D, 82nd MEDICAL DETACHMENT, 121st ASSAULT HELICOPTER CO, US ARMY, SOC TRANG, VIETNAM, 1967
Clearly marked with the time-honored red cross marking, this was a special medevac machine with space for six stretchers in the cabin. When the newer "Deltas" and "Hotel" versions first arrived in Vietnam they were assigned to the medevac units.

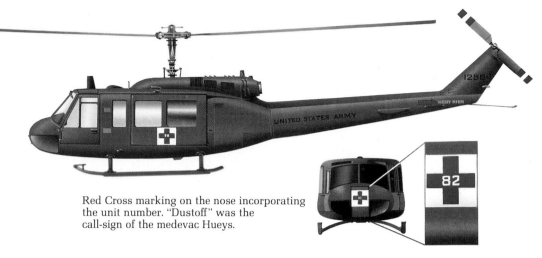

Red Cross marking on the nose incorporating the unit number. "Dustoff" was the call-sign of the medevac Hueys.

UH-1B, 1st LIFT PLATOON, 117th AVIATION CO (AIRMOBILE LIGHT), 52nd AVN BATTALION, US ARMY, QUI NHON, VIETNAM, 1964
Black and brown tiger-stripe finish on a basic "slick" in the early days of the US involvement in the war. In the doorway is a 7.62mm MG to give suppressive fire during the assault phase.

UH-1D/H, 260th COMBAT AVN BATTALION, US ARMY CU CHI, VIETNAM, 1967
Black Baron was the Battalion commander's command and control flight machine. In it he had a range of radio equipment with which he could direct air landing operations.

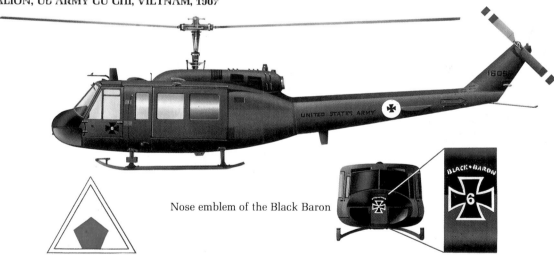

Nose emblem of the Black Baron

UH-1D, 3 SQUADRON, ROYAL NEW ZEALAND AIR FORCE, HOBSONVILLE, NEW ZEALAND, 1980
First of five for the RNZAF, NZ3801 arrived in 1966 finished in the standard US Army scheme of overall Olive Drab with white serial numbers and the then official fern insignia. This was later replaced by the Kiwi marking, and in the mid 1970s the machine itself was repainted green.

NORTH AMERICAN A-5

As a Mach 2 carrier-based strike aircraft, the Vigilante was not very successful. Its biggest problem, which remained unsolved, concerned the linear bomb-bay located in the center of the fuselage between the engines. This should have ejected a Mk 28 nuclear weapon rearwards, but it proved unreliable in a series of trials. Instead, 59 early production A-5As and Bs were converted to RA-5C multi-sensor recce aircraft and gave valuable service during the Vietnam war. Total production reached 156, and the type was retired from USN service in the late 1970s.

A3J-1 (A-5A), VAH-7, US NAVY, USS *ENTERPRISE*, AUGUST 1962
The first full squadron deployment at sea saw this early version aboard *Enterprise*. The bomber had a noticeably flat-topped fuselage compared with the humped appearance of the later RA-5C. Colors were Light Gull Gray and Gloss White, with the unit badge on the side of the engine intake.

A3J-2, US NAVY, NAVAL AIR TEST CENTER, PATUXENT RIVER, USA, 1962
Trials aircraft used for the re-configured airframe of the YA-5C which became the reconnaissance RA-5C. Bureau Number was 149300 applied small under the tailplane, with the last three digits painted in black on the nose. The re-fueling probe housing can be seen above the number.

RA-5C, RVAH-6 "FLEURS," US NAVY, USS *CONSTELLATION*, LATE 1960s
Built as an A-5A bomber this machine was assigned to the Pacific Fleet, as indicated by the NL tail code. Under the fuselage is a side-looking radar pod which also contained cameras. The nose number denotes the squadron and aircraft number (4) within the squadron.

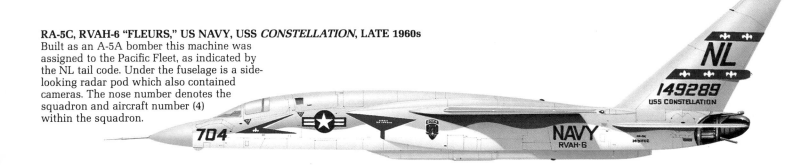

RA-5C, RVAH-5, US NAVY, USS *CONSTELLATION*, SE ASIA, 1968
During the Vietnam war, the recce "Vigis" operated around the clock from carriers in the Gulf of Tonkin, gathering information on targets in the North for future strikes by bombers. Some Vigilantes also acted as aerial tankers supporting the "snoopers."

RA-5C, RVAH-13, US NAVY, USS *INDEPENDENCE*, SE ASIA, EARLY 1970s
For over-land recce operations, a coat of standard SE Asia camouflage was deemed advisable, and late in the Vietnam conflict, aircraft like this became a familiar sight on Yankee Station in the Gulf.

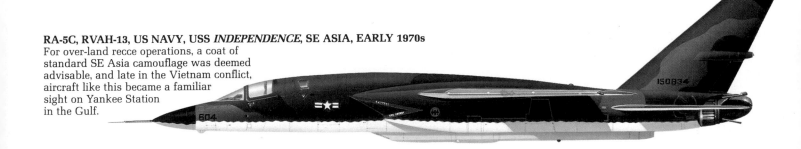

The tadpole-shaped Intruder has been a familiar sight on US Navy carriers since it entered service in the mid 1960s. An all-weather attack aircraft with a crew of two, the A-6 is capable of delivering 18,000lb of bombs over a 1000-mile range, a feat regularly demonstrated during the Vietnam war. From the basic A-6 design, Grumman developed the four-seat EA-6B Prowler electronic-warfare aircraft, the first of more than 149 flying in May 1968. Production of both types continues.

A-6E, VA-65 "TIGERS," US NAVY, USS *INDEPENDENCE* (CVW-7), 1974
Shown before the addition of the chin-mounted sensor turret known as TRAM (Target Recognition And Multi-sensor), which is on most E versions, this example is in the standard scheme of non-specular Light Gull Gray with Glossy White undersides. Bright unit markings were still part of the operational scene.

EA-6A, VMCJ-2, US MARINES, DA NANG, VIETNAM, 1972
Replacing the EF-10B Skyknight, this Intruder version provided tactical ECM for Marine strike operations in SE Asia. Unlike other A-6s, the EA-6A had no wingtip speed brakes, relying instead on one on each side of the rear fuselage for aerodynamic braking (seen here under the word "MARINES").

A-6E, VA-128, US NAVY, NAS WHIDBEY ISLAND, USA, MID 1980s
The low-visibility finish had really taken effect by this time and units were allowed to display their markings only in outline form, usually on the tail. This squadron was the Pacific Fleet replacement training unit. The grays used are 36320 (dark) on the upper surface and 36375 (light) on the undersides.

EA-6B, VAQ-134, US NAVY, USS *ENTERPRISE* (CVW-14), LATE 1970s
In the lengthened fuselage the Prowler carries a four-man crew which includes two ECM operators in the rear seats. Under the wings and belly are powerful jamming pods. The unusual "rhino-horn" in front of the cockpit is the aerial refuelling probe and is on all versions of the A-6.

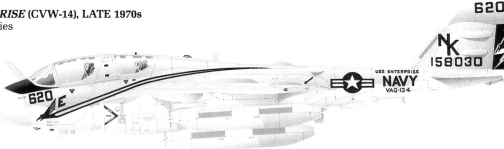

EA-6B, VMAQ-2, US MARINES, MCAS EL TORO, USA, MID 1980s
The official low-visibility gray scheme for the Prowler uses three different shades, but they are hard to detect at more than a few yards, their merging into an overall tone being the object of the finish. Production of this aircraft in updated form is planned to continue until 1992.

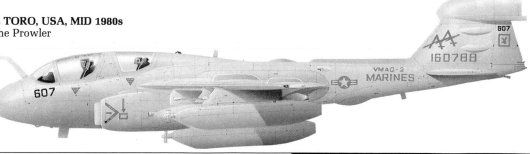

SEPECAT JAGUAR

BAC in the UK and Dassault-Breguet in France jointly developed the Jaguar from separate requirements issued by the RAF and the French Air Force. Both single-seat all-weather attack and two-seat trainer versions were produced, the first aircraft flying on 8 September 1968. Each country ordered some 200 aircraft, and overseas sales have been made to India (where it is license-built), Ecuador, Nigeria and Oman. The Jaguar has seen combat with the French Air Force in Mauretania in 1977 and more recently in Chad. Total sales to date amount to 573 aircraft.

GR Mk 1, 14 SQUADRON, RAF BRÜGGEN, WEST GERMANY, 1984
The RAF received 202 Jaguars, almost all camouflaged in Dark Green and Dark Sea Gray. Low visibility national markings were somewhat compromised by the brightness of the squadron badge, but this would have been toned down or removed in wartime. Under the wing is a 264 Imp gal drop-tank.

JAGUAR A, EC 1/7 "PROVENCE," FRENCH AIR FORCE, ST DIZIER, FRANCE, 1983
Armée de l'Air purchased 160 single-seat As and 40 two-seat Es to equip nine Escadrons in 3, 7 and 11 Escadres de Chasse. Aircraft deployed overseas to Africa had their European camouflage oversprayed in a sand and stone coloring.

JAGUAR INTERNATIONAL, 8 SQUADRON, SULTAN OF OMAN'S AIR FORCE, THRUMRAYT, OMAN, 1981
Dark Earth and Light Stone applied over all surfaces is the scheme adopted for the low-level attack role in this barren country. In recent years the small tail insignia has been changed, with blue replacing the red.

JAGUAR INTERNATIONAL, 5 SQUADRON, INDIAN AIR FORCE, 1982
Shemsher (an assault sword) is the Indian name for the aircraft and 5 Sqn "The Tuskers" was the first unit to receive UK-built machines to the full Indian standard. A maritime strike version is also in service armed with Sea Eagle missiles and a French Agave radar.

JAGUAR INTERNATIONAL, FEDERAL NIGERIAN AIR FORCE, MAKURDI, NIGERIA, 1985
Devoid of any unit markings, the 13 single and five two-seaters delivered in the mid-1980s carry only national insignia and the aircraft number on the fin, prefixed with the Air Force abbreviation.

M-B-B
BO105

Armed with six HOT or eight TOW anti-tank missiles, the small BO105 can be a deadly opponent to enemy armor. Initially developed for the civil market, this Messerschmitt-Bolkow-Blohm design found favor with the West German Army in its BO105M form for liaison and comms duties. The later BO105P with uprated transmission and improved rotors was selected for A-T use. Other operators include Indonesia (where it is built under license), Iraq, the Netherlands, Spain and Sweden (designated HKP 9A). Military production exceeds 650.

BO105P, WEST GERMAN ARMY AVIATION, 1985
Three *Panzerabwehrregiments* home-based at Celle, Roth and Fritzlar are equipped with the anti-tank version of the BO105. Each of the 212 machines can carry six HOT wire-guided missiles, the gunner using a roof-mounted sight to acquire the targets.

BO105GSH, BATTALION DE HELICOPTEROS DE ATAQUE I, SPANISH ARMY AVIATION, SPAIN, 1986
Assembled in Spain by CASA, the BO105 operates with the Army in three main roles, anti-tank (Spanish designation HA.15), reconnaissance (HR.15) and attack with a 20mm cannon installation under the fuselage (also HR.15).

BO105CBS, F6 WING, SWEDISH AIR FORCE, KARLSBORG, SWEDEN, 1986
Four examples are in service for search and rescue duties, two with F6 Wing shown here and two with F7 at Satenas, hence the orange high-visibility areas on the fuselage and tail unit. Swedish type designation is HKP 9B.

BO105CBS, FUERZA AEREA DE CHILE, 1986
The first of some 30 machines for the FACh was delivered early in 1986. Assembly is being undertaken in Santiago by ENAER. The bright paint scheme using the Chilean national colors indicates a VIP/Government machine bearing the standard H = helicopter prefix used on FACh rotary-wing craft.

SIKORSKY CH-53/S-65

Together with the Chinook, the largest Western helicopter in service, the CH-53 is best remembered for its rescue and recovery operations during the Vietnam war. Less successful was its involvement in the abortive Iranian hostage rescue mission in April 1980. The first CH-53 flew in October 1964 and entered US Marine service on 20 September 1966. Subsequent versions included the HH-53B/C (USAF) CH-53D (USMC), the three-engined CH-53E (USMC, USN), CH-53G (W German Army) and the specialized mine-countermeasures MH-53E.

S-65C-3, ISRAELI DEFENSE FORCE/AIR FORCE, ISRAEL, 1971
Sikorsky camouflaged the 33 machines supplied to the IDF/AF in this scheme of sand, brown and green. However, the Middle East climate faded the colors considerably and the machines took on a much lighter finish.
Continuing Israeli security prevents unit badges, squadrons and bases to be stated with any degree of certainty.

CH-53G, MHFTR-35, III KORPS, W GERMAN ARMY, NIEDERMENDIG, W GERMANY, 1980
Dark olive green overall, *Heersflieger* CH-53Gs carry a four-digit code ranging between 8401 and 8512, making this example the 66th machine of 112 purchased. Three Regiments operate the type, one attached to each Army Corps.

HH-53C, 37th ARRS, US AIR FORCE, DA NANG AB, SOUTH VIETNAM, 1971
The premier rescue helicopter in SE Asia, Super Jolly Green Giants roamed across the jungles of North and South Vietnam.
The long nose refuelling probe for air-to-air refueling allowed extended missions to be flown in search of downed aircrew. Miniguns were often the only defensive armament for these large machines.

CH-53D, HMH-462, US MARINE CORPS, FUTENMA, OKINAWA, LATE 1970s
Dark olive drab made these helicopters often appear almost black in daylight. Apart from the rescue and warning markings, all other insignia was applied in black. Sea Stallion is the official name of Marine-operated CH-53A/Ds.

CH-53C, 601st TASS, USAF, SEMBACH AB, W GERMANY, EARLY 1980s
'European 1' camouflage pattern was sprayed on the small force of USAF CH-53C Super Jollies based in W Germany and New Mexico, USA. Official Tech Order color names are Gunship Greens 34092 and 34102 and Gunship Gray 36118, the numbers relating to the Federal Standard 595a list.

HH-53C, 67th AEROSPACE RESCUE & RECOVERY SERVICE, USAF, RAF WOODBRIDGE, UK, 1983
Designed for long-range rescue operations, 44 of these specialized machines were built, each protected by armor, and fitted with an inflight refueling probe, advanced avionics, auxiliary fuel tanks and uprated engines. 'European 1' camouflage includes black outline national markings.

RH-53D, HM-12, US NAVY, NAS NORFOLK, USA, 1975
The tremendous power of the H-53 prompted the USN to order a minesweeping version, the RH-53A. The later D variant, of which 30 were built, succeeded it and HM-12 was the first Helicopter Mine Countermeasures Squadron. The structure under the rear fuselage is used to tow the mine sweep gear.

MH-53H, 1st SPECIAL OPERATIONS WING, USAF, HURLBURT FIELD, USA, 1987
Night and adverse weather operations called for this modification of the HH-53C. Equipment includes Forward-Looking Infra-Red, Doppler navigation system and, in the nose thimble, radar taken from the A-7D Corsair II.

CH-53E, US MARINE CORPS, 1987
Four Marine units operate this three-engined version of the H-53 series. Anonymous in its dark olive drab finish with no insignia readily apparent, this giant can carry 55 combat-ready troops or lift most types of Marine artillery as well as downed aircraft and helicopters.

CH-53E, HC-1, US NAVY, NORTH ISLAND, CALIF, 1985
USN Super Stallions adopted this very dark gray finish principally for night operations although it is also effective coloring against the sea. All markings appear pale blue with just the machine number (441) in white. The external fuel tanks on the E version each carry 650 US gal.

Developed from the Jet Provost basic trainer, the Strikemaster two-seat, light attack and training aircraft made its first flight on 26 October 1967, the first deliveries being made (to Saudi Arabia) the following year. Powered by a Rolls-Royce Viper engine, this functional design proved particularly robust when used on ground-attack duties in the harsh climate of the Middle East. Total Strikemaster production was 15.

Mk 87, KENYA AIR FORCE, KENYA, 1971
Six were delivered in 1971 with Dark Green, Dark Sea Gray and Light Aircraft Gray undersides. Five were still in use in 1988.

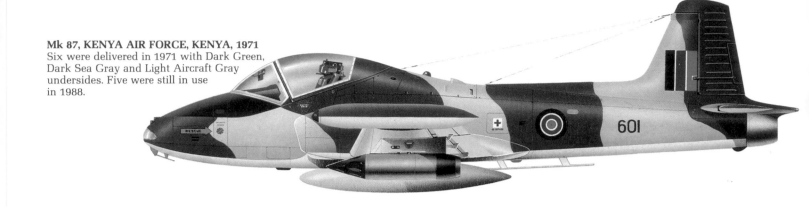

Mk 88, 14 SQUADRON, ROYAL NEW ZEALAND AIR FORCE, OHAKEA, NEW ZEALAND, 1972
One of 16 delivered, NZ6361 was camouflaged in Dark Green, Olive Drab and Light Brown. The wing roundel is marked on the top of the port and the bottom of the starboard wing.

Mk 84, 130 "EAGLE" SQUADRON, REPUBLIC OF SINGAPORE AIR FORCE, SINGAPORE, 1982
Sixteen were delivered in 1969 for training; hence the dayglo markings over the Dark Green, Mid-Bronze Green and Dark Earth scheme.

Mk 80, ROYAL SAUDI AIR FORCE, RIYADH, SAUDI ARABIA, 1973
The white on green flag inscription on the fin reads "There is no God but Allah, and Muhammad is the Prophet of Allah." Unit codes are in both Arabic and Roman numerals.

Since the stormy days of its development the F-111 has consistently proved itself to be an admirable all-weather attack aircraft, capable of delivering guided weapons on to a target thousands of miles from its base. Following the first flight in December 1964, GD developed the design from the initial F-111A, which saw action in Vietnam, through the C for Australia and the D, E and F for the USAF. The carrier-based F-111B for the Navy was canceled, but SAC introduced 76 FB-111As, taking the total production to 562.

F-111F, 493rd TACTICAL FIGHTER SQUADRON, 48th TFW, USAF, LAKENHEATH, UK, 1983
The ultimate model, with more powerful engines than previous versions and more advanced avionics. In the April 1986 attack on Libya, 13 F-111Fs took part, some using 2000lb laser-guided bombs carried underwing, as shown in this view. One aircraft was lost on the operation, code-named "El Dorado Canyon."

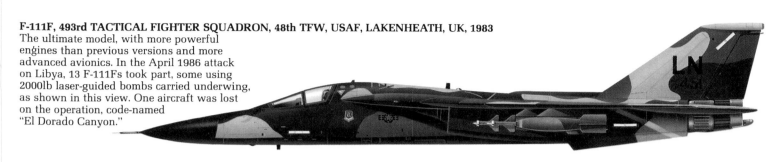

F-111C, 1 and 6 SQUADRONS, ROYAL AUSTRALIAN AIR FORCE, AMBERLEY, AUSTRALIA, 1984
A8-146 is one of 24 C versions purchased by the RAAF. It combines the basic F-111A airframe, engines and avionics with the long-span wings of the FB-111A bomber. This example has SE Asia camouflage with miniaturized insignia and unit lightning flash on the fin.

FB-111A, 33rd BOMB SQUADRON, 509th BOMB WING, USAF, PEASE AFB, USA, 1974
The "New Hampshire Special" marking on the nose, SAC badge under the cockpit and Second Air Force insignia on the fin brighten this camouflaged strategic bomber version. Like the TAC-operated aircraft, it has an ejectable cockpit module for the two crew.

EF-111A, 366th TACTICAL FIGHTER WING, USAF, MOUNTAIN HOME AFB, USA, 1982
Grumman converted 42 F-111As into the defense and electronic-warfare EF-111A nicknamed "Electric Fox" and officially called Raven. Finished in the two-tone gray scheme, a number of aircraft are also based in the UK to support European F-111A operations. Note the TAC badge on the rudder and unit badge by the cockpit.

F-111A, NATIONAL AERONAUTICS AND SPACE ADMINISTRATION, EDWARDS AFB, USA, 1973
An example of a trials aircraft for aerodynamic research, the 13th F-111 built received a new wing of shorter span and other refinements under the NASA Transonic Aircraft Technology (TACT) program. This aircraft was further modified and flown in 1985 with a Mission Adaptive Wing for the Advanced Fighter Technology Integration program.

MIKOYAN-GUREVICH
MiG-23/MiG-27

Introduced into regiments of the Soviet Air Force in the early Seventies, the variable-geometry MiG-23 was a logical step for the MiG Bureau to take, given that a number of Western aircraft manufacturers were incorporating swing wings to get better airfield performance while retaining an acceptable combat capability. The initial fighter version dubbed Flogger B has been developed through the G and K, while the dedicated attack MiG-27 Flogger D is now also found in J form. In between other types have ensured a considerable production run for this versatile design.

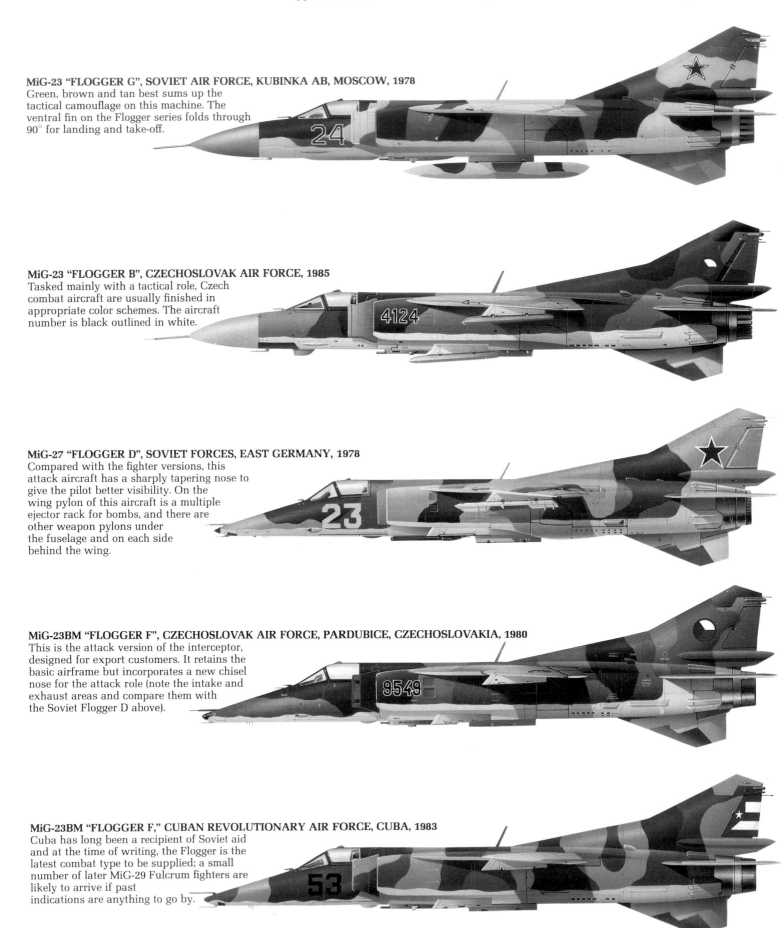

MiG-23 "FLOGGER G", SOVIET AIR FORCE, KUBINKA AB, MOSCOW, 1978
Green, brown and tan best sums up the tactical camouflage on this machine. The ventral fin on the Flogger series folds through 90° for landing and take-off.

MiG-23 "FLOGGER B", CZECHOSLOVAK AIR FORCE, 1985
Tasked mainly with a tactical role, Czech combat aircraft are usually finished in appropriate color schemes. The aircraft number is black outlined in white.

MiG-27 "FLOGGER D", SOVIET FORCES, EAST GERMANY, 1978
Compared with the fighter versions, this attack aircraft has a sharply tapering nose to give the pilot better visibility. On the wing pylon of this aircraft is a multiple ejector rack for bombs, and there are other weapon pylons under the fuselage and on each side behind the wing.

MiG-23BM "FLOGGER F", CZECHOSLOVAK AIR FORCE, PARDUBICE, CZECHOSLOVAKIA, 1980
This is the attack version of the interceptor, designed for export customers. It retains the basic airframe but incorporates a new chisel nose for the attack role (note the intake and exhaust areas and compare them with the Soviet Flogger D above).

MiG-23BM "FLOGGER F," CUBAN REVOLUTIONARY AIR FORCE, CUBA, 1983
Cuba has long been a recipient of Soviet aid and at the time of writing, the Flogger is the latest combat type to be supplied; a small number of later MiG-29 Fulcrum fighters are likely to arrive if past indications are anything to go by.

FOKKER F27

With a pedigree which stretches back to the famous Fokker airliners of the Twenties, the F27 Friendship achieved sales of some 760 to operators in 63 countries. Military users of this turbine-engined transport totaled more than 25 and most still use the type on troop-carrying, freight, VIP or maritime patrol duties. The name Troopship is generally only associated with the F27s flown by the Dutch AF, while Maritime is the official Fokker name of a dedicated over-water patrol variant.

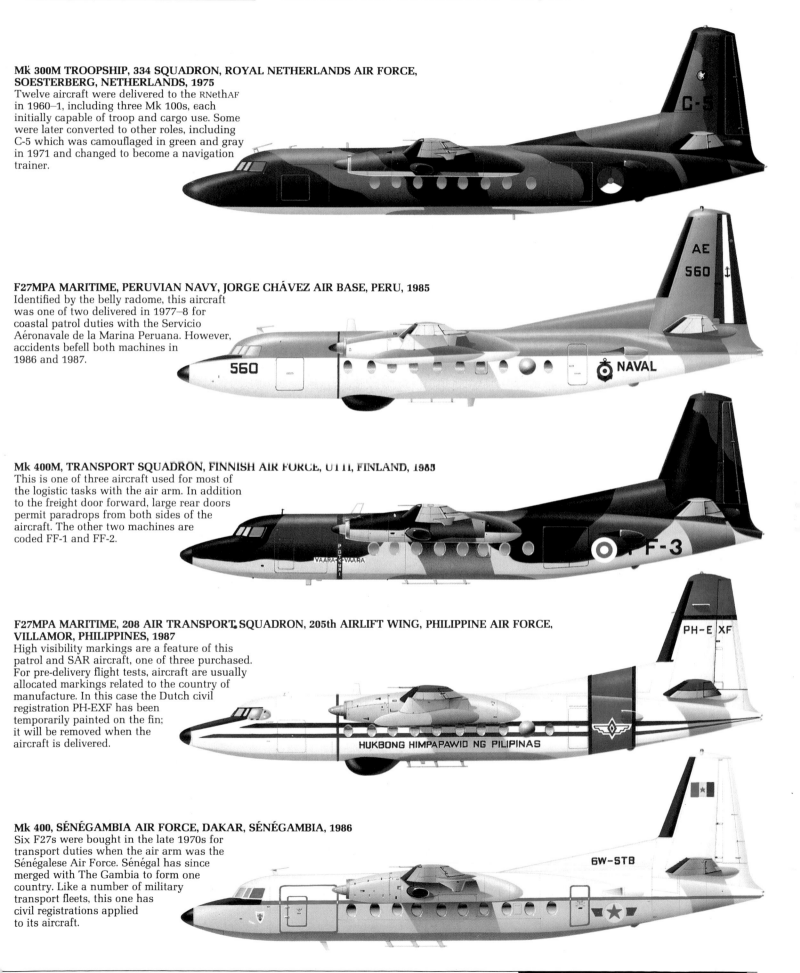

Mk 300M TROOPSHIP, 334 SQUADRON, ROYAL NETHERLANDS AIR FORCE, SOESTERBERG, NETHERLANDS, 1975
Twelve aircraft were delivered to the RNethAF in 1960–1, including three Mk 100s, each initially capable of troop and cargo use. Some were later converted to other roles, including C-5 which was camouflaged in green and gray in 1971 and changed to become a navigation trainer.

F27MPA MARITIME, PERUVIAN NAVY, JORGE CHÁVEZ AIR BASE, PERU, 1985
Identified by the belly radome, this aircraft was one of two delivered in 1977–8 for coastal patrol duties with the Servicio Aéronavale de la Marina Peruana. However, accidents befell both machines in 1986 and 1987.

Mk 400M, TRANSPORT SQUADRON, FINNISH AIR FORCE, UTTI, FINLAND, 1985
This is one of three aircraft used for most of the logistic tasks with the air arm. In addition to the freight door forward, large rear doors permit paradrops from both sides of the aircraft. The other two machines are coded FF-1 and FF-2.

F27MPA MARITIME, 208 AIR TRANSPORT SQUADRON, 205th AIRLIFT WING, PHILIPPINE AIR FORCE, VILLAMOR, PHILIPPINES, 1987
High visibility markings are a feature of this patrol and SAR aircraft, one of three purchased. For pre-delivery flight tests, aircraft are usually allocated markings related to the country of manufacture. In this case the Dutch civil registration PH-EXF has been temporarily painted on the fin; it will be removed when the aircraft is delivered.

Mk 400, SÉNÉGAMBIA AIR FORCE, DAKAR, SÉNÉGAMBIA, 1986
Six F27s were bought in the late 1970s for transport duties when the air arm was the Sénégalese Air Force. Sénégal has since merged with The Gambia to form one country. Like a number of military transport fleets, this one has civil registrations applied to its aircraft.

AEROSPATIALE/ WESTLAND PUMA

The prototype Puma first flew on 15 April 1965, the type being designed to meet a French Army requirement for a tactical helicopter. Entering service four years later, the Puma was subsequently adopted by the armed forces of more than 25 countries. The cabin has seating for up to 16 troops, the RAF version being designated HC Mk 1. Later developments center on the Super Puma, which is similar in appearance but has major changes to increase its performance. Production of both types totals more than 1000.

HC Mk 1, 230 SQUADRON, RAF GÜTERSLOH, WEST GERMANY, 1982

Special events call for special markings. In this case, the tiger motif in its badge qualified the squadron for attendance at the 1982 Tiger Meet, calling for a color scheme with a difference. A good effort by the ground crew – who had to return the aircraft to its standard scheme after the event.

AS.332L, EJERCITO DE CHILE, TOBALADA, CHILE, 1986

Main identifying features of the Super Puma are the additional fin under the tail, larger main wheel sponsons and a more pointed nose. This is one of three purchased in 1983, of which two survive.

SA.330J, IRISH AIR CORPS, BALDONNEL, EIRE, 1983

Sprayed in an olive drab scheme, this radar and flotation-equipped machine was trialed by the Irish Army during the early 1980s. It was later returned to Aérospatiale.

SA.330L, 3 ESCUADRON, 8 GRUPO DE AVIAÇÃO, BRAZILIAN AIR FORCE, CAMP DOS AFONSOS, 1986

Locally designated CH-33s, six Pumas were delivered to the Força Aerea Brasileira. Insignia on the boom is a combined squadron and group number, while on the cockpit door is the unit badge.

BOEING CH-47 CHINOOK

Since its first flight in September 1961 the twin-rotor Chinook has enjoyed steady sales success, with some 16 armed forces taking deliveries of this medium transport helicopter. The US Army, which set the initial requirement for a battlefield-mobility helicopter, has received more than 730, using and losing a few during the Vietnam war. License-built in Italy and Japan, production now is centered on the CH-47D and derivatives such as the MH-47E special-forces version.

CH-47C, UNITED STATES ARMY, TAN SON NHUT, VIETNAM, 1972
Dubbed "The Hook" (and less printable nicknames) by the GIs in SE Asia, the Chinook provided the important heavy airlift required by the war in the South. Olive Drab overall was standard, as was the forward hatch-mounted MG.

HC Mk 1, 18 SQUADRON, RAF, PORT SAN CARLOS, FALKLAND ISLANDS, JUNE 1982
"Bravo November" was the sole survivor of the Exocet attack on the *Atlantic Conveyor* container ship on 25 May 1982. Camouflaged in Dark Green and Dark Sea Gray, this machine flew almost continuously until the Argentine surrender some three weeks later. The call-sign letters BN appeared on the front and rear rotor pylon in black.

CH-47C, ITALIAN ARMY LIGHT AVIATION, VITERBO, ITALY, 1982
With camouflage not too dissimilar to those flown by the RAF, the Italian Army machines are built by Elicotteri Meridionali and some 30 are currently in use. Two units are equipped with Chinooks, No 11 and 12 Gruppo Squadroni, both based at Viterbo.

CH-47C, 12 SQUADRON, ROYAL AUSTRALIAN AIR FORCE, AMBERLEY, AUSTRALIA, EARLY 1980s
Eleven of 12 machines have been in service since they were delivered in 1974. A white top was added to the Olive Drab coloring of this example, but they have recently all been re-camouflaged in a green scheme. This machine is serialed A15 (indicating the Chinook) -008 (the eighth to be purchased).

CH-47C, ROYAL MOROCCAN AIR FORCE, RABAT, MOROCCO, 1988
A desert sand and stone camouflage was applied to the 12 Italian-built Chinooks delivered for logistic support along the country's borders. Note the five-letter code above the tail emblem.

SUKHOI Su-7

Rugged simplicity is the Su-7s greatest asset, because as a combat aircraft it lacks range and weapon load, two vital factors as far as attack aircraft are concerned. Code-named "Fitter" by the West, the prototype of this single seat warplane flew in 1955, with production launched in 1958. Service variants include Su-7B, -7BM, -7BKL and the -7UM two-seat conversion trainer. Supplied to 12 air arms, including some in the Warsaw Pact. It was later developed into the current and more efficient swing-wing Su-17, -20 and -22 series.

Su-7BMK, V-VS (SOVIET AIR FORCE), TRANS-BAIKAL MILITARY DISTRICT, USSR, 1978
Wearing a tactical camouflage of dark green, earth and light blue, this Soviet-operated "Fitter A" carries two 600-liter drop-tanks on the fuselage pylons and UV-16-57 rocket pods under the wings.

Su-7BMK, CZECHOSLOVAK AIR FORCE, 10th AIR ARMY, 1980
About 70 of the "Fitter A" version were in Czech service at this time. With four fuel tanks the range becomes almost respectable. The Aircraft has two wing-root NR-30 cannon to fight with, plus two additional underwing pylons fitted on late-production aircraft.

Su-7UM, EGYPTIAN AIR FORCE, CAIRO WEST AIRFIELD, EGYPT, 1976
To give conversion training on the type, the two-seat -7UM was produced. The instructor in the rear seat uses a periscope to see ahead, but his view remains limited. "Moujik" (peasant) is the West's name for the trainer version.

Su-7BM, EGYPTIAN AIR FORCE, 1976
Desert camouflage in disruptive patterns was the standard finish for these machines, of which some 120 were used by Egypt. The Arabic number on the nose is 7664. These aircraft made many attacks on Israeli ground forces during the Yom Kippur war of 1973.

Su-7BM, ALGERIAN AIR FORCE, 1977
Another of the Soviet Union's Middle Eastern export clients, Algeria received about 20 of the "Fitter A" version. The pod at the base of the rudder is the tail parachute housing; by the wing-root gun is a steel anti-blast panel to protect the fuselage skin.

Latest and most powerful of Grumman's "cat" family, the F-14 entered US Navy service in October 1972 and more than 600 have been delivered. Current plans are centered on the F-14A Plus, which involves replacing the TF30 engines with more powerful and advanced F110 turbofans. A further upgrade, known as the F-14D, has the later engine as well as new radar and avionics, plus the AIM-54C digital Phoenix air-to-air missile. More than 400 A versions will be converted to Ds by 1998.

F-14A, VF-32, US NAVY, USS *JOHN F. KENNEDY*, MID 1970s
Combat proven and victor in a few short, sharp exchanges with Libyan Soviet-made MiG-23 Floggers and Su-22 Fitters, the F-14 is heavily advantaged with its long-range radar and associated Phoenix missiles. Ever safety-conscious, the Navy insisted on a whole range of stencil instructions to be applied to the airframe, an example of which is visible on the nose.

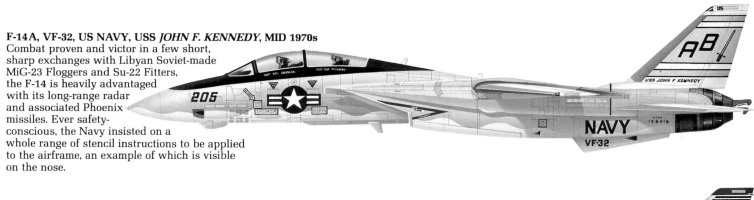

F-14A, VF-143 "THE WORLD FAMOUS PUKIN' DOGS", USS *AMERICA*, 1976
The Tomcat incorporates a Mach Sweep Programer. This automatically varies the wing-sweep angle according to the mission requirements, such as efficient cruise (unswept), supersonic combat (swept), etc. Maximum in-flight sweep angle is 68°, but 75° is possible for deck stowage.

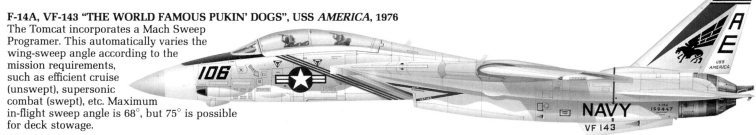

F-14A, VF-14 "TOP HATTERS," US NAVY, EARLY 1980s
Light Gull Gray overall appears on this aircraft, which has much subdued tail markings but retains all insignia in original coloring. In 1986 the unit's gray-painted aircraft displayed the hat in a white circle on the fin, with the carrier code on the inboard surfaces.

F-14A, VF-1 "WOLFPACK," US NAVY, NELLIS AFB, USA, 1977
Aviation artist Keith Ferris devised this experimental finish, designed to break up the outline of the F-14. Three shades of gray in hard-edged splinter style were used, and in some cases no markings were applied. Several aircraft took part in the trials, others coming from VF-2 and VX-4. The schemes have not been adopted to date.

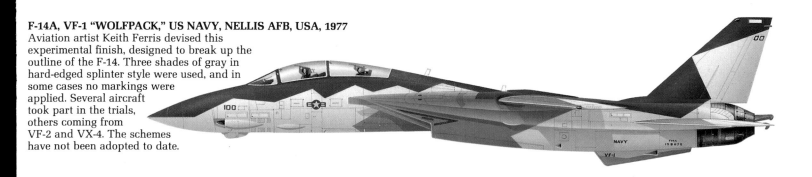

F-14A, VF-103 "SLUGGERS", US NAVY, USS *SARATOGA*, 1983
Gray outline markings, subdued unit tail insignia, but a black 211 on the nose with the last two digits repeated at the tip of the fin for identification when parked on deck. The number is also repeated on the flaps, so that "flyco" on the island can identify the aircraft as it moves to the catapult for launching.

MIL Mi-24 HIND

Currently the largest anti-tank helicopter in the world, the Mi-24 bore the brunt of the hill fighting against the *Mujahideen* in Afghanistan, and many hundreds equip Soviet-Warsaw Pact helicopter regiments. Armament comprises either a 12.7mm MG in a chin turret or a twin-barrel 30mm cannon on the right-hand fuselage side, plus a range of air-to-ground ordnance carried under the stub wings. The double cockpit houses the gunner at the front with the pilot above and behind. Eight equipped troops can be carried in the cabin.

Mi-24 (HIND D), SOVIET ARMEISKAYA AVIATSIYA, USSR, 1984
Factory-applied sand and stone camouflage appears as standard on most Soviet-operated Hinds, although green sometimes replaces the darker color. A tail-rotor warning is applied on the rear fuselage, and on the boom is the aircraft number in yellow.

Mi-24 (HIND D), AFGHAN REPUBLICAN AIR FORCE, KABUL, AFGHANISTAN, 1985
Hinds are flown extensively in the convoy escort role as well as on search-and-destroy missions in the mountains. The advent of Stinger and Blowpipe SAMs, called for different tactics and the crews have put these into effect by staying outside the envelope of the missiles.

Mi-24 (HIND D), POLISH AIR FORCE, 1986
A darker color scheme is a feature of this and a number of other Polish Hinds. About 30 are reported to be in service and they have been seen carrying Aphid infra-red homing air-to-air missiles in addition to the standard weaponry.

Mi-24 (HIND D), IRAQI AIR FORCE, BAGHDAD, IRAQ, 1985
For operations against Iranian forces this Iraqi Hind has been given an additional national flag marking on the forward fuselage, presumably to aid identification over the battlefield and reduce the chances of being attacked by friendly forces. There is only one instance of an Iraqi Hind shooting down a passing Iranian Phantom.

DASSAULT MIRAGE F.1

Like its delta-winged Mirage III predecessor, the Mirage F.1 has enjoyed considerable export success and now flies with 10 air arms as well as with the French Air Force. It was developed as a multi-role aircraft. Main variants are a dedicated fighter (F.1C), an all-weather fighter and ground-attack (F.1E) and trainer (F.1B). The type has been flown on combat operations in the Middle East with the Iraqi AF and in North Africa with the Moroccan AF. Production exceeds 730.

F.1CE, ESCUADRON 141, ALA DE CAZA 14, SPANISH AIR FORCE, ALBACETE, SPAIN, 1980
May 1975 and 04 was one of the first batch of aircraft delivered to Spain, the second nation to order the interceptor. Internal armament of the F.1 consists of two 30mm cannon located under the intakes.

Ala 14 badge applied to the engine intake area of the Spanish aircraft. It shows Don Quijote saluting a flight of Mirages.

Plan view of the Spanish F.1 camouflage scheme. The yellow lines on the wings mark the limit for maintenance personnel to walk.

F.1CZ, 3 SQUADRON, SOUTH AFRICAN AIR FORCE, WATERKLOOF, SA, 1980
The first Mirage F.1s for South Africa arrived in April 1975, but not until 19 months later were they publicly acknowledged to be in service. As well as the fighters, some ground-attack versions were also received, both types having this Olive Drab, Deep Buff, Light Admiralty Gray scheme.

F.1CH, ROYAL MOROCCAN AIR FORCE, 1980
A basic green, brown and tan finish was applied to the 50 Mirages acquired by Morocco from 1978. It is believed about 10 have been lost to ground fire during attacks on Polisario guerillas.

F.1EQ, IRAQI AIR FORCE, BAGHDAD, IRAQ, 1987
More than 120 Mirages have been purchased by Iraq and the type conducted thousands of sorties against Iran. Some were specially equipped to fire Exocet missiles; others have been adapted to use Soviet armaments in the air-to-ground role. This example carries a French Magic AAM.

MCDONNELL DOUGLAS F-15 EAGLE

Designed to replace the Phantom, the F-15 is the USAF's primary air-superiority fighter and planned production to date of all models totals 1266 aircraft in addition to 20 development machines. Since the prototype flew on 27 July 1972, five versions have been produced, the F-15A and C single-seaters, F-15B and D two-seaters and the F-15E two seat dual-role figher and interdiction aircraft. Eagles also fly with the air forces of Japan, Saudi Arabia and Israel.

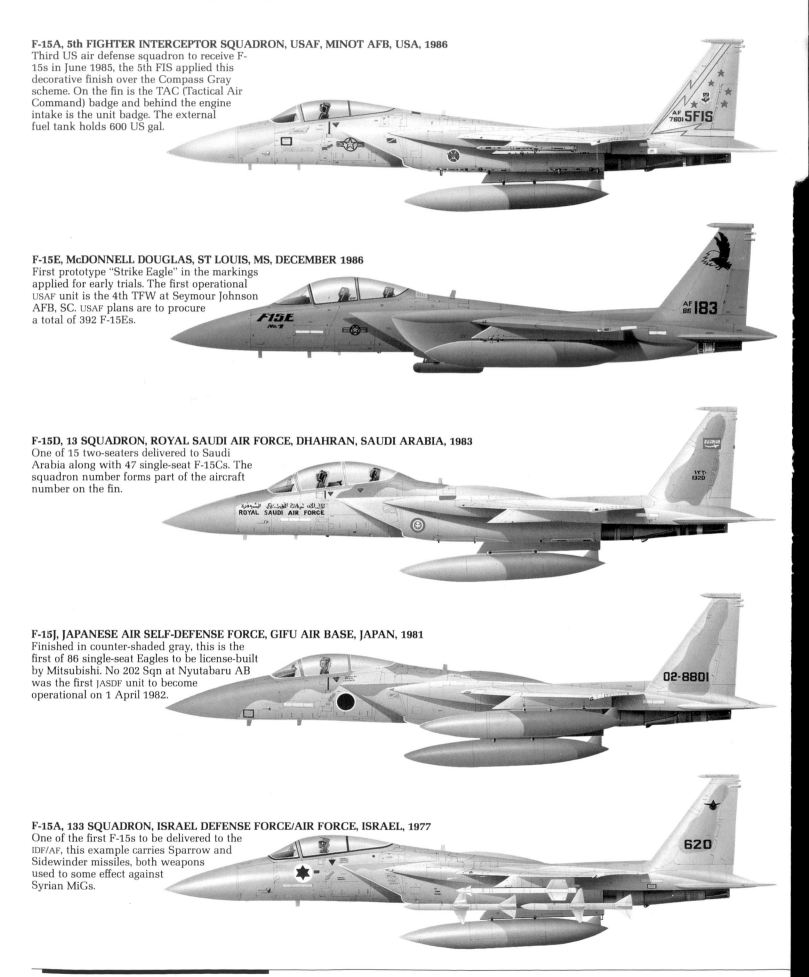

F-15A, 5th FIGHTER INTERCEPTOR SQUADRON, USAF, MINOT AFB, USA, 1986
Third US air defense squadron to receive F-15s in June 1985, the 5th FIS applied this decorative finish over the Compass Gray scheme. On the fin is the TAC (Tactical Air Command) badge and behind the engine intake is the unit badge. The external fuel tank holds 600 US gal.

F-15E, McDONNELL DOUGLAS, ST LOUIS, MS, DECEMBER 1986
First prototype "Strike Eagle" in the markings applied for early trials. The first operational USAF unit is the 4th TFW at Seymour Johnson AFB, SC. USAF plans are to procure a total of 392 F-15Es.

F-15D, 13 SQUADRON, ROYAL SAUDI AIR FORCE, DHAHRAN, SAUDI ARABIA, 1983
One of 15 two-seaters delivered to Saudi Arabia along with 47 single-seat F-15Cs. The squadron number forms part of the aircraft number on the fin.

F-15J, JAPANESE AIR SELF-DEFENSE FORCE, GIFU AIR BASE, JAPAN, 1981
Finished in counter-shaded gray, this is the first of 86 single-seat Eagles to be license-built by Mitsubishi. No 202 Sqn at Nyutabaru AB was the first JASDF unit to become operational on 1 April 1982.

F-15A, 133 SQUADRON, ISRAEL DEFENSE FORCE/AIR FORCE, ISRAEL, 1977
One of the first F-15s to be delivered to the IDF/AF, this example carries Sparrow and Sidewinder missiles, both weapons used to some effect against Syrian MiGs.

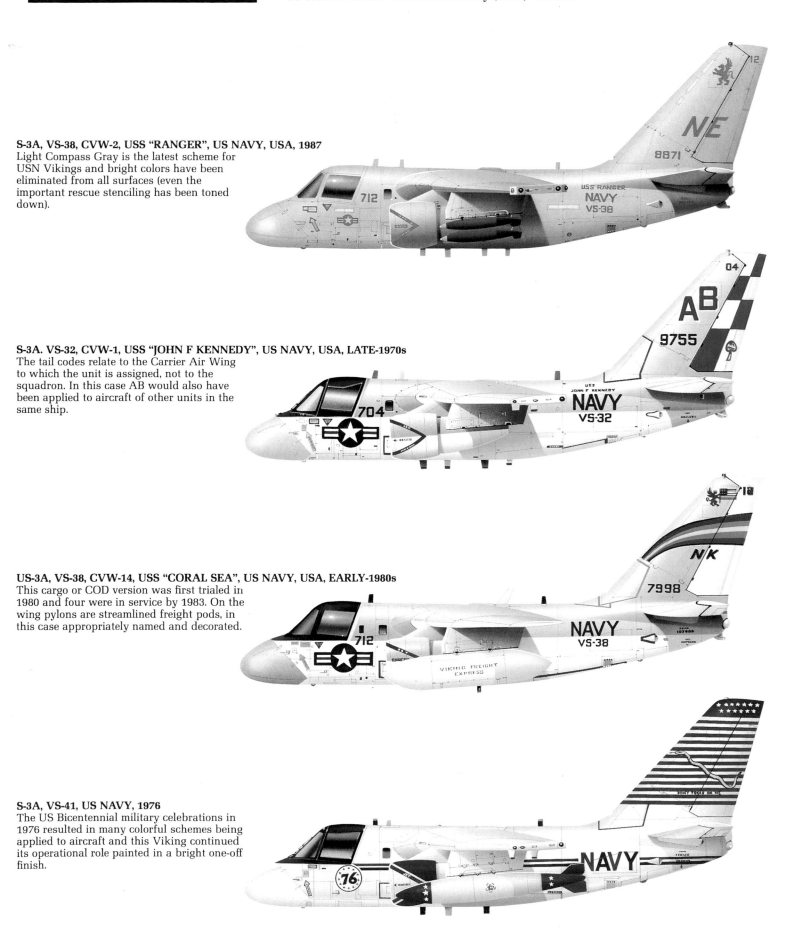

LOCKHEED S-3 VIKING

The standard fixed-wing carrier-based aircraft with US Navy ASW squadrons, the Viking is a highly advanced sub-hunting "computer with wings." It entered service in 1974 and production ended in 1978 following completion of the 187th aircraft. For carrier stowage, the wings and fin fold and there is also a retractable MAD boom at the tail and a refuelling probe above the cockpit. S-3Bs are modified S-3As while the US-3A is a Carrier On-Board Delivery (COD) version.

S-3A, VS-38, CVW-2, USS "RANGER", US NAVY, USA, 1987
Light Compass Gray is the latest scheme for USN Vikings and bright colors have been eliminated from all surfaces (even the important rescue stenciling has been toned down).

S-3A. VS-32, CVW-1, USS "JOHN F KENNEDY", US NAVY, USA, LATE-1970s
The tail codes relate to the Carrier Air Wing to which the unit is assigned, not to the squadron. In this case AB would also have been applied to aircraft of other units in the same ship.

US-3A, VS-38, CVW-14, USS "CORAL SEA", US NAVY, USA, EARLY-1980s
This cargo or COD version was first trialed in 1980 and four were in service by 1983. On the wing pylons are streamlined freight pods, in this case appropriately named and decorated.

S-3A, VS-41, US NAVY, 1976
The US Bicentennial military celebrations in 1976 resulted in many colorful schemes being applied to aircraft and this Viking continued its operational role painted in a bright one-off finish.

BRITISH AEROSPACE HAWK

Firm contracts for more than 350 Hawk advanced trainer and attack aircraft have been placed since the type made its first flight on 21 August 1974. The RAF introduced the Hawk into service in November 1976 to replace the Gnat and Hunter for advanced flying, weapon and navigation training. Orders were subsequently placed by Finland, Indonesia, Kenya, Zimbabwe, Abu Dhabi, Kuwait, Dubai, Saudi Arabia, Switzerland and the UAE. Some 300 T-45 Goshawks have been ordered for the US Navy and the Hawk 200 single-seater has been developed.

T Mk 1, NO 1 TACTICAL WEAPONS UNIT, RAF BRAWDY, UK, 1980
Bearing the "shadow squadron" insignia of 234 Sqn, this aircraft has the standard matt Dark Green and Dark Sea Gray camouflage for the low-level tactical training role. The serial number is repeated in white on the fin.

Crest of the Tactical Weapons Unit.

Hawk T Mk 1 XX192 upper surface camouflage pattern.

Rear fuselage of a "79 Sqn", No 1, TWU, aircraft. Note that in this case the serial number and the fin number do not tie-up.

The camouflage wraps around the fuselage, wing and tailplanes to give an overall scheme. All color demarcation is kept clear of access panels. Wheel bay color is Gloss White.

Across the Bristol Channel from the Welsh base at Brawdy, Chivenor is the home of "63 Sqn," No 2, TWU, one of whose aircraft is seen here.

Mk 50, BRITISH AEROSPACE DEMONSTRATOR, DUNSFOLD, UK, LATE 1970s
Dark Earth, Stone and Azure Blue undersides were applied for a series of demonstration flights in the Middle East. Serialed ZA101, the aircraft also has an out-of-sequence registration G-HAWK.

T Mk 1A, NO 2 TACTICAL WEAPONS UNIT, RAF CHIVENOR, UK, 1985
Satin-finish Medium Sea Gray with Barley Gray undersides is the low-visibility finish for this Sidewinder-armed aircraft. The insignia is pink and light blue. Note that Hawks wired to fire Sidewinder missiles are designated T Mk 1A.

T-45 GOSHAWK, US NAVY, 1987
Early impression of the Gloss White and Orange-colored future Navy trainer. The actual machine has undergone a number of changes to the airframe since this drawing, but the colors are believed to be substantially correct.

186

FAIRCHILD A-10

From almost any angle the A-10 has an easily-recognizable shape. The unorthodox positioning of the two engines to reduce the effect of heat emissions attracting infra-red missiles, the widely-spaced fins, and the massive wing able to carry some seven tons of ordnance are features which make the aircraft unique. The USAF received 713 by 1984 and these equip close-support wings in Europe, South Korea and the USA. Extensive armor plating protects the aircraft's vital parts, including the pilot.

A-10A, 333rd SQUADRON, 355th TACTICAL FIGHTER WING, USAF, DAVIS-MONTHAN, USA, 1976
Serialed 75–269, this is the 20th A-10 built and carries the first of a number of "standard" finishes, applied when the aircraft was undergoing trials and tests, some of which were aimed at determining the most effective scheme to adopt; 17 aircraft were finished like this.

A-10A, 57th TACTICAL TRAINING WING, USAF, NELLIS AFB, USA, 1977
A random pattern of two greens and a brown daubed over the light gray base color was an experimental scheme trialed in a "Jaws II" exercise held in November 1977. It was not adopted.

A-10A, 354th TACTICAL FIGHTER WING, USAF, MYRTLE BEACH, USA, 1977
This was the scheme chosen after the camouflage trials as standard for all production aircraft from serial No 75–280 onwards. All markings were dulled with black outline "star and bar," badges, rescue and maintenance stenciling and the unit/base code on the fin.

YA-10, US AIR FORCE, EDWARDS AFB, USA, LATE 1976
The second prototype, with the port wing and outside port fins painted white for photographic orientation in spinning tests. On the nose is a test probe, and the fin shape is different from that eventually adopted for production aircraft.

A-10A, 23rd TACTICAL FIGHTER WING, USAF, ENGLAND AFB, USA, 1983
When the light gray finish was found to be too contrasting "down among the trees," the so-called Lizard scheme was adopted and still exists on A-10s. The shark-mouth surrounds the 30mm seven-barreled cannon, while on the fin tip is the squadron color. Lizard color reference to FS595a: Green (34103), Green (34092), Gray (36081).

187

SIKORSKY H-60

Intended as a combat survivable replacement for the thousands of UH-1 Hueys in the US Army, the prototype UH-60 flew on 17 October 1974 and entered service in 1978. While the US Army alone requires 2253 by the year 2007, the Navy plans to order 432 SH-60 Seahawk versions for ASW and SAR duties and current export orders stand at over 100 for 11 countries. US Army Black Hawks can carry 11 soldiers or an 8000lb underslung load.

UH-60A, US ARMY, FORT BENNING, USA, 1980
Dark Olive Drab is the basic colour scheme applied to all Army Black Hawks and few carry unit identification. An external stores support system (ESSS) can be fitted allowing the carriage of additional fuel or weapons on four pylons.

UH-60A, 421ST AVIATION BATTALION, US ARMY, W GERMANY, 1983
In a medevac-configuration, a four-litter assembly is mounted around a centrally-located pedestal which rotates to facilitate loading and unloading. Black Hawks received their baptism of fire during the US invasion of Grenada in 1983, sustaining ground-fire damage on a number of occasions. Of 32 deployed, only one was lost.

SH-60B, SEAHAWK PROTOTYPE FOR US NAVY, STRATFORD, USA, 1980
Painted in the then-standard Gull Gray and White USN colors, the first Seahawk flew on 12 December 1979. It carries a dummy Mk 46 lightweight torpedo and has an instrumented probe in the nose. Just in front of the fuselage insignia is the sonobuoy launch rack while behind the marking is the port-side AN/ALQ-142 electronic support measures aerial.

SH-60B, HSL-43, US NAVY, NORTH ISLAND, USA, 1986
Low visibility Compass Gray is the current scheme for Seahawks with compatible insignia such as the TT unit code on the fin and aircraft number on the nose. In the main cabin is a highly-skilled sensor operator working a range of electronic equipment designed to detect and kill submarines, while the pilot and co-pilot share the front cockpit.

XSH-60J, JAPANESE MARITIME SELF-DEFENSE FORCE, MITSUBISHI WORKS, JAPAN, 1987
To begin replacing the current fleet of Sea Kings, the JMSDF has ordered an initial batch of 12 Seahawks following delivery of two machines from Sikorsky for trials purposes. Coded 01, this is the first of the two helicopters and carries the Gloss White–Gull Gray USN scheme.

Since its first flight, on 21 March 1971, the Lynx has become established as one of the most versatile military helicopters in front-line service. In the Royal Navy, the Lynx equips the Small Ship Flights for anti-submarine warfare and anti-surface vessel duties, while the British Army Air Corps uses it as a tank-hunting battlefield helicopter armed with TOW anti-armor missiles. Nearly 400 Lynx have been built and overseas users include Denmark, South Korea, Nigeria, the Netherlands, Norway and West Germany.

HAS. Mk 3, 815 SQUADRON, RNAS PORTLAND, UK, 1988
The overall scheme of semi-gloss Dark Sea Gray has proved ideal for over-water flying. The letters "PO" are Portland base initials.

AH. Mk 1, ARMY AIR CORPS, MIDDLE WALLOP, UK, 1988
This green-gray disruptive scheme was recently adopted for its nap-of-the earth ambush-style tactics against enemy tanks.

HAS. Mk 2 (FN) FLOTTILLE 31F, FRENCH AERONAVALE, LANVEOC-POULMIC, 1987
This example has an overall dark blue-grey finish, with the unit badge beneath the cockpit side window.

Mk 21, 1 ESQUADRAO DE HELICOPTEROS ANTI-SUBMARINOS, BRAZILIAN NAVY, SAO PAULO DE ALDEIA, 1987
Nine Lynx were bought by Brazil of which eight are in service. The finish is semi-matt.

GENERAL DYNAMICS F-16

In aerospace history, the F-16 will probably go down as the fighter of the 1980s. Its diminutive-tailed delta shape symbolizes western air defense more than any other type and by 1990 more than 3000 had been ordered for 16 air forces. The prototype YF-16 flew on 20 January 1974 and the F-16A entered USAF service in 1979. This was followed by the first export order the following year. Single and two-seat versions operate side by side, both being combat capable.

F-16A, 8th TACTICAL FIGHTER WING, USAF, KUNSAN AB, SOUTH KOREA, 1986
The C is steadily replacing the older A series aircraft and this unit has now re-equipped. By the cockpit is the "Wolfpack" marking next to the unit badge. National markings are toned down although the tail codes and serial remain black. Camouflage colors:
(dark) Gray (36118),
(medium) Gray (36270),
(light) Gray (36375).

Plan view of the top color demarcation used by most F-16 operators.

F-16B, TACTICAL AIR COMMAND, USAF, HILL AFB, USA, 1980
Aircraft 78-0096 was used to evaluate the "Lizard" camouflage scheme of two greens and gray for possible use by F-16 units in Europe. To date this has not been adopted.

F-16A, 306 SQUADRON, ROYAL NETHERLANDS AIR FORCE, VOLKEL, NETHERLANDS, 1982
This unit is assigned the tactical reconnaissance role alongside 311 and 312 Sqn at the same base. The unit's eagle head badge is applied to the fin, and below is the aircraft number prefixed by the letter J which relates specifically to the F-16 in RNethAF nomenclature.

F-16C, REPUBLIC OF KOREA AIR FORCE, SOUTH KOREA, 1988
Pending a decision on its future fighter, the ROKAF has ordered 30 single seat C versions and six D combat-trainers. To date, the aircraft have been delivered in the gray air-superiority scheme, but this SE Asia finish is likely if the aircraft revert to the attack role.

F-16A, ISRAEL DEFENSE FORCE/AIR FORCE, ISRAEL, 1980
"Café-au-lait" is the IDF/AF nickname for this disruptive desert finish applied to a number of types including the F-16s. For security purposes the aircraft numbers are regularly changed to prevent strength assessment by unfriendly neighbors. To date, 210 F-16s have been ordered by Israel.

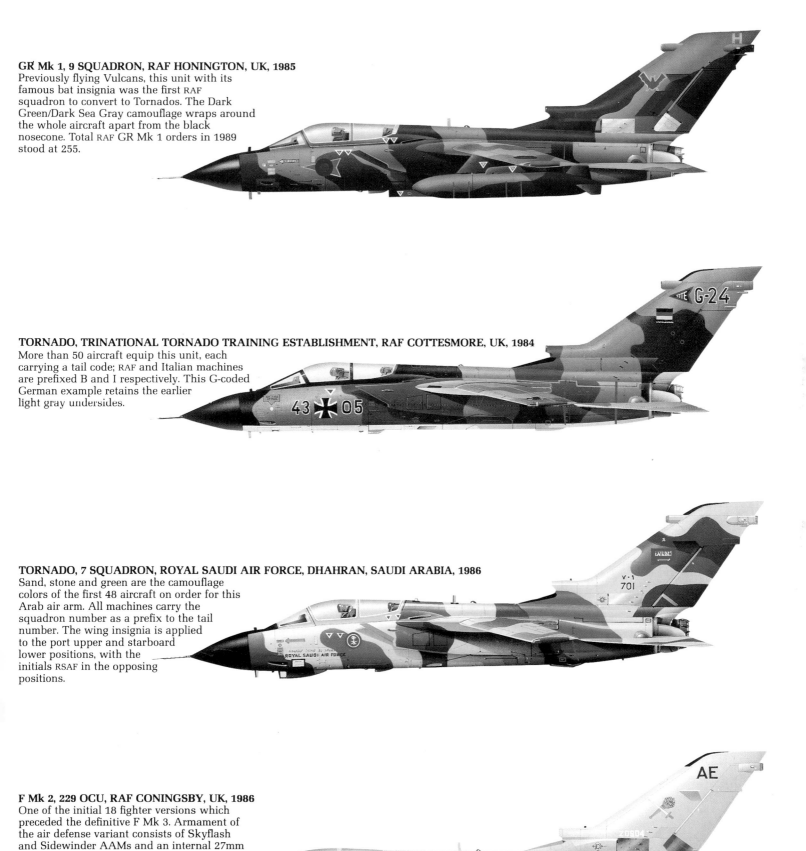

PANAVIA TORNADO

One of the most successful international programs in aerospace, the Tornado was developed by the UK, West Germany and Italy to meet a joint low-level attack aircraft requirement. The first prototype flew on 14 August 1974 and by late 1989, contracts had been placed for a total of 929 aircraft for the three nation's air forces (including 180 F.3 fighters for the RAF), the Royal Saudi Air Force, and Oman (temporarily suspended).

GR Mk 1, 9 SQUADRON, RAF HONINGTON, UK, 1985
Previously flying Vulcans, this unit with its famous bat insignia was the first RAF squadron to convert to Tornados. The Dark Green/Dark Sea Gray camouflage wraps around the whole aircraft apart from the black nosecone. Total RAF GR Mk 1 orders in 1989 stood at 255.

TORNADO, TRINATIONAL TORNADO TRAINING ESTABLISHMENT, RAF COTTESMORE, UK, 1984
More than 50 aircraft equip this unit, each carrying a tail code; RAF and Italian machines are prefixed B and I respectively. This G-coded German example retains the earlier light gray undersides.

TORNADO, 7 SQUADRON, ROYAL SAUDI AIR FORCE, DHAHRAN, SAUDI ARABIA, 1986
Sand, stone and green are the camouflage colors of the first 48 aircraft on order for this Arab air arm. All machines carry the squadron number as a prefix to the tail number. The wing insignia is applied to the port upper and starboard lower positions, with the initials RSAF in the opposing positions.

F Mk 2, 229 OCU, RAF CONINGSBY, UK, 1986
One of the initial 18 fighter versions which preceded the definitive F Mk 3. Armament of the air defense variant consists of Skyflash and Sidewinder AAMs and an internal 27mm cannon. The pale Barley Gray finish is standard on all operational machines. The F.2s will be updated to F.3 standard and will be redesignated F.2As.

Acknowledgements

The Author and Publishers wish to thank William Green and Gordon Swanborough of Pilot Press, without whose help this book could not have been produced. To Dennis Punnett for his help with the artworks, to Hussain Mohamed for assembling them and designing the book and to Michael Bowyer, Richard Gardner, Harry Holmes, Dave Howley, Joe Merchant, Bruce Robertson, Roy Sanders, Mike Stroud and Dick Ward.

PHOTOGRAPHIC AND ILLUSTRATION CREDITS:
All material is copyright: Nigel Bradley endpapers, 1–6, 13 (center left), 14 (insert), 21 (top right); Imperial War Museum 8–9, 13 (top left), 15 (top); USAF/IWM 14 (top), USAF 15 (bottom), Barry Wheeler 9 (center), 19 (top); Pilot Press 9 (top), 13 (top), 16 (bottom), 21 (top left); US Navy 10, 12; Octopus Publishing Group Library 11 (top), 16 (top and center), 18 (top); Flight International 11 (bottom), 15 (center left and right); British Aerospace 13 (right and bottom), 20 (top and center); Boeing Aircraft Corporation 17 (top); McDonnell Douglas 17 (bottom); Westland Helicopters 18 (bottom); Lockheed Corporation 19 (right), 21 (bottom); Patrick Allen 19 (left), 21 (center); Ministry of Defence 20 (bottom); Aerospace Publishing 151 (third from top).